Refugees Are (NOT) Welcome Here

Law and Society Series
W. Wesley Pue, Founding Editor

We pay tribute to the late Wes Pue, under whose broad vision, extraordinary leadership, and unwavering commitment to socio-legal studies our Law and Society Series was established and rose to prominence.

The Law and Society Series explores law as a socially embedded phenomenon. It is premised on the understanding that the conventional division of law from society creates false dichotomies in thinking, scholarship, educational practice, and social life. Books in the series treat law and society as mutually constitutive and seek to bridge scholarship emerging from interdisciplinary engagement of law with disciplines such as politics, social theory, history, political economy, and gender studies.

Recent books in the series:

Emilie Biland, translated by Annelies Fryberger and Miranda Richmond Mouillot, *Family Law in Action: Divorce and Inequality in Quebec and France* (2023)
Kate Puddister and Emmett Macfarlane, eds., *Constitutional Crossroads: Reflections on Charter Rights, Reconciliation, and Change* (2022)
Derek Silva and Liam Kennedy, eds., *Power Played: A Critical Criminology of Sport* (2022)
Erez Aloni and Régine Tremblay, eds., *House Rules: Changing Families, Evolving Norms, and the Role of the Law* (2022)
Florence Ashley, *Banning Transgender Conversion Practices: A Legal and Policy Analysis* (2022)
Dia Dabby, *Religious Diversity in Canadian Public Schools: Rethinking the Role of Law* (2022)
Kim Stanton, *Reconciling Truths: Reimagining Public Inquiries in Canada* (2021)
Daniel Rück, *The Laws and the Land: The Settler Colonial Invasion of Kahnawà:ke in Nineteenth-Century Canada* (2021)
Suzanne Bouclin, *Women, Film, and Law: Cinematic Representations of Female Incarceration* (2021)
Amanda Nelund, *A Better Justice? Community Programs for Criminalized Women* (2020)
Trevor C.W. Farrow and Lesley A. Jacobs, eds., *The Justice Crisis: The Cost and Value of Accessing Law* (2020)
Jamie Baxter, *Inalienable Properties: The Political Economy of Indigenous Land Reform* (2020)
Jeremy Patrick, *Faith or Fraud: Fortune-Telling, Spirituality, and the Law* (2020)
Obiora Chinedu Okafor, *Refugee Law after 9/11: Sanctuary and Security in Canada and the United States* (2020)
Anna Jane Samis Lund, *Trustees at Work: Financial Pressures, Emotional Labour, and Canadian Bankruptcy Law* (2019)
Shauna Labman, *Crossing Law's Border: Canada's Refugee Resettlement Program* (2019)
Peter McCormick and Marc D. Zanoni, *By the Court: Anonymous Judgments at the Supreme Court of Canada* (2019)

For a complete list of the titles in the series, see the UBC Press website, www.ubcpress.ca.

Refugees Are (NOT) Welcome Here

The Paradox of Protection in Canada

Azar Masoumi

UBCPress · Vancouver

33 32 31 30 29 28 27 26 25 24   5 4 3 2 1

Printed in Canada on FSC-certified ancient-forest-free paper (100% post-consumer recycled) that is processed chlorine- and acid-free.

Library and Archives Canada Cataloguing in Publication

Title: Refugees are (not) welcome here : the paradox of protection in Canada / Azar Masoumi.

Names: Masoumi, Azar, author.

Series: Law and society series (Vancouver, B.C.)

Description: Series statement: Law and society | Includes bibliographical references and index.

Identifiers: Canadiana (print) 2023053029X | Canadiana (ebook) 20230530397 | ISBN 9780774868716 (hardcover) | ISBN 9780774868730 (PDF) | ISBN 9780774868747 (EPUB)

Subjects: LCSH: Refugees – Government policy – Canada. | LCSH: Refugees – Legal status, laws, etc. – Canada.

Classification: LCC JV7282 .M37 2023 | DDC 325/.2140971 – dc23

BRITISH COLUMBIA ARTS COUNCIL | BRITISH COLUMBIA

UBC Press gratefully acknowledges the financial support for our publishing program of the Government of Canada and the British Columbia Arts Council.

This book has been published with the help of the UBC Press First Time Authors Fund.

UBC Press
The University of British Columbia
2029 West Mall
Vancouver, BC V6T 1Z2
www.ubcpress.ca

To all those who have been turned away
from relative safety and prosperity in Canada

Contents

Figures

Acknowledgments

I have the blessing of the knowledge that I have many, many people to thank.

First and foremost, heart-felt thanks to Andil Gosine, Radhika Mongia, and David Murray, who saw this project since its inception and through several reincarnations. Thank you for encouraging and challenging me all in the same breath. Thanks also for years of guidance, mentorship, and genuine human connection.

Many thanks to all those who agreed to be interviewed for this research, taught me about the Canadian system, and helped me make key research connections. Special thanks to Andrew Brouwer and Michael Creal for their warm support of my research and to all the phenomenal activists involved with the Canadian Council for Refugees for their inspiring work.

I am grateful for the network of exceptional friends and colleagues who enrich my life to no limit: Ronak Ghorbani, William Hébert, Asha Jeffers, Hollis Moore, Kate Pinder, Vivian Solana, Meera Sethi, Matthu Strang, Alison Fisher, Danielle Landry, Sareh Serajelahi, Angela Allen, Gulay Kilicaslan, Rana Sukarieh, Rawan Abdelbaki, Hilary Cameron, and Parisa Moosavi. Thanks also to my childhood friends who continue to cheer me on across oceans and continents: Laleh Hosseini and Sanaz Poursabri.

Thanks to Abu Rami, Um Rami, and Huthaifa for taking me into their family and for filling my fridge, pantry, and belly with many delicious Syrian meals while I worked through this project.

Thank you to all my cousins, across all continents, particularly Najmeh Masoumi, Minoo Ghassemi, and Pouya Gharahdaghi, for bringing so much joy, comradery, and love to my life.

To my many aunties and uncles, biological or otherwise, in all corners of the world, who are too many to recount: thank you for your spectacular humour and unending warmth.

To my long-time mentors Alan Sears and Andie Noack: thank you for your wisdom and compassion. I have not made a single important career decision without your advice since I met you, and I have the good sense not to do so in the future. Also, warm thanks to my friend and mentor David Moffette: your generosity and dynamism never fail to astound me.

To Arash and Arman, my two brothers: you are my comrades in life. Thank you for being there through all the highs and the lows. *Khabardari vallah kheili sakhte! À ma chérie Marie-Ève: merci d'avoir été la meilleure compagnie que je pouvais espérer pendant que je finissais ce livre. Et de me permettre de parler autant de sociologie!* To my mom, Mahvash: thank you Maman jaan, for everything. I know it has been lots. Thank you also for all the rides, all the food, and all the hugs. I'm also thankful to the memory of my dad, Ali: Baba, I know you would have been proud to see this day.

I dedicate this book to Grise, discussed in Chapter 6, and all those, known and unknown, who have been turned away from relative safety and prosperity in Canada and sent to poverty, danger, or death.

Chronology of Significant Events

1951	The *Refugee Convention* is presented for signature
1969	Canada signs the *Refugee Convention*
1969	Anal intercourse between consenting adults is decriminalized in Canada
1976	The *Immigration Act* legislates the category "refugee"
1982	The *Canadian Charter of Rights and Freedoms* is established
1985	The Supreme Court *Singh* decision extends charter rights to non-citizen residents
1989	The IRB is instituted
1993	Bill C-86 introduces procedural restrictions to access to refugee status
1993	The *Gender Guidelines* are released by the IRB
1998	The Lead case against Roma Hungarians is released by the IRB
2001	The *Immigration and Refugee Protection Act* passes
2003	The Canada Border Services Agency is established
2004	The *Safe Third Country Agreement* is signed with the United States

2006 The Lead case is overturned by Federal Court

2010 The *Balanced Refugee Reform Act* passes

2012 The *Protecting Canada's Immigration System Act* passes

2012 The designated countries of origin policy is established

2012 The UNHCR guidelines on SOGIE protection are released

2012 The Refugee Appeal Division is established

2017 The *SOGIE Guidelines* are released by the IRB

Refugees Are (NOT) Welcome Here

Introduction
States of Paradox, the Paradox of States

During a casual dinner-table conversation, I once explained my research to a middle-aged American man. He immediately broke into a giggle that expressed both amusement and shock at what he had just heard: that gay folk can now become refugees too. Although he had the good sense not to make the point openly, I knew that he found me absurd for suggesting that there remained any problem with how wealthy Western countries handled refugee protection: If gays are counted in, who is not?

The state of refugee protection may seem understandably perplexing to casual observers. On the one hand, refugee rights have become as inclusive as one can imagine. The protective scope of the 1951 *Convention Relating to the Status of Refugees (Refugee Convention)* has now stretched far beyond its original parameters.[1] As a result, groups that previously had no ground for protection, such as domestically abused women or LGBT persons, are now commonly accepted as legitimate refugees.[2] On the other hand, refugee advocates, lawyers, and scholars are unified in their claim that refugee rights have become increasingly difficult to access (see Bohmer and Shuman 2008). As the United Nations High Commissioner for Refugees (UNHCR) (2022) reports, only 17 percent of the world's 21.3 million refugees and 4.4 million displaced Venezuelans are resettled in the global North. The vast majority (83 percent) of the displaced live in developing countries where chances of acquiring full citizenship and permanent legal residence are low. Meanwhile, wealthy liberal countries actively repel those who search for rights in their territories. Reports of legally questionable and inhumane treatment of refugee claimants – for instance, in Australia's islands of detention (British Broadcasting Corporation 2016; Jones 2017; Williams 2017) – paint a dim picture of the state of refugee protection in the liberal states of the developed world. How can refugee rights have expanded and yet become more restrictive over the course of that expansion?

This book studies the administration of inland[3] refugee claim processing in Canada in order to answer this question. Through a multi-method genealogical study, I show that over the last thirty years, access to Canadian refugee protection has been simultaneously, and systemically, expanded and restricted. Indeed, I argue that the Canadian regime of refugee protection is a dynamic, complex, and conflicted articulation of an expansionist humanitarian impetus as well as a pragmatic restrictionist compulsion.[4] I suggest that these contradictory impulses are symptomatic of the paradox of state-controlled refugee protection: that of ensuring the universal equality of rights through the exclusionary mechanisms of the nation-state. In this book, I offer a topology of the larger paradox of universal rights by sketching the mechanisms and processes that achieve and maintain Canadian refugee protection. I argue that despite its internal paradoxes, the Canadian regime of refugee protection maintains its overall stability by way of two systemic arrangements. First, while expansions are primarily, although not exclusively, achieved in the field of legislation and jurisprudence, restrictions are, in large part, accomplished in administrative and bureaucratic fields. This means that legislative and jurisprudential expansions are continually counterbalanced by policy interventions, institutional practices, and bureaucratic procedures. I refer here to below-legislative level interventions introduced by administrators and ministers, such as the desginated countries of origin policy, which are not technically legislation (and in fact can be challenged in court), but systemic interventions at the hands-on policy level that impose restrictive boundaries on refugee protection. As a result, the Canadian regime both expands and restricts without losing its overall stability.

Second, while expansions in refugee rights emerge around tightly bounded categories, such as those of the convention refugee, gender-based claimant, and sexual orientation and gender identity and expression (SOGIE) refugee, restrictions target flexible groups of excludable claimants that are often demarcated by their (racialized) nationality. With every instance of legislative or jurisprudential expansion, these nationally demarcated scapegoats are mobilized to produce the administrative threshold of Canadian refugee protection: when the law expands rights for women and SOGIE refugees, government bureaucracies find other groups to exclude from protection. Of course, the scapegoated national groups encompass the very classes of claimants that are now afforded protection. Yet, the dynamic production of targets of exclusion as supposedly distinct from the newly protected and rightful subjects, allows paradoxical developments to emerge side by side.

While this book juxtaposes the expansionist desires of the law with the restrictionist impulses of the administrative and bureaucratic forces, it does not suggest that the law is purely expansionist,[5] nor that the bureaucracy is exclusively restrictive. With its direly limited terms of application, refugee law, without doubt, provides the basis for many adaptable forms of restrictionism. Yet it is commonly the bureaucracy that translates abstract legal notions into actual mechanics of exclusion. In fact, as I will show throughout this book, the various configurations of excludable subjects are produced in accordance with the situated needs and interests of the claim-processing bureaucracy. Thus, I argue that in the three decades of systematic refugee protection in Canada, the articulation of expansionist and restrictionist impulses, mostly in these separate fields and in relation to supposedly distinct subjects, has allowed the Canadian regime of refugee protection to advance contradictory agendas without losing its overall stability. In short, these articulated arrangements have sustained this regime despite, and through, its paradoxes. But why is Canadian refugee protection paradoxical? And, importantly, why does this paradox persist?

Failure, Articulation, and the Promise of Protection

The Canadian regime of refugee protection is founded on a paradox. On the one hand, this regime is based on the premise that all humans are equal bearers of natural rights and, consequently, are entitled to protection against violations of their natural liberty. The right to asylum, therefore, is closely associated with the concept of natural human liberty (Bashford and McAdam 2014), a notion that emerged from the writings of thinkers such as Thomas Hobbes ([1651] 1996) and John Locke ([1689] 1988) and constitutes the basis of liberal philosophy and politics (Gray 1995). Thus, as an entity that administers the right to asylum, the Canadian regime is centrally organized around the universal equality of humans.[6] On the other hand, Canadian refugee protection is part of the larger apparatus of state-controlled migration regulation and, as such, directly contributes to the exercise of exclusionist control. For instance, the Canadian regime is premised on ahistorical assumptions that non-nationals have no legitimate claim to enter or reside in national territories (Malkki 1992) and that regulating migration should be the exclusive prerogative of the state (Balibar 1991; Torpey 2000; Mongia 2007, 2018). As such, the Canadian regime labours to (re)produce citizenship as social closure (Brubaker 1992): non-citizens, particularly those from poor countries,[7] are not meant to have unhampered access to residency rights in Canada. In fact, in and beyond Canada, state-controlled migration regulation produces the desire, the subjects, the logics, and the apparatus for systematic discrimination (Loescher 1993; Soguk 1999; Haddad 2008). In this global system, as Hannah Arendt ([1951] 1973) notes, those who fall outside of the bounds of the imagined community of the nation (Anderson 1991), such as refugees, are simply rightless and unequal. In other words, the paradox of refugee protection in Canada is, at its core, the difficulty of administering universal equality while exercising exclusivist control.

The paradox of state-controlled refugee protection creates highly qualified notions of "universal" rights, which are reflected in the international refugee law itself. The *Refugee Convention* defines the refugee as a person who "owing to well-founded fear of being persecuted for reasons of race, religion, nationality, membership of a particular social group or political opinion, is outside the country of his nationality and is unable or, owing to such fear, is unwilling to avail himself of the protection of that country."[8] Aside from the obvious assumption of masculine subjecthood here (hence, the pronoun "he"), this definition was originally qualified by geographic and historical specifications that made refugee protection largely for and about Europeans: as initially drafted, refugee protection pertained to those displaced as the result of "events occurring in Europe before 1 January 1951."[9] To be sure, signatory states had the option to pursue more universal parameters of application by opting for the clause "events occurring in Europe *or elsewhere* before 1 January 1951."[10] In either option, of course, Europe remained the unquestioned focus of protection obligations, while protecting those displaced "elsewhere" was only a voluntary choice that could, if they so wished, be taken up by individual states. Refugee protection was truly, at least initially, created for Europe.

The historical Eurocentricism of the *Refugee Convention,* as Laura Madokoro (2016, 2022) insightfully suggests, is at once a reflection of long-standing racial hierarchies of protection and the ubiquitous anti-refugee sentiments that conceived of the displaced as "burdens" and, consequently, deliberated to limit the scope of protection asked of signatory states. Indeed, the state representatives who drafted the *Convention,* particularly those representing the United States, were adamant about this geographical restriction, fearing that a wider definition would impose considerable financial costs and erode state control over who and how many people became entitled to rights (Glynn 2011). These concerns were particularly acute in the increasingly tense context of the Cold War, in which liberal states became invested in both maintaining unhampered control over their borders and resettling Eastern European political refugees as a way to discredit communism (Loescher 1993). In sum, preoccupied with their own racial, exclusivist, and geopolitical considerations, liberal states were not keen on making rights universal. The *Convention* reflected this political intent.

The Eurocentric terms of the *Refugee Convention* were eventually amended by the 1967 *Protocol Relating to the Status of Refugees (Refugee Protocol),* normalizing the universal application of refugee protection.[11] While somewhat generative, the protocol was a rather conservative response to the much more expansive conceptualization of protection proposed by the Organization of African Unity (OAU) (Loescher 1993). Unlike the *Convention,* which only recognizes individualized state-sanctioned persecution, the OAU's definition also regarded as refugees those affected by generalized forms of violence such as war, occupation, foreign domination, or other events that seriously disturb public order. In lieu of adopting this wider and more universally relevant definition, the *Refugee Protocol* only removed the geographic and historical limitations of the *Convention*. Hence, while now globally applicable, the protocol limits rights to cases involving violations of individual civil and political liberties. This limitation continues to make refugee protection inaccessible to the majority of the world's displaced populations: according to the UNHCR, only 21.3 million of the 89.3 million people forcibly displaced from their homes qualify as convention refugees (UNHCR 2022). The remaining 76 percent are considered displaced but not refugees.

Importantly, the failure of the *Refugee Convention* to account for the fuller array of issues that produce forced displacement is only a reflection of the wider problem of liberal rights, a problem that Karl Marx ([1844] 2002) conceptualizes as an erroneous separation between the political and the social in liberal philosophy. Although the political, the civil, the social, and the economic realms cannot be practically separated, except in the most abstract of liberal fantasies, liberal law consistently advances political and civil rights in distinction from, and to the marginalization of, economic and social rights.[12] In this split vision, as Fritjof Capra and Ugo Mattei (2015) show, law emerges in a dichotomy between the individual right (to private property) and the state right (to sovereignty). Thus, the penchant of refugee law for prioritizing the violation of citizens by states (civil and political rights) over and beyond, for instance, the violation of workers by capitalists (economic rights) or of farmers by ecological devastation (ecological rights) should be considered in direct lineage from the narrow liberal conception of rights and rightful subjects.

The geopolitics, and geopolitical blind spots, of this limited vision of rightfulness in the refugee protection context are noteworthy. As Susan Koshy (1999) has shown, in establishing parameters of human rights internationally, liberal countries successfully promoted civil and political rights over economic, social, and cultural rights, despite and against the efforts of Third World and socialist states. This geopolitical divide, of course, had been long rooted in spatially dichotomized political histories:

while civil and political rights are commonly considered the outcome of the French and American bourgeois revolutions in the late eighteenth century, economic and social rights are often traced back to the socialist revolutions of the early twentieth century (Marks 1981). Despite its many inaccuracies,[13] the spatial dichotomization of rights along the West-East fracture fuelled geopolitical divisions at the time of the drafting of the *Refugee Convention*. Devised and promoted primarily by the liberal "bloc," refugee rights came to be narrowly defined in terms of the breakdown of political and civil relations between an individually violated citizen and a sovereign violating state. Rights, in other words, became largely about political and civil persecution. As a result, to this day, the emaciated and the dispossessed may well become displaced, but they do not become rightful.

The rightfulness of the displaced is further qualified by the hefty requirement that they must be outside of their country of nationality or habitual residence before they may be recognized as a refugee at all.[14] This means that signatory states have no obligation to those who do not, or cannot, cross international borders, regardless of their circumstances. Thus, rightfulness is turned into a function of the resources and life opportunities (such as money, time, and internationally respected passports) that are, somewhat ironically, most common to citizens of wealthy, politically stable countries: the very people who are least likely to need international protection. Of course, those without such means cannot be penalized in refugee proceedings if they cross borders without authorization. But absence of penalization does not equal the presence of rights: asylum seekers may cross borders without state authorization (if they can), but they do not have the right to do so. Indeed, unauthorized border crossing is stringently prohibited by states, even if it is undertaken by legitimate convention refugees. In the words of Catherine Dauvergne (2004, 71), "rights follow that crossing [of borders], they do not precede it." Those seeking protection only become rightful after they cross borders; yet refugee law does not guarantee a right to border crossing. In effect, refugees have certain rights, but they possibly have no means to reach them.

These qualified universalities of refugee protection are further intensified in the more recent iterations of neoliberalism: a fiscally conservative and austerity-promoting logic of governance that has, since the 1980s, aggressively rolled back much of the equality-inducing measures of the Keynesian welfare state model across the globe (McCluskey 2003; Hartman 2005). Importantly, neoliberalism is not only an aggressively austere political trend but also a distinct mode of governance that to quote Wendy Brown (2015, 17), "configures all aspects of existence in economic terms." This means that neoliberalism converts "the distinctly *political* character, meaning, and operation of democracy's constituent elements into *economic* ones" (17; emphasis in original). Consequently, politics and public administration become largely conceived, and evaluated, based on economic logics and their accompanying calculations.

The overwhelming "'economization' of political life" (Brown 2015, 17) has had significant implications for the state of refugee protection in Canada. The advent of systematic refugee protection in Canada has coincided with the neoliberalization of Canadian public administration, whereby economic logics came to centrally frame the operations and assessments of the Canadian regime. As a result, refugee protection became, and continues to be, perceived in large part in terms of its productivity credentials: the viability of state-controlled refugee protection relies heavily on the ability to maximize the ratio of output to operating costs. In this economized context, concerns with the quality and equality of humanitarian conduct are, inevitably, relegated to the back seat. Notably, the current economized neoliberal logic qualifies equality not based on (gendered and racialized) assumptions of natural and rational inferiority, as the liberal logic once did,[15] but, rather, because of its supposed sheer economic unfeasibility: universal equality simply costs too much. There are too many people displaced by material deprivation, political instability, and ecological devastation to resettle into equality. Hence, refugee protection remains limited to the far less likely culprit of forced displacement: individualized state-sanctioned persecution. A wider protection framework, the neoliberal state deduces, would be economically unsound.

Unsurprisingly, thus, neoliberal governance fails to deliver the universal equality that it claims.[16] This failure, however, is much more than a simple, unfortunate flaw; indeed, I suggest that this "failure" is a functional condition of neoliberal continuity.[17] As Elizabeth Povinelli (1998) argues, the perpetually unfulfilled promise of equality works to present liberal justice as a project always in the making and, by consequence, always requiring our patient waiting. The perpetually unfulfilled promise, thus, becomes the pretext for our hopeful anticipation. In effect, neoliberal rule sustains its own futurity by promising and never fulfilling – by promising the equality that it shall not fulfill.

In this book, I use the concept of articulation, as developed by sociologist and cultural theorist Stuart Hall (1980, 1985), to understand the paradox of state-controlled refugee protection as a similarly functional failure. In Hall's theory, articulation is the joining of distinct and disparate elements in contingent and historically specific unities. As such, articulation provides the possibility of "thinking unity *and* difference; difference *in* complex unity" (Hall 1985, 93). Importantly, for Hall, articulations are not predetermined, necessary, or eternal. Neither are the joined elements of an articulated unity, despite their connectedness, reduceable to one another or to any other singular force (325). In fact, articulations may involve the joining of disparate and, at times, surprisingly inconsistent elements. Thus, citing Louis Althusser, Hall describes articulations as fusions "into a *ruptural* unity" (95; emphasis added). Ruptures, however, do not make articulations random and unstructured associations. To the contrary, Hall describes articulations as "complex *structures*" that however internally fraught, exhibit systemic patterns of joining and tendencies and configurations (Hall 1980, 325; 1985, 91; emphasis added). Neither wholly agentic nor inescapably predetermined, articulations are the results of "previously structured practices" (Grossberg 1986, 95). For, as Hall suggests, "we make history, but on the basis of anterior conditions which are not of our making" (Grossberg 1986, 95). In other words, articulations are dynamic, systemic, and political.

Hall's concept of articulation allows us to conceive the Canadian regime of refugee protection as functionally ruptured and incoherent. This is to suggest that the paradoxical impulses of this regime are integral to its overall stability and continuity. In the dynamic inner workings of this regime, for instance, the expansionist impetus for humanitarianism repeats the liberal promise of universal equality, while the restrictionist impulses supply the qualifying conditions that ensure this promise is not fulfilled. Together, these paradoxical impulses produce incoherently functional notions of protection and regimes for administrating them. They make it possible to propose, for example, that refugees deserve protection (because they are equal humans) but not at the expense of Canadians (who are somehow more human). It is perhaps because of this cooperative incoherence that despite its repeated failure to protect refugees, state-controlled refugee protection remains in place in Canada.

It is important to note that my use of the term "failure" is not meant to undermine the unquestionably life-altering role of refugee protection regimes for many displaced peoples. While acknowledging their importance, I suggest that conceptualizing the existing regimes in the unforgiving terms of failure allows us to highlight the astonishing absence of protection for the majority of those who are in need of refuge. Failure presents the urgency to ponder why only a fraction of the world's displaced population (24 percent) can be protected under the mandate of the UNHCR and why only a fraction of recognized convention refugees (17 percent) is resettled in countries that offer the most prosperity, stability, and rights. How is it that Canadian refugee protection fails at protecting refugees and yet persists in doing so? Contemplating these vast shortcomings encourages a structural analysis of the forces that make effective refugee protection largely inviable, and viable refugee protection widely ineffective. It is in the spirit of such analysis that I propose that state-controlled refugee protection persists not despite its failures but, rather, because of them. Put differently, the existing regimes are meant not to fully protect refugees.

Bureaucratic Autonomy and the Administration of (Immigration) Law

Many of the failures and injustices of systems of refugee protection and migration control, particularly their racialized and colonial forms and implications, have been capably explored by critical analyses of immigration law and policy. The foundational works of scholars such as Sherene Razack (1995, 1999), Yasmeen Abu-Laban (1998), Sunera Thobani (2000, 2007), and Peter Li (2001) in Canada, for example, have exposed the role of immigration and refugee law in reinstating racial and (settler) colonial hierarchies, albeit under seemingly benign guises.[18] While I strongly concur with these scholars, this book makes a case for considering the failures of state-controlled refugee protection also in terms of the operations of the bureaucracy. As Christopher Anderson (2010) and Sule Tomkinson (2018) also show, a close examination of the institutional contexts in which refugee law and policy are developed and implemented is critical to understanding the, at times, perplexing outcomes of migration control regimes.

I suggest that examining migration control regimes at the material (rather than discursive) and meso- (rather than macro-) level of the bureaucracy (rather than the law) elucidates some of the nuances of migration exclusion, such as the positioning of some racialized subjects as rightful and others as rightless. How is it that in the early 1990s, for instance, Somalian refugees were accepted at extremely high rates in Canada, while Jamaicans were nearly completely rejected (see Chapter 2)? A close view of the bureaucratic operation may reveal that racialized exclusion is less a function of perfect mappings of absolute categories of race and more a method of furthering administrative interest in restricting the access of target groups whose intended exclusion is, nonetheless, partially informed by their racialization (see Masoumi 2020). In short, the bureaucracy is as influential as the law in materializing (racialized) failures in protection.

In conceptualizing the relationship between law and migration-control bureaucracies, critical scholars have, in broad strokes, taken two approaches. The first approach, largely influenced by Michel Foucault ([1965] 1988, [1976] 1990, [1975] 1995, [1978–79] 2008), has considered bureaucracies active and cooperative partners with law in regulating migrant and refugee movements. This scholarship has explored, to cite only a few examples, how migration-regulation bureaucracies produce subjects (Soguk 1999; Murray 2011; Park 2015), occasions (Razack 1998; Rajaram 2013), and technologies (Mongia 2018; Lee-An 2020) of regulation.[19] Thus, in this approach, bureaucracies work to operationalize, enable, and even expand the regulation envisioned, initiated, or aspired to by law. Law and bureaucracies, in short, seamlessly work toward the same goals.

The second approach, conversely, has placed bureaucracies in a relation of perpetual reaction to law. Most notably, although not exclusively, informed by Michael Lipsky's (1980) study of front-line public servants, scholars have presented bureaucratic work as a set of never-ending practical and moral dilemmas imperfectly resolved through, for instance, affective and personalized styles (Fuglerud 2004; Feldman 2008; Jubany 2011; Murray 2014; Tomkinson 2018) or institutionalized methods (Kim 2011; Cabot 2014; Saltsman 2014; Mukhtar et al. 2016) in everyday or exceptional circumstances (Mountz 2010; Satzewich 2015). In outlining the troubled and troubling work of bureaucrats in applying legal ambiguities to actual cases, this approach has presented bureaucracies as active and innovative, yet strained by the need to appease the law. In sum, the existing scholarship considers bureaucracies either as active partners with the law or in frustrated subjugation to it.

This book takes a third approach to the study of law and bureaucracies, one that regards bureaucracies not in cooperation with, or in reaction to, the law but, rather, in a position of relative autonomy from it. My conceptualization of bureaucratic autonomy is aided by scholarship on the implementation of employment and civil rights law (Dobbin et al. 1988, 1993; Edelman 1990, 1992; Edelman, Abraham, and Erlanger 1992; Edelman, Erlanger, and Lande 1993; Sutton et al. 1994), organizational theory (Meyer and Rowan 1977; DiMaggio and Powell 1983; Friedland and Alford 1991; W. Scott 1991; Greenwood et al. 2010, 2011), and institutional change (Streeck and Thelen 2005; Mahoney and Thelen 2010). These bodies of scholarships emphasize, respectively, the agentic role of bureaucracies in undermining progressive legal change, organizations' internally competing and contradictory logics, and the capability of institutions to produce substantive outcomes through subtle and gradual change. In doing so, they afford the bureaucracy a degree of complex agency that in my view, is largely neglected in critical studies of state-controlled migration regulation.[20]

Considering the bureaucracy in a position of relative autonomy, of course, does not mean that bureaucracies have, in any way, absolute autonomy in the conduct of their operations. Bureaucracies are, after all, deeply entangled in tight webs of relations with legal and political regimes and, thus, cannot move freely without disturbing these networks or inciting reactions. Moreover, this is not to suggest that bureaucracies always and necessarily resist the law. To the contrary, this book offers multiple examples of bureaucratic cooperation, reaction, and subordination. To cite one example, in Chapter 6, I document the wilful cooperation of the Canadian refugee claim-processing bureaucracy in implementing the designated countries of origin policy as well as its disenchanted reaction to the imposition of short adjudication timelines by the *Protecting Canada's Immigration System Act*.[21] As these examples suggest, the bureaucracy remains vulnerable to the power of more forceful agents, and, consequently, cooperation and reaction are among its common features.

Nonetheless, bureaucracies do far more than simply cooperate with, or react to, the law. As Max Weber ([1922] 1978) argued close to a century ago, bureaucracies are not neutral devices but, rather, structures with specific ingrained tendencies. For Weber, the bureaucracy is rigidly regulated by, and faithfully reproduces, modern rationality, even at the risk of generating meaningless irrationality. Therefore, irrespective of its situational mandate, the bureaucracy is internally structured to prioritize rational conduct and administrative control. This attachment to rationality, as George Ritzer ([1993] 2013) has argued, permeates and orients much of contemporary life, including, in this case, the moral and humanitarian work of refugee protection. While inland refugee protection, in Canada, is conducted by an administrative tribunal and not a state bureaucracy, the work of refugee-claim processing is governed by principles, such as regulation-bound decision-making, formalized and specialized conduct, and hierarchical organization that according to Weber, define bureaucratic structure. In this sense, therefore, the operations of the Canadian regime can be categorized as bureaucratic, even if they are not conducted, strictly speaking, by a bureaucracy.

A Weberian view of the bureaucratic structure suggests that bureaucracies have, at least to some extent, a mind and logic of their own. The structural distinction of the bureaucracy, I propose, warrants understanding it as a field in its own right: a structured and relatively autonomous domain that according to Pierre Bourdieu (1993a, 1993b, 1996; Hilgers and Mangez 2015), features distinct internal rules, logics, actors, forms of capital, and hierarchies. Thus, while interdependent with, and connected to, the law, the bureaucracy is at once somewhat separate and independent from it.[22] Hence, the bureaucracy works most loyally not in servitude to the law but, rather, toward its own goals and interests.[23] The distinct interests of the bureaucracy, furthermore, put the bureaucratic agenda in dynamic convergence and divergence with those of other forces: bureaucracies full-heartedly cooperate with the law when it is in their self-interest, desperately react to it when they are overpowered, or manipulate and resist it when possible and preferable. In short, the bureaucracy dynamically plays the game of immigration control, making strategic alignments with and against the law where necessary. Somewhat expectedly, thus, conflicts of agendas, logics, and interests regularly erupt in state-controlled refugee protection.

Although bureaucratic autonomy is a source of conflict and paradox in Canadian refugee protection, it is also the reason for its stability. It is, in part, due to the distinction and relative autonomy of the bureaucracy from the law that the Canadian regime may pursue contradictory agendas concurrently without losing its stability: the paradoxical urges of the Canadian regime are, conveniently so, conceived, pursued, and materialized in distinct fields and by relatively autonomous sets of institutions, actors, and logics. Indeed, bureaucratic autonomy should be considered for its contribution to sustaining regimes of governance far beyond the relatively small realm of refugee protection. As Katerina Rozakou (2017) has argued, statecraft relies on bureaucratic irregularity and malfunction; bureaucracies are not meant to fully cooperate with, or capably administer, the law. In other words, the bureaucratic capacity to undermine the law is not an accidental hurdle in the way of an otherwise functionally expansive system of governance but, rather, a key component in how equality-inducing laws perpetually fail to work.

Context, Methodologies, and Terminologies

The paradoxes of state-controlled refugee protection are difficult to miss in Canada. Although only a very minor recipient of the world's refugees, Canada revels in international praise: the only country to have ever received the prestigious Nansen medal for its commitment to refugee protection (CCR 2009), Canada is applauded globally on account of its independent and non-adversarial system of refugee status determination and for having inaugurated the formal recognition of gender-based persecution (Hamlin 2014). On the SOGIE front, Canadian refugee protection remains progressively inclusive, having both featured comparatively strong rates of SOGIE acceptance (Swink 2005) and advanced well-respected policies on the adjudication of these claims. For these reasons, Canada is often taken as a bright example of refugee protection.

Yet, like much of the global North, Canada has also modelled aggressive anti-refugee restrictionism. Canada, for example, pioneered restrictive border control strategies such as penalizing airlines for carrying unauthorized passengers and stopping travellers at airports abroad (Mountz 2010; Hamlin 2014; Satzewich 2015). In the case of unauthorized boat arrivals, Canadian authorities have intercepted travellers in ad hoc zones of legal exception in order to preclude their access to the fuller range of rights that stepping on Canadian soil normally confers (Mountz 2010). Furthermore, the Canadian state operates multiple immigration holding centres and detains thousands of foreign nationals, including prospective and failed refugee claimants, each year.[24] On several occasions, the Canadian government has even run overseas campaigns to dissuade specific groups from travelling to, and making refugee claims in, Canada.[25]

In addition, over the past three decades, acceptance rates of inland refugee claims have dropped notably in Canada. Consider Figure 1, which presents the acceptance rates of inland refugee claims adjudicated by Canada's quasi-judicial, non-adversarial, and politically independent tribunal, the Immigration and Refugee Board of Canada (IRB). Since 1989, the IRB has adjudicated refugee claims made inside Canada using the same legal definitions and standards of administrative justice and procedural fairness. Yet not only have the yearly acceptance rates diverged widely across time (for example, nearly 70 percent in 1989 and only 29 percent in 2009), but, up until the legislative overhaul in 2012[26] and the election of the Liberal Party in 2015,[27] the rates were declining considerably, as the statistical trend line in Figure 2 demonstrates.[28] This trend means that notwithstanding a few periods, claimants' chances of receiving positive refugee decisions in Canada generally declined since the IRB was established. Most surprisingly, acceptance rates dropped despite the recognition of additional forms of persecution in this period –

Figure 1 Refugee Claims Accepted by the IRB, 1989–2021

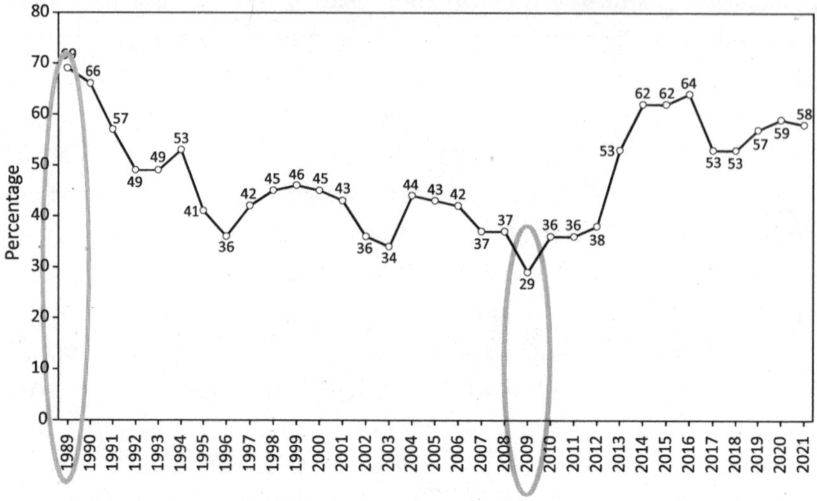

Note: This figure was created by the author based on data acquired from the IRB through ATIP requests. The acceptance rates were calculated based on the number of claims accepted each year divided by the total number of claims referred, including those withdrawn and abandoned. The numbers were rounded to the closest whole number for ease of presentation.

for example, although persecution based on gender, gender identity, and sexual orientation began to be widely acknowledged in Canada in the early 1990s, refugee acceptance rates went through a general decline between 1993 and 2012. In effect, while the number of legitimate grounds for refugee protection increased, the overall likelihood of receiving protection decreased. Curiously, thus, despite the gains in refugee rights since 1989, it has become both harder to access Canada's inland refugee protection regime and to receive protection from it.

This book presents a genealogical view of the inner workings of the Canadian regime of refugee protection to understand these perplexing developments and to trace their evolving formulations. Originating from the works of Friedrich Nietzsche and Michel Foucault, genealogy refers to a "historical-philosophical account of how reality comes into being" (Vucetic 2011, 1295). Put differently, genealogical research explores, to borrow from William Walters (2012, 12), "the conditions of possibility" of its subject of investigation. As such, genealogical studies

Figure 2 Trend Line of Refugee Claims Accepted by the IRB, 1989–2012

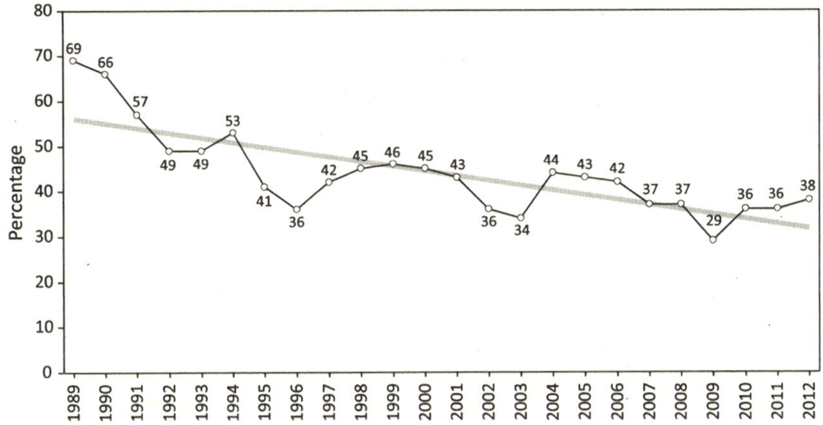

Note: This figure was created by the author based on data acquired from the IRB through ATIP requests. The acceptance rates were calculated based on the number of claims accepted each year divided by the total number of claims referred, including those withdrawn and abandoned. The numbers were rounded to the closest whole number for ease of presentation.

work to denaturalize social and political reality and expose the contingency of existing systems of truth and power (Tatum 2018). The account in this book, similarly, aims to historicize the existing regime of refugee protection in Canada and, by consequence, question its largely unquestioned form and existence.

This book is based on over twenty months of primary research involving textual, interview, and observational material. Much of the data on the earlier years of the Canadian regime was derived from published and commissioned reviews of the Canadian refugee status determination system, annual reports of the IRB, media and newspaper articles, and archival documents. Published studies and annual reports are available in print or online. Newspaper articles were located through the Factiva search engine using keywords and relevant time frames. Archival documents were acquired through access to information and privacy (ATIP) requests to Library and Archives Canada. Where necessary, I also acquired unpublished statistical information through requests to the IRB's ATIP division. I used this data to complement the official accounts that were featured in the IRB's annual reports, both in early and recent years.

Despite my best attempts at exhaustive empirical research, the methodological limitations of this study, particularly on the earlier years of Canadian refugee protection, are noteworthy. Most of the archival documents consulted for this study are protected government files and cannot be freely reviewed by researchers or archivists before being vetted by ATIP specialists. In the absence of the possibility of open review, I selected the files based on their indexes. Unfortunately, many of the indexes were vague and poorly maintained. As a result, admittedly, the choice of files frequently devolved to pure guesswork. Moreover, given the enormous volume of archived documents on the Canadian regime, I was only allowed access to a fraction of the files. Thus, I have certainly not seen all the relevant documents on the topics I explore. Nonetheless, through multiple requests, I acquired over forty-five hundred pages of documents. Some of these were heavily redacted, and a large portion was not of use for this project.

To complement the textual material, I conducted seventeen interviews with refugee lawyers, former IRB adjudicators, community support workers, advocates, and language interpreters between July 2016 and January 2017. Many of these participants had multiple intersecting roles within the Canadian regime – for instance, some lawyers had also served as former adjudicators, and many were heavily involved in refugee advocacy. Since IRB adjudicators are not permitted to speak about their work to researchers or the media, I only interviewed former adjudicators. All of those who chose to participate in this study held progressive views on refugee protection and were eager to share their first-hand experiences. Interviews provided valuable insights into the operations of the inland refugee protection regime, both as a workplace and as an administrative body.

I also attempted, over several months of eager contact, to secure interviews with IRB officials and employees, with the hopes of gleaning insight into the work of refugee claim processing beyond the focus on hearing rooms and adjudications. These efforts, as I detail in the concluding chapter of this book, were widely unsuccessful; as also observed by Sule Tomkinson (2015a, 2015b), gaining research access to democratic states is, rather ironically, extremely difficult. The IRB workers and officials I contacted either refused interview requests out of fear, I imagine, of repercussions for their careers or only provided exorbitantly superficial and formalistic responses. The data derived from my two "interviews" with IRB authorities, both of which were conducted in written format as per the interviewees' request, are provided in full in the two appendices of this book: Appendix A: Information Received from the IRB Communications Office in Ottawa and Appendix B: Written Interview with an IRB Manager. These appendices provide the content of the interviews exactly as they were received, minus small modifications to conceal the identity of one interviewee. While these interviews produced little meaningful data beyond the material already available publicly on the IRB's website, my communications with the IRB bureaucrats were, nevertheless, immensely generative for my analysis of the paradoxes of bureaucratic refugee protection. These will be discussed more fully in the conclusion of this book.

In addition to research interviews, I attended two orientation sessions held by the IRB and several consultation sessions organized by the Canadian Council for Refugees (CCR) in 2016 and 2017. The IRB's orientation sessions, which are designed to familiarize prospective claimants with the refugee status determination process and are held in actual hearing rooms, provided a grounded understanding of the process of claim making in Canada. These sessions were also unique opportunities to observe the interactions between IRB officials and prospective claimants and their advocates. The CCR's consultation sessions offered intensive education on the recent and ongoing struggles in Canadian refugee protection. Some of these sessions included presentations and speeches by ministers, Canada Border Services Agency authorities, and IRB officials, allowing first-hand observation of the relationships between state officials and the public, refugee advocates, and officials from other departments and offices. Informal conversations with long-standing refugee advocates at consultation sessions proved invaluable in pointing me to key moments in the development of the existing regime. ATIP statistics, interviews, and observations formed much of my analysis of the recent years of Canadian refugee protection.

The methodological choices in this study were informed by a sociological commitment to denaturalizing the seemingly ordinary and benign bureaucratic procedures that make up refugee protection administration in Canada. Throughout this book, I use the empirical data to place the operations and procedures of the Canadian regime in specific material, historical, political, and organizational contexts. The multiplicity of sources of data in this project required a dynamic and eclectic approach to data analysis. I studied various sources against one another to produce a fuller account of the paradoxical developments of the Canadian regime. For instance, I often complemented the limited and carefully crafted official accounts of annual reports with the much more revealing data in the media and archival documents. In studying the media, I was minimally concerned with representational analysis (Hall 1997, 2001); rather, I used the media content to track the trajectories of the IRB's many public relations crises over time. Reading the official accounts of the Canadian regime through the more candid lens of archived documents, media reports, and interviews revealed much about the unspoken goals and priorities of refugee protection at various historical moments.

In this book, I call the object of my analysis the "Canadian regime of refugee protection" to delineate the composition of the entities that administer refugee protection in Canada. The empirical process of this study made it indisputably clear to me that the entity that one might offhandedly call "the state" in theoretical talk is, in fact, far from monolithic. As bodies that are designed to accumulate and administer control, states are inevitable sites of tense power struggles. They are, further, made up of several departments that are often implicitly arranged in complex hierarchies; run by different managerial styles; and have distinct cultures, mandates, and structures. Consequently, departments with overlapping zones of operation are likely to develop involved histories of competition over jurisdictional authority and resources. Moreover, given that most state departments rely on others in their day-to-day operations, interdepartmental politics are constantly formed and reworked. Conflict is an everyday reality within states. States are, in short, far from simple and simply unified.

In delineating my subject of study, I have intentionally avoided the commonly used term "system" because of its monolithic connotations. I have also decided against using the terms "apparatus" and "assemblage" despite their productive and nuanced use in the scholarship. These terms have been aptly invoked to complicate conceptualizations of states as self-contained and insular, highlighting instead the reality that state operations are commonly accomplished by and through bodies that may be classified as non-governmental (Goldring and Landolt 2013; Cabot 2014; Murray 2016). While I, too, consider states to be deeply enmeshed with civil and non-governmental society, this study is primarily concerned with the practices, procedures, and strategies of state departments that administer refugee protection in Canada. Of course, this does not mean that these practices, procedures, and strategies are ever carried out without reliance on, or interventions from, non-governmental bodies. To the contrary, at many points, I point to the ways in which non-governmental actors, such as advocacy groups and lawyers, have shaped refugee protection administration in Canada. The primary focus of this study, nevertheless, remains on the operations of Canadian state departments. For this reason, I use the term "regime" to delineate a narrower field of analysis than "apparatus" and "assemblage" signify. Unlike the much broader and (deliberately) undefined connotations of the latter terms, "regime" directly cites the governing state as its subject. In its literal meaning, "regime" is defined by the *Canadian Oxford Dictionary* as "a method of government or domination of a country or state." Hence, it cites the systematic, formalized, and centralized constellation of forces that this book examines.

In the context of this study, the Canadian regime of refugee protection is understood to primarily consist of three bodies: the IRB, Immigration, Refugees and Citizenship Canada (IRCC),[29] and the Canada Border Services Agency (CBSA). These three entities are distinct in their structure, size, resources, mandate, jurisdiction, relative authority, and organizational culture. For example, as the department that is charged with border control and security, the CBSA has a highly stern culture, can operate in great obscurity, and holds great sway over when and how claimants are cleared to enter refugee adjudication proceedings. The IRB, in contrast, is a quasi-judicial tribunal tasked with a humanitarian mandate that requires projecting a much more genial and tender image. Internally, however, the IRB has cultivated an extremely reserved and cautious culture that reflects its sense of vulnerability following years of intense public scrutiny. While smaller than the other two departments that make up the Canadian regime, the IRB is not without its own exclusive organizational advantages: since the board holds the ultimate and exclusive authority over refugee decisions, the IRB adjudicators can out-rule any political will, including that of the immigration minister, in refugee adjudications. Despite this advantage, the IRB can be controlled by the minister and the IRCC indirectly through legislation and budgetary pressures. Thus, all three bodies have unique jurisdictional powers that place them in complex relations of authority with one another and shape their organizational cultures, aspirations, and struggles. Given its centrality to the processing of inland refugee claims, the IRB features most prominently in this book.

Two notes on the political positioning and analytical aspirations of this book are in order. First, although this book is inspired and concerned by the injustices of Canadian refugee protection, it is not a contemplation of how Canada, or any other state for that matter, may administer refugee protection well or more justly. As many would argue, Canada offers one of the better regimes of refugee protection in the world, but perhaps there is not much competition to beat; to cite a prominent refugee law scholar, "Canada is the best player on a bad team" (Oziewicz 1993, A13). Thus, instead of intending to tweak Canada's performance, my hope is to show that the game itself is one of perpetual injustice: even the seemingly humanitarian factions of state-controlled migration regimes systematically and inevitably qualify universal equality. The aim here, therefore, is not to fix the existing regimes of state-controlled refugee protection but, rather, to reconsider the primacy of state control over migration regulation altogether.

Second, and lastly, while this study examines the specificities of the Canadian regime of refugee protection in great detail, it is my goal to present Canada also beyond its local or geopolitical distinctiveness. For while this study is about Canadian refugee protection, it is also, and much more broadly, about the struggles and strategies of public administration in an age of economic restructuring, the ongoing paradoxes of liberal humanitarianism, and the relationship between law, bureaucracies, and justice. There are no easy conclusions to offer: it is not that the Canadian regime is dysfunctional or unjust, although it can be reasonably described as both. Neither is it that the failures of Canadian protection are due to a wanting of competence, vision, or political commitment. Rather, Canada administers refugee protection in the ways that it does because it is part of a larger global arrangement that intends to restrict access to the rich and richly rightful world of liberal democratic states. The paradox of refugee protection in Canada, in other words, is not just about Canada but also about the larger problem with the promises and failures of liberal universality.

Book Outline

This book provides a chronological account of systematic refugee protection in Canada in three parts. Part 1 considers the genesis and early years of systematic refugee protection in Canada (1946–92). Part 2 examines the Canadian regime as it matures beyond its early years (1993–2006). Part 3 is a critical examination of more recent times in Canadian refugee protection (2007–17). Each part consists of two chapters, dedicated respectively to exploring the developments in the fields of law and bureaucracy. The first chapter of each part examines the legal, legislative, and jurisprudential changes in refugee rights in Canada. The subsequent chapter explores the bureaucratic developments in the same time frame. Together, the two chapters present the articulated arrangements of Canadian refugee protection in each period: notable expansions in law for some subjects and systematic restrictions by the bureaucracy against others.

Chapter 1 provides a contextualized account of the genesis of the contemporary regime of refugee protection in Canada. Examining, in particular, Canada's oscillating involvement in the creation and ratification of the *Refugee Convention*, I retrace the paradox of Canadian refugee protection to the conflictual agendas of the multitude of forces that sought to establish or resist refugee protection as a formalized state obligation. I show that systematic refugee protection was ultimately imposed by a sweep of unprecedented legislative and jurisprudential expansions against the reservations of bureaucratic authorities. The emerging regime, thus, was entrenched from the outset with tensions between a desire to expand refugee rights and to maintain unhampered state control over immigration.

Chapter 2 offers a view into the early years of the newly established IRB to understand how restrictionism was articulated in a regime founded on remarkable legal protections. As we will see, the bureaucratic realities of refugee claim processing necessitated exerting restrictive control on the number of those who entered the Canadian regime; indeed, had the IRB not actively deterred and rejected claims, it would have quickly collapsed under the volume of its caseload. The necessities of institutional survival, hence, primed the bureaucracy for restrictionism and countered the gains in legal expansions.

Chapter 3 explores the development of Canada's Guidelines on Women Refugee Claimants Fearing Gender-Related Persecution in the 1990s as a significant feminist intervention in refugee jurisprudence. Although these guidelines instituted a basis for extending refugee protection to previously unrecognized forms of (gender-based) violence, they did not, in practice, increase access to refugee protection in Canada. Canada's expanding policy on gender-based refugees was formulated in administrative terms that ensured its minimal impact: the expansionist drive of refugee jurisprudence, in other words, was articulated in and through the impulse for restrictionist control.

Chapter 4 contextualizes the struggles of bureaucratic refugee claim processing in the 1990s and early 2000s to understand the IRB's continuing interest and active role in limiting the number of individuals who could be recognized as refugees in Canada. Pressed by unrelenting and contradictory demands, the bureaucracy operationalized progressively involved strategies of restrictionism, at times in collaboration with other departments. These strategies were diverse, adaptive, and consequential: thousands of refugee claimants were cut out of access to refugee protection by the bureaucracy.

Chapter 5 takes the Canadian protection of gender and sexually nonconforming refugees as the focus of its investigation. I juxtapose the emerging expansions in SOGIE rights with the intensification of Canadian border and migration control in the 2000s to highlight the continuing paradoxes of state-controlled refugee protection. Situating Canada's strong record of SOGIE protection in the largely homo- and transphobic history of the Canadian state, this chapter further examines the rapid transformation of non-normative persons from subjects of criminalization to subjects of rights.

Chapter 6 explores and contextualizes the restrictionist operations of the Canadian regime in the era of growing SOGIE rights. In the late 2000s, austerity and political neglect made bureaucratic refugee claim processing exceptionally challenging. As a result, the IRB remained unequivocally invested in reducing the number of individuals who accessed Canadian refugee protection. This drive for restrictionism, moreover, led to complex patterns of SOGIE inclusion: despite the generally high rates of SOGIE acceptance, SOGIE claimants who belonged to national groups that were primed for exclusion rarely received refugee status in Canada. Hence, the efficacy of Canada's progressive SOGIE jurisprudence needs to be evaluated with a measure of intersectional skepticism.

The six chapters of this book sketch the paradoxical operations of the Canadian regime of refugee protection and map their systemic arrangements over the past three decades. Together, the chapters document the processes and mechanisms by which Canadian refugee protection has both expanded rights and restricted access to them. In the concluding chapter, I situate the Canadian paradox of refugee protection in the global regime of liberal states and their ironically ineffective refugee protections. Considering the astounding failures of liberal regimes to protect refugees, I offer speculations on the subject that is best protected by these regimes: the regime of state-controlled refugee protection itself.

Part 1

The Early Years, 1946–92

1 Forty Years of Beginnings
The Origins of Systematic Refugee Protection in Canada

There are several points of origin to Canada's history of systematic refugee protection. Despite, or perhaps because of, its tragic record of inhospitality to refugees during and before the Second World War,[1] Canada became heavily involved in the international efforts to develop universal standards for refugee protection through the 1951 *Convention Relating to the Status of Refugees (Refugee Convention)* in the late 1940s.[2] Yet Canadian political authorities refused to join the *Refugee Convention* for nearly two decades after it was opened for signing. Even after Canada signed the *Convention* in 1969, it took several years to harmonize domestic immigration laws with the international provisions of refugee protection, a task finally achieved by the 1976 *Immigration Act*.[3] Canada's first cohesive system of refugee protection was established over a decade later in 1989. In short, systematic refugee protection in Canada emerged over forty years of stacked beginnings.

This chapter traces the paradoxical articulation of Canadian refugee protection back to this staggered history. I place the genesis of the contemporary regime decades prior to its formal establishment to highlight the foundational paradoxes of state-controlled refugee protection. As I will show, the confused and confusing lags between Canadian enthusiasm for, and hesitation about, refugee protection were the result of involved histories of tension between several incommensurable agendas. These included a statist desire for political control, a humanitarian aspiration for universal rights, a judicial interest in administrative justice, and an administrative attachment to pragmatic feasibility. Far from a pre-determined historical outcome, the Canadian regime was the product of decades of conflictual struggle between these competing and relatively autonomous forces.

This chapter provides a genealogical account of the contemporary regime of refugee protection in Canada. The first section explores Canada's ambivalent relationship with universal refugee rights. I show that the ongoing paradoxes of Canadian refugee protection find their roots in Canada's convoluted relationship with the *Refugee Convention:* a co-creation of Canada that was, nonetheless, not formally adopted for nearly two decades. As this historical analysis demonstrates, the desire for unhampered immigration control disrupted years of international leadership in devising a universal framework for refugee rights. Canada's ambivalence toward the *Convention* in these early years encapsulated a much larger paradox: the irreconcilability of statist desires for exclusionary migration control with the universalist impulses for equality of rights and international cooperation.

The second section examines the developments that eventually led to the establishment of systematic refugee protection in Canada. I show that the exceptionally expansive legislative and jurisprudential environment of the late 1970s and the 1980s were instrumental to the creation of a cohesive regime of refugee protection. These legal developments provided unprecedented levels of protection for refugees. In this new era of refugee rights, the practices and preferences of bureaucratic authorities were drastically disjointed. Hence, Canada's regime of refugee protection came at the cost of enduring tensions between legal and bureaucratic forces. These tensions were even further exacerbated by the advent of economic logics of neoliberal governance. Thus, the Canadian regime emerged from structurally paradoxical demands that were to haunt it for decades to come.

Paradoxical Origins (1946–69): Canada and the Genesis of International Refugee Law

Days into the United Nations (UN) conference in Geneva where the *Refugee Convention* was first presented for signature in July 1951, Leslie G. Chance, the consular official and Canadian delegate, was obliged to perform a spectacular act of pivoting. Having led the drafting of the *Convention* the previous winter, Chance had arrived in Geneva with the understanding that he was soon to sign the instrument on behalf of his government, albeit subject to minor modifications.[4] Of course, he had not anticipated the quick turn of events that were to lead to a suspenseful week of uncomfortable diplomatic manoeuvrings, followed by an eventual retraction from the *Convention*. Chance's career never fully recovered from this acrobatic episode (Girard 2019). Canada's last-minute pivoting during the 1951 conference was particularly surprising because it followed years of active Canadian participation in developing global cooperation on matters of displacement and statelessness. In the immediate postwar years, Canada joined efforts to resettle displaced Europeans[5] and advocated for the establishment of an international refugee organization in the UN's Social and Economic Council.[6] When the International Refugee Organization (IRO), the precursor to the UN High Commissioner for Refugees (UNHCR), began its five-year mandate in 1946–47, Canada was an early and avid member.[7]

Of course, Canadian enthusiasm for global cooperation on refugee matters was neither uniform nor unconditional. In the late 1940s, Liberal Cabinet members periodically haggled over the amount of financial contribution asked of Canada for the upkeep of the IRO[8] and restated every desire to prevent an erosion of state control over who and how many migrants entered Canada as refugees.[9] These concerns, however, did not override the broader support for a formalized international initiative, particularly when such an initiative was unlikely to clash with Canadian foreign policy.[10] In these years, Canada freely advanced its own geopolitical interests through refugee protection and resettlement – for instance, by prioritizing the resettlement of "democratic anti-communist refugees."[11]

The closing years of the 1940s imposed an urgency on the international collaborations for refugee protection. While the temporary mandate of the IRO was scheduled to draw to a close by the end of 1951, the "refugee problem" was nowhere near a permanent resolution. With growing realization that statelessness and displacement had become persistent global problems, the UN was keen to establish a permanent framework that would ensure a universal minimum of rights for those outside of the bounds of a nation-state. In this spirit, the UN Social and Economic Council mandated an ad hoc, multinational committee to draft an instrument of refugee rights, a document that was to become the cornerstone of refugee law. Canada participated fully in this international collaboration, and its delegate, Consular Chance, was elected as the chair of the ad hoc committee. The committee met for five weeks in Lake Success, New York, in 1950 and produced a draft convention that was then presented for evaluation.[12] After eighteen months of study by the UN and its member states, the *Refugee Convention* was opened for final drafting and signature at the 1951 UN conference in Geneva. As expected, Canada was represented by Chance, who was soon instructed to abandon his previous position as an ardent supporter of the *Convention*.[13]

Canadian commitment to the *Refugee Convention* crumbled over the first week of the Geneva conference. In the weeks preceding the conference, Canada appeared to be on an uncomplicated path to acceding to the *Convention*. In their meeting on June 20th, Canadian cabinet ministers believed it largely "possible and desirable" for Canada to become a signatory, pending relatively minor reservations.[14] The following week, Cabinet continued to believe the *Convention* to involve no "points of substance that need cause concern" except for one.[15] Hence, the Canadian delegation was authorized to attend the conference in Geneva and contribute to the drafting of the final text of the *Convention*, while the minister of citizenship and immigration examined the instrument more closely. However, soon thereafter, the tone of deliberations changed dramatically. On June 29th, only three days after Canada's participation in the conference had been approved, the minister of immigration and citizenship announced to his Cabinet colleagues that "it would be inadvisable for Canada to accept [specific articles of the *Refugee Convention*] in their present form."[16] As a result of the minister's reservations, the decision to accede was postponed pending further investigation.

The Cabinet's hesitation in committing to the *Refugee Convention* was expressed in a telegram dispatched from Ottawa on June 30th to Consular Chance. Chance, who had just arrived in Geneva, was instructed to withhold any definitive indication on Canada's position until further notice.[17] Having received this disheartening instruction at the opening of the conference,[18] Chance tactfully resisted the expectation that he would, following his leadership in drafting the *Convention,* also chair the conference. While awaiting final instructions, Chance pleaded for approval, writing in a telegram on July 3, 1951, to the secretary of state for external affairs: "I hope, however, that you may shortly be able to tell me that the Cabinet will approve of the signing of the Convention." "Any turning back on our part now," Chance telegraphed, "might create very unhappy situation [sic]," particularly as Canada had been "regarded throughout as taking forward attitude, somewhat in contrast to that of the United States."[19] Chance further suggested that most other delegates had been authorized to sign the document. These pleas, however, were unsuccessful in turning the quickly rising tide of political opposition. By July 4th, the decision to refrain from signing the *Refugee Convention* was firmly made.[20] Canada was to drop the *Convention* as swiftly as it had joined its drafting. Chance was not even allowed to press for amendments that would potentially resolve concerns and make the *Convention* acceptable for Canada's accession.[21] As Chance later recounted in his report to the Privy Council, this put him in a position that was "a little embarassing."[22]

The Cabinet's decision to withdraw from the *Refugee Convention* was, in general terms, due to growing concern about the implications of the *Convention* for existing laws and practices in Canadian migration control. From the Cabinet's perspective, joining the *Convention* had always been contingent on the assumed possibility of doing so "without making any changes in Canadian law."[23] In effect, somewhat paradoxically, Cabinet was only prepared to commit to making no commitments: the *Convention* was acceptable so long as it made no demands on the status quo of refugee policy or practice. As the Geneva conference drew near, the Canadian Cabinet grappled with the implausibility of undertaking a consequence-free commitment to universal refugee rights. Suddenly, the *Convention* began to be regarded as far more than a simple statesman's agreement between party countries. In fact, cabinet ministers came to suspect that the *Convention* was likely to "give rise to misunderstanding" about the legal entitlements of refugees; as they noted, "there would almost certainly be a general feeling that [the *Convention*] *did confer individual rights* [to refugees] or, alternatively, that *legislation should be passed* giving parallel individual rights under domestic law."[24] Acceding to the *Refugee Convention* seemed out of course with a state unprepared to confer rights to refugees or change existing statutes and protocols. Ironically, the main goal of the *Convention* in establishing a minimum standard of universal rights for refugees was precisely why it could not be adopted: universal equality of rights was incongruent with the interests and priorities of the exclusivist state.

The general incommensurability of state interest and refugee rights was anchored in reservations about specific articles of the *Refugee Convention*. In particular, the stipulated prohibition against deportation to countries of persecution was a significant source of anxiety. In addition to constraining the state's hand in immigration matters, this prohibition complicated the geopolitical and ideological interests of the Canadian government in the Cold War era. If deportations and removals were prohibited, Canada could, in theory, become a haven for communists fleeing the United States; by signing the *Convention*, the Cabinet feared that "Canada would be undertaking an obligation not to expel a communist, for example, to a country which has declared the Communist party illegal or [where, like in the United States] ... communists have recently been sentenced to imprisonment." This level of protection for "communists or other persons who believe in the destruction of fundamental human rights and freedoms" was unfathomable to the political and ideological sensibilities of the Canadian state.[25] Universal refugee rights could not be adopted precisely because they were universal. The equality of rights was predicated, ultimately, on the condition of liberal political opinion and, arguably, subjecthood.

Canada was not alone in objecting to the protections proposed by the *Refugee Convention*. By 1951, the spirit of international conversations on refugee matters had shifted considerably from the immediate postwar years. In the increasingly security-concerned climate of the Cold War, states insisted on control over borders and migration and were unwilling to relinquish the authority to impose restrictions against foreigners at will. Concerns about security and border control were raised so widely at the Geneva conference that some advocates considered the international atmosphere "just not right" for the introduction of a universal instrument on refugee rights (Hoffman 1951, 3). Refugee rights, in short, were emerging at a bad time.

The first few days of the 1951 conference made the implausibility of achieving global consensus on refugee rights plainly evident: only twenty-four of the forty-one countries that had originally supported the idea had sent delegates (*Globe and Mail* 1951). To make matters worse, nearly every government found some aspect of the *Refugee Convention* objectionable. Yet the promise of universal refugee rights had been in the making for years, and the *Convention* could not be flatly rejected without risking moral reprimand. Thus, state parties manoeuvred the moralized politics of refugee protection in a general atmosphere of "obfuscation and dilatoriness" (*Ibid.*, 2). The extent and volume of negotiations was such that the conference had to be extended five additional days beyond the original schedule. At the end, twelve countries signed the *Refugee Convention* in Geneva.[26] Canada was not one of the twelve.

Canadian authorities continued to examine the repercussions of joining the *Convention* the following year and came close to signing the instrument while it remained open for signature at the UN headquarters until December 31, 1952.[27] By this time, the concerns that had originally prevented the adoption of the *Convention* were considered largely resolved, invalid, or inconsequential, particularly as it was correctly understood that delegatory signature, unlike formal ratification, did not impose immediate legal obligations on Canada.[28] Furthermore, it was considered possible to mitigate the few remaining issues via formal instruments of reservation.[29] Despite this possibility, immigration officials resisted adopting the *Convention* without a more thorough study of both the *Convention* itself[30] and the reservations made by other countries.[31] The unending processes of study and examination continually deferred the calls for accession.[32] The *Convention* eventually came into force in 1954 when Australia became the sixth country to deposit its instruments of ratification.[33] Canada was yet to become a party.

Canadian accession to the *Refugee Convention* remained an open topic that periodically resurfaced in political and administrative discussions throughout the 1950s and early 1960s.[34] Accession was often encouraged, if not actively pursued, by the Department of External Affairs (DEA), particularly following news of other countries' accessions.[35] Some delegates of the DEA, not unlike Consular Chance himself, were especially keen on brokering Canada's accession, particularly because, in their eyes, accession improved Canada's international standing.[36] For instance, the Canadian delegate to Geneva in 1957 wrote passionately to the DEA about the virtues of accession, concluding that "it would not cost us very much and would add to Canada's good name in the refugee field if Canada were to accede."[37] Despite these pressures, the Department of Immigration remained unapproving of any accord that could impose restrictions on migration control practices or legislation.[38] In fact, immigration officials repeatedly ignored or flatly refused the early attempts of the head (or the high commissioner) of the UNHCR to encourage Canadian accession. Following a meeting with the deputy minister of citizenship and immigration in 1953 in Ottawa, the high commissioner reported that he had been told that "there was not the slightest chance of Canada acceding to the Convention."[39] In effect, the Canadian state was of two conflicting minds on the question of accession: the fractions of the state concerned with Canada's international reputation in the realm of humanitarianism were firmly in favour of becoming a party, yet the portion of the state in charge of immigration control wished to retain as exclusive and unhampered authority as possible. These internally paradoxical interests kept accession in chronic suspense, propelled by unending arrays of studies and investigations.

Canada eventually signed the *Refugee Convention* in 1969, nearly two decades after the Geneva conference. The decision to accede was made without controversy in the Liberal Cabinet of the newly elected Prime Minister Pierre Elliott Trudeau.[40] By then, Trudeau had generated great public appetite for universalist human rights. In fact, at that time, the Canadian government was in the process of acceding to a whole host of international treaties, including the *Refugee Convention* (see *Globe and Mail* 1968, 6). The concurrence of growing interest in international humanitarianism and a unified political will at last eclipsed state-centric reservations.

Canada finally became a party to the *Convention* that it had actively worked to create. Nonetheless, signing the *Convention* did not put an end to the dissonances between international refugee rights and Canadian immigration control. Although by the late 1960s much of Canada's actual practices were in line with the provisions of international refugee law, the *Convention* still involved significant discords with existing legislation. Most notably, the *Refugee Convention* considered persecution based on race and political opinion as grounds for protection (Article I) and required state parties to apply protection provisions irrespective of race, religion, or country of origin (Article III). However, the 1952 *Immigration Act* (formally in force until 1978), allowed the exclusion of non-Euro-Americans as well as (communist) political dissidents from admission to Canada.[41] In other words, the *Convention* offered protection based on forms of racial and political exclusion that were endemic to the Canadian law itself.

The discord between the racially inclusive sentiments of international refugee law and the racist provisions of Canadian immigration legislation did not evade the notice of Canadian officials. In 1953, the director of immigration noted one such discord in an internal memorandum to the deputy minister of citizenship and migration; the director wrote that "refugee, defined in Article I A [of the *Refugee Convention*], could include some Asiatics; in such event the provisions of P. C. 2115 [the 1923 *Chinese Immigration Act*[42]] would be applicable and they may be deemed to conflict with the provisions of Article III [of the *Convention*]."[43] The director's assessments were, to be sure, somewhat erroneous: the *Chinese Immigration Act* had been repealed in 1947, six years prior to this correspondence and, hence, did not pose a problem to the implementation of the *Convention*. However, the director was correct to register a larger unease between refugee law and immigration legislation. While the 1962 and 1967 Orders in Council Immigration Regulations had notably reduced the weight of race in the selection of immigrants, the *Immigration Act* itself remained unequivocally racist (and anti-communist). Curiously, race had become a basis of refugee protection before it was removed as a category of immigration exclusion. Thus, from a purely legalistic standpoint, protecting refugees of non-European origins was somewhat oxymoronic. Canadian immigration law was yet to be brought in line with the universal equality of refugee rights.

Refugees Enter the Law (1970–89): The Irony of Neoliberal Refugee Protection

However painfully achieved, acceding to the 1951 *Refugee Convention* had little immediate effect on the state of refugee rights in Canada. Canada was still decades away from establishing a cohesive system to administer refugee protection. In fact, for much of the 1970s, the term "refugee" did not even exist in Canadian law. As a result, refugee rights were outlined solely in the text of the *Convention* and, hence, were largely unenforceable in the Canadian judicial system (Dirks 1984). In other words, refugee rights existed in theory (and as a matter of international stance), but they were largely inaccessible in practice (and in the context of the judicial system). In the absence of legally binding standards, refugee protection amounted to little more than the sum of the administrative practices that government officials could be convinced to implement. And these were minimal: there did not even exist a formal procedure for making refugee claims outside of an immigration inquiry. This meant that refugee claims could only be made as a last resort against deportation and removal after migrants had already found themselves in trouble with immigration law.

In the immediate years following accession, refugee claims were processed much in the same way as they had been before: on an ad hoc basis and through makeshift procedures that granted refugee status by way of Cabinet Orders in Council (Dirks 1984). Over the ensuing years, some improvements were made to the claim-processing proceedings. In 1973, refugee claim adjudications were formalized through the establishment of an interdepartmental advisory committee comprised of officials from the Department of Immigration (then called the Department of Manpower and Immigration) and the DEA (Plaut 1985). The committee reviewed refugee cases without any direct contact with the claimants and based solely on second-hand textual accounts prepared by senior immigration officers who interviewed applicants under oath. The committee's recommendations were then sent to the minister of immigration.[44] The minister held the ultimate authority over refugee decisions (Dirks 1984) and could deny refugee status based on security or related concerns (Plaut 1985). This procedure, of course, left refugee decisions open to the influence of political and foreign policy interests and lacked gravely in transparency, oversight, and consistency.[45]

To ameliorate these issues, multiple levels of review and oversight were added to the adjudication process over the years (Plaut 1985; Dirks 1995). While well-intentioned, these alterations made for increasingly convoluted proceedings. By the mid-1980s, the procedures had grown excessively inefficient and slow: it took from two to five years to process refugee claims. Lengthy processing times generated a large and growing backlog. The inefficiency and inadequacy of the ad hoc system reflected poorly on the Canadian state and its humanitarian agenda. Canadian refugee protection was in dire need of an overhaul.

The persisting problems of Canada's makeshift refugee status determination system was in large part due to the precarious status of refugees in Canadian law. Without the force of law, there was simply not enough urgency to tackle the complex task of refugee protection in a more systematic fashion. The need for legislative change was not lost on Canadian political authorities. Since the late 1960s, immigration ministers had flirted with the idea of defining the refugee category in immigration law and producing a cohesive protection policy (Goldblatt 1969). However, formalizing refugee protection through legislation was a contentious political endeavour (Hawkins 1988). Change required strong public support and even stronger political will. With growing public interest in humanitarianism and the appointment of Robert Andras as the minister of manpower and immigration in 1972, the scene was set for legislative change; Andras and his team of immigration authorities took to the task of revising and liberalizing Canadian immigration through the 1976 *Immigration Act* (Dirks 1984).[46]

The 1976 *Immigration Act* changed the legal landscape for refugees substantially. By defining the term "refugee" in Canadian law, the *Act* made refugees a relevant judicial category. Furthermore, the *Act* granted full legislative force to the provisions of the *Refugee Convention*, including stipulations of political and racial neutrality. While greatly influential, the 1976 *Act* was not alone in revolutionizing the state of refugee rights in Canada. Another decade of expansive legal and jurisprudential change was on its way to permanently reconfigure Canadian refugee protection.

In the 1980s, procedural fairness and administrative justice were gaining more weight than ever in Canadian jurisprudence and the judicial system. While the 1982 *Canadian Charter of Rights and Freedoms* established due process as a constitutional right for citizens (Hamlin 2014),[47] the Supreme Court of Canada decision in *Singh v Minister of Employment and Immigration* in 1985 extended *Charter* rights to all persons residing inside Canada, irrespective of their citizenship status.[48] Consequently, inland refugee claimants became entitled to standards of administrative justice that were on par with those of Canadian citizens. Procedural fairness, consistency, and transparency became legal requirements of refugee status determination. The ad hoc system, which sorely failed on these grounds, was effectively ruled out of line with the Canadian Constitution.

In addition to upholding standards of administrative justice, the *Singh* decision forced significant changes on the existing system of refugee status determination. Most importantly, the decision established in-person hearings as a necessary component for refugee status adjudications. Refugee decisions, the Supreme Court of Canada argued, could not be made with sufficient fairness without direct contact between claimants and adjudicators, particularly because documentary evidence is rarely enough to substantiate the merit of claims.[49] Thus, refugee adjudication proceedings were obliged to allow claimants to present their cases in hearings.

The *Singh* ruling found a disgruntled audience in state officials, who considered in-person hearings grossly impractical, inefficient, and cumbersome (Dirks 1995). Indeed, the judicial and bureaucratic forces diverged widely in their visions of refugee protection. While legal actors prioritized safeguarding principles of procedural justice, bureaucrats were preoccupied with considerations of administrative convenience and feasibility. The *Singh* decision delivered a determinative strike in this battle of priorities; perhaps anticipating the dismay of administrators, the decision concluded that "a balance of administrative convenience does not override the need to adhere to [principles of natural justice and procedural fairness]."[50] The law had ruled, and state bureaucrats had no choice but to comply.

Thanks to these successive legislative and jurisprudential changes, refugee claimants became unprecedentedly rightful subjects in Canada.

Forms of protection that were until then haphazardly administered as matters of discretional authority were now legal entitlements. The old system of refugee-claim processing had become virtually untenable. The legal expansions of the late 1970s and early 1980s had created a normative legal environment (Edelman 1990) that prioritized the quest for universal equality above and beyond administrative and statist interests. In this new environment, an independent and non-adversarial model of refugee status determination was endorsed and eventually accepted.[51] The new model brought an abrupt end to the largely unhampered reign of immigration officials over refugee admissions. As such, the new system was created at the cost of considerable loss of jurisdictional authority for the Department of Immigration (Hathaway 1993). By prioritizing refugee justice, the law had inadvertently sown the seeds of long-standing tensions between the agendas of refugee protection and immigration control.

The tensions between legal and bureaucratic forces unfolded in a context of rapid economic and political change. Although Canadian law was resolutely expanding refugee rights, the drive for inclusivity was not unfettered. The 1976 *Immigration Act* itself encapsulated the paradoxical impulses for universal equality and statist restrictionism. On the one hand, the *Act* made refugees a legal category and removed race as a criterion of immigration exclusion. On the other hand, it heavily imbricated economic calculations in immigration admissions. In the newly liberalized vision of Canadian immigration, racial logics were replaced by economic ones (Bauder 2008); skills, education, profession, language proficiency, and compatibility with the occupational needs of Canada became the criteria for immigration admission. Canada was no longer blatantly racist, but, arguably, no less exclusivist.

The increasing prominence of economic logics in Canadian immigration was not an isolated or exceptional phenomenon. Across the globe, governments of advanced industrial countries were overtaken by neoliberal economic-centred rationalities. With the full-blown rise of Thatcherism and Reaganism only a few years ahead, governments were reformulating how they operated and perceived their functions. The New Public Management was on its way to restructure the welfare state (Aucoin 1995; Ferlie 1996; Lane 2000; Connell, Fawcett, and

Meagher 2009). Fiscal responsibility, cost-revenue analysis, and lean management were emerging as buzzwords in public administration discourses. It was in this rapidly neoliberalizing context that the Immigration and Refugee Board of Canada (IRB) was set up to begin the work of systematic refugee protection on January 1, 1989.

It is perhaps a historical irony that the legislative and jurisprudential push for systematic refugee protection in Canada came at a time poorly suited to the task of unreserved humanitarianism. The law had established refugee protection as a humanitarian obligation, detached from economic and political considerations. Thus, unlike immigrants, refugees could not be admitted or rejected based on their professional and educational skills, their compatibility with the Canadian labour market, or their ability to become self-supporting residents without prolonged public support. Moreover, the cost and inconvenience of administering a well-conceived system of refugee protection was ruled insignificant compared to the weight of the ideal of universal equality. Yet this normative vision of refugee protection was at odds with the neoliberal logics that were rapidly restructuring government operations. A non-revenue generating, costly, and unpredictable operation for the good of non-taxpaying, non-voting non-citizens was not an easy fit with the demands of fiscal restraint. Indeed, refugee protection presented an opening outside of the economy-centred streams of neoliberal immigration. Hence, it created a delicate dilemma: to administer a strong corpus of refugee rights (as imposed by the law) and, simultaneously, to diminish the economic cost of protection (as required of and by the bureaucratic actors). Although the new regime was in large part the result of the overpowering force of the law in exercising expansions, state bureaucrats continued to exert considerable restrictive influence on Canadian refugee protection. The new regime was, from the outset, stretched between these contradictory forces and had no choice but to find articulations that allowed their mutual, if negotiated, fulfillment.

2 With Rights Came the Rightless

Bureaucracy and Restrictionism

On the eve of the 1976 *Immigration Act* passing into Canadian law, the Liberal immigration minister J.S.G. Cullen formulated the paradoxical arrangements that were to articulate the emerging regime of refugee protection.[1] After highlighting some unprecedented expansions in refugee protection, the minister emphasized that Canadian protection was not open to all. In particular, protection was not for those who fled economic hardship: "We cannot open our borders to all economic refugees, *such as citizens of third-world countries,* and we can't do anybody a favor if we bring people to Canada who will not be able to establish themselves" (*Globe and Mail* 1978, 8; emphasis added). Although remarkably expansive, Canadian refugee protection was not boundless. Indeed, the limits of Canadian protection were delineated by an exclusive focus on the civil and political sphere of citizen-state relations; hence, economic refugees, identified offhandedly by the minister's classed and racialized reference to "citizens of third-world countries," were excluded from the otherwise expanding realm of rights. This classed and racialized exclusion constituted systemic avenues for articulation of restrictionism in the Canadian regime of refugee protection.

This chapter provides a close account of the bureaucratic operations of Canada's first systematic regime of refugee protection in its earliest years to explore how restrictionism was operationalized despite, against, and through the legal expansions of the preceding years. Systematic refugee protection in Canada was born out of exceptional legislative and jurisprudential expansions in refugee rights. These expansions, nonetheless, were at odds with the emerging neoliberal logics of governance and the long-standing bureaucratic visions of protection. Thus, despite the exceptionally expansive legal environment that created the new regime, restrictionism remained a central impulse in Canadian refugee protection. In fact, restrictionism became a matter of structural necessity: the claim-processing bureaucracy actively and effectively limited the impact of legal expansions only to ensure its own survival. In other words, restrictionism was articulated in and through the bureaucracy.

Shortly after its establishment in 1989, the IRB faced major administrative challenges in its handling of large and growing volumes of caseloads. These challenges primed the claim processing bureaucracy to pursue systemic deterrence and rejections. In these early years, the new regime's chances of survival relied heavily on administering restrictive control over who and how many claimants could access the inland refugee system. Thereby, despite the normative legal quest that had fuelled the new regime, the pragmatic requirements of claim processing articulated a clear impetus and need for restriction.

The need for systemic restrictionism, in turn, mobilized bureaucratic procedures and practices that aimed to curb access to Canadian refugee protection. The emerging administrative methods of mass deterrence and rejection were often formulated around claimants' nationality. These methods had devastating consequences for those who became their targets. Importantly, in administering these methods, the bureaucracy diverged from standards of refugee law, in particular undermining the supposedly "universal" right of the displaced to seek protection. The restrictionist bureaucracy, in short, acted of its own accord and in relative autonomy from the law.

The Battle of Numbers: The Bureaucracy and the Necessity of Restrictionism

During a seminar with the Canadian press in 1989, Gordon Fairweather, the chairperson of the newly formed Immigration and Refugee Board of Canada (IRB), offered a response to an anticipated question: "You are entitled, of course, and will be asking us what are the challenges [sic] in the next couple of years. They are just one word, *numbers*."[2] Fairweather's remark accurately summarized the most significant and chronic challenge of systematic refugee protection in Canada: processing the large number of claims that continuously inundated the claim-processing bureaucracy since the earliest days of its operation. The young IRB's battle with numbers was situated in a charged moral and political context. Given the growing humanitarian consciousness in Canada, the work of refugee protection was steeped in a heightened sense of morality. Operating a morally cogent system of refugee protection was critical to the legitimacy of the new regime. Therefore, the IRB officials laboured to establish and maintain a laudable record that advanced Canada's humanitarian reputation. For instance, the IRB regularly participated in shaping the refugee systems of other countries[3] and boasted of international praise from the United Nations High Commissioner for Refugees (UNHCR) and other states where possible (see IRB 1991, 11; 1992, 32; 1993, 34; 1994, 6–7). These moral contributions in part substantiated the value of the new bureaucracy.

Yet the IRB's institutional worth was not exclusively assessed on moral terms. Despite its highly moralized agenda, the IRB was, at its core, an administrative body. As a new and somewhat precariously placed state entity in the era of neoliberal restructuring and cutbacks, the young IRB had yet to earn its full standing as a member of the federal government of Canada.[4] The IRB's taxed relationship with the Department of Immigration only exacerbated these political pressures. To solidify its status, the IRB had to deliver a strong performance under the scrutiny of politicians and government officials who were yet to be convinced that the board was worth the resources devoted to it. In short, the IRB was expected to be both laudably humanitarian and administratively reasoned.

As the young IRB soon learned, handling the administrative realities of inland refugee claim processing was a daunting task. The work was challenging from the outset: on the day that the IRB began its work, it inherited a monumental backlog of eighty-five thousand cases from the previous system. Some of these cases had already been in the processing pipelines for several years (IRB 1990, 19). Unfortunately, clearing the backlogs was only one small part of the IRB's troubles. The much larger issue was the unpredictable and unrestrained flow of freshly made claims that entered the adjudication procedures.[5] It did not take long before the trouble with caseloads reached a crisis point. Before the end of its first year of operations, the IRB found itself confronted with an incoming stream of cases almost double the number it had the capacity to handle: while the IRB had been designed to process about fifteen hundred claims per month, the last three months of 1989 produced caseloads that averaged around three thousand claims per month (IRB 1990, 15). The young bureaucracy was wildly unprepared to manage this volume of input. The situation suddenly became grim: by the end of 1989, eight thousand new claims had not even entered the first stage of the then two-staged adjudication process. The second stage of adjudication was also completely overrun by pending cases. To make matters worse, and as the IRB officials had correctly forecasted, the high rates of incoming claims were to continue into the following year. The IRB was quickly losing ground in its battle with unfavourable odds.

The IRB's struggles with the unexpectedly high volume of incoming claims were cause for serious anxiety about the future of the board. These struggles betrayed the high hopes invested in the IRB's ability to end the chronic dysfunctionalities of Canadian refugee protection (Dirks 1995). Officials across the immigration regime watched the growing caseloads with fearful eyes. As the immigration deputy minister warned in an interdepartmental letter in January 1990, "total current volumes are such ... that, unless we make changes, the system could again be totally overloaded in about a year."[6] Like its predecessor, the IRB was at risk of collapse.

The IRB's administrators monitored the flow of incoming claims with anxious vigilance. They were keenly aware of the need to absorb the unexpected volume of work. Officials employed multiple strategies: they increased the number of hearing rooms in their busiest offices, enhanced hearing room booking practices, and explored expeditious methods of reviewing and adjudicating claims (IRB 1991). Much attention, analysis, and creativity were devoted to running the IRB against the threat of accumulating backlogs. Practically every stage of the claim adjudication process came under scrutiny and surveillance. Regular statistical reports closely monitored the flow of claims through all stages of the adjudication process; reports were issued weekly, monthly, and quarterly, allowing analysis of the IRB's performance, workload, and progress in short and long terms.[7]

To cope with the strain caused by the increased workloads, the IRB requested additional funds before the end of its first year of operation. In 1989, the IRB's $42,297,000 operating budget was increased by supplementary funds of $10,643,000 (IRB 1990, 25). The following year's $61,788,000 budget was supplemented by $18,112,000 (IRB 1991, 32). These supplementary funds were critical to increasing the IRB's adjudication output. The funds were used to hire new adjudicators and open a new office in Toronto (IRB 1992, 12). However, these funds did not increase the IRB's budget in proportion to the rise in the volume of claims. As a result, the IRB's operations had to be substantially modified to cope with the increase in caseloads. Naturally, the IRB officials turned their attention to increasing the productivity of adjudication procedures. Two procedures – the "expedited process" and the "simplified inquiry process" – were designed and implemented in 1989 to alleviate the work of claim processing. These procedures allowed positive decisions to be issued via informal meetings rather than through full two-person adjudications, enabling the IRB to conclude a larger number of cases more quickly and with fewer resources.[8] The two procedures were further developed and heavily utilized in the following years (IRB 1990, 15; 1991; 1992, 17–18).

Although improving productivity was integral to managing workloads, procedural efficiency alone was not enough to resolve the IRB's larger trouble with numbers. The volume of caseloads was simply too large to be sustainably handled by the new regime. Orderly bureaucratic conduct required exercising restrictive control over the number of claims that entered the Canadian system. Of course, the IRB had no way of controlling the global events that produced displacement. However, as state officials believed, Canada could be made less attractive as a destination for the displaced (see, for instance, IRB 1991). In other words, to protect the IRB against collapse, refugees needed to be deterred from making claims in Canada. As the strain from workloads grew, deterrence became a more pronounced objective in discussions of refugee claim processing.[9] Of course, the emphasis on deterrence was a far cry from the humanitarian mandate of the IRB. In the moralized logics of refugee protection, persecuted individuals could not be justifiably deterred from making claims in Canada. Deterrence required subjects who could be relegated to positions of excludability.

In this fraught context, the IRB began to promote a rigid dichotomy between "real" refugees (who deserved protection) and "fraudulent" claimants (who needed to be deterred). The narrow provisions of refugee law provided easy avenues for this polarization. The law's exclusive focus on the individualized realm of citizen-state relations meant that experiences of generalized violence, such as those of poverty and dispossession, could be dismissed as grounds for protection. Hence, those suspected or accused of making claims based on economic motivations, however desperate their circumstances, were considered legitimate targets of deterrence. Despite occasional acknowledgment of the connection between economic deprivation and displacement (IRB 1990, 12; 1993, 12), the IRB officials remained largely unsympathetic to economically deprived groups of claimants. Economic refugees, as Cullen had suggested, had no claim to the expanding regime of rights in Canada. In fact, rejecting these claimants was considered integral to minimizing the "abuse" of the Canadian system: swift rejection of these claims, Canadian officials believed, sent a clear message to those who were supposedly using the refugee protection system to buy themselves time in Canada.[10]

The growing emphasis on deterrence in Canadian refugee protection coalesced with and mobilized concerted interest in immigration restrictionism and border control. The IRB (1991, 11, 25; 1992, 23) even began to call for the stronger enforcement of removal and deportation provisions in regard to rejected refugee claimants; the lack of rigorous border enforcement, the IRB officials pleaded, undermined attempts to deter "fraudulent" claims. Deterrence could only be achieved through well-coordinated interdepartmental cooperation.[11] "Fraudulent" claimants needed to be rejected and quickly removed from Canada.

The growing interest in deterrence and restrictionism anchored emerging politics around refugee acceptance rates. The first year of the IRB's (1990, 15) work had produced an acceptance rate of 76 percent, which was considerably higher than the approximately 30 percent rate of the previous ad hoc system.[12] Officials across the immigration regime considered the new acceptance rates a "problem area" that needed management. In their eyes, high acceptance rates were a "pull factor" that attracted overwhelming numbers of claims to Canada.[13] Controlling the flow of incoming claims required dropping acceptance rates considerably. Canada had to become less attractive as a humanitarian destination for the displaced.

Under immense political and administrative pressure, the Canadian regime of refugee protection became increasingly restrictionist. The impact on acceptance rates was immediate and substantial. In 1990, the overall acceptance rates dropped to 70.3 percent (IRB 1991, 19).[14] The following two years saw steady declines to 64 percent and 57 percent respectively (IRB 1992, 21; 1993, 20). Acceptance rates at the full hearing stage of adjudications, which was under the exclusive authority of the IRB, also declined rapidly.[15] In the span of only six months, these rates dropped from 88 percent in 1989 to 75 percent in July 1990.[16] Evidently, the IRB adjudicators had begun to reject lager portions of claims even when they were not directly pressed by immigration officials; restrictionism was not simply imposed from above but also internalized and ingrained in the bureaucratic operations of refugee claim processing. The bureaucracy had become an independent force of restrictionism.

Whom to Reject: National Groupings and Systemic Deterrence

Restricting the flow of incoming claims required the administrative ability to identify those who could be rejected and deterred. Of course, from a strictly legal perspective, claims could only be rejected based on individual assessments of their merits within the parameters of refugee law. However, as the first year of the IRB's work had evidenced, independent and individual adjudications were not by themselves conducive to a strong program of restrictionism. Turning the tides of rising numbers called for more systematic methods that would ensure not only fast claim processing but also larger rates of rejection. Rejections had to be systematized.

To fulfill the need for systemic rejections, the IRB turned to classifying "fraudulent" claimants based on their countries of origin. National groupings proved a workable means to restrictionist ends; not only did a claimant's nationality offer an administratively convenient way of categorizing caseloads in large blocks, but national classifications could be made with some consideration for the provisions of refugee law. After all, the determination of refugee status routinely involved assessing conditions in countries of origin. These assessments, as the IRB administrators discovered, could facilitate wholesale rejection of claims from some of the countries that featured prominently in the IRB's statistics. For instance, an absence of well-documented political and civil crises in poor countries could be taken to invalidate claims of persecution. Of course, using country conditions as the method for determining refugee status was hardly consistent with the law. In fact, refugee law mandated that claims be evaluated based solely on individual merits and without regard to race, ethnicity, and nationality.[17] Yet country conditions could be framed as the (systemically disadvantaging) background for (supposedly individualized) adjudications. Hence, the IRB could reject large numbers of claims without blatantly violating the legal requirement of individual assessment; country conditions, in other words, offered the struggling bureaucracy a way to negotiate the stringent standards of the law with the administrative need for restrictionist control.

In the early years of its operation, the IRB relied heavily on country conditions to process caseloads. A UNHCR visiting consultant to the IRB's documentation centre in August 1989 reported concern over how IRB adjudicators were approaching and using documentation on country conditions. To the consultant's alarm, Canadian adjudicators were commonly treating country reports as clear and straightforward measures of credibility.[18] Instead of using these reports as the broad backdrop for examining the unique circumstances of each claim, adjudicators were looking to country documentation for directions on whether to decide for or against claimants. Consequently, acceptance rates were highly polarized: nearly all claimants from some countries were accepted as refugees, while claimants from other countries were rejected en masse. Refugee status was practically decided based on the country of origin rather than the content of claims.

The use of country conditions in refugee claim processing was intimately in sync with the administrative needs of the IRB: at any given time and across geographical jurisdictions, administrators focused their restrictionist efforts most intensely on countries that posed a risk to the orderly conduct of refugee claim processing. Thus, the first countries that became targets of systemic rejection were those that had long been considered threats to Canadian refugee protection. Chief among these were Jamaica, Trinidad, and Portugal.[19] Given that claimants from these countries were considered to have contributed to the collapse of the previous system, the IRB administrators were strongly inclined to reject and deter them. The work of refugee protection was to begin, somewhat ironically, with protecting the bureaucracy against refugees.

The early years of the IRB were dark times for refugee claimants from Jamaica and Trinidad. At the end of 1989, the IRB (1990, 15) reported an acceptance rate of 0 percent for both groups.[20] Notably, Jamaican and Trinidadian claimants were overwhelmingly rejected at the initial stage[21] of adjudications: in the first half of 1990, 0 percent of Trinidadian and only 17 percent of Jamaican claimants were even referred to a full hearing. In contrast, 95 percent of all claims were allowed to proceed to full adjudications.[22] Rejecting Jamaican and Trinidadian claimants at the initial stage made for quick and inexpensive case processing: claimants were removed from the adjudication process before they had a chance to present their cases fully. This left claimants with minimal recourse to legal protection and appeal. Thus, despite the expansive array of rights, Jamaican and Trinidadian claimants were kept away from the new regime and in a state of near rightlessness. Importantly, their rightlessness was achieved through the multilayered stages of the bureaucratic process. Not only had the IRB become a force of restrictionism, but restrictionism was also advanced in and through decidedly administrative means.

Remarkably, despite the moralized politics of refugee protection, the harsh treatment of Jamaican and Trinidadian claimants in refugee claim proceedings came at no cost to the legitimacy of the IRB. In fact, rejecting these claimants was not considered a contentious matter; Jamaicans and Trinidadians were widely disbelieved across the immigration regime. Indeed, in the initial stage of assessments, most Jamaican and Trinidadian claimants were rejected based on the credibility of their claims rather than their ineligibility to receive refugee status.[23] In 1990, out of the fifty-nine Jamaican claims concluded at the initial stage, only one was rejected based on ineligibility; conversely, forty-two eligible Jamaican claims were rejected for supposedly lacking a credible basis. Similarly, only three of the fifty-one concluded initial claims by Trinidadian claimants were found to be ineligible; thirty-seven eligible claimants were rejected due to credibility issues.[24] In other words, Jamaicans and Trinidadians were not necessarily ineligible for protection; rather, they were simply not believed to be "real" refugees.

To make matters worse, in the rare instances when a claimant from Jamaica or Trinidad received an initial positive assessment, the immigration minister was keen to intervene and challenge the decision.[25] While 95 percent of positive initial decisions from the so-called legitimate countries were conceded, ministerial representatives were steadfast in opposing positive outcomes for Trinidadians and Jamaicans: in 1990, no cases from Trinidad and only one positive initial decision from Jamaica was conceded by the minister.[26] In short, several actors across the multi-staged adjudication process worked to ensure Trinidadians and Jamaicans had nearly no chance of acquiring refugee status in Canada. The resolve to reject and deter these claimants was held in wide administrative consensus.

Because of the widespread disbelief of Trinidadian and Jamaican claimants, the claim-processing bureaucracy had much to gain from their wholesale rejection. Indeed, the plummeting chances of Jamaicans and Trinidadians in securing refugee status in Canada was endorsed as evidence of the IRB's administrative competence. A review of the adjudication procedures in July 1990 reported the low referral rates and concluded: "So, the initial hearing stage is continuing to perform its basic function of culling out claims from countries that are clearly not sources of convention refugees and ensuring that claimants from countries that are known to be in upheaval get sent on for a full hearing."[27] Similarly, in his letter to the clerk of the Privy Council and the secretary to the Cabinet in January 1990, the associated deputy minister of the Department of Immigration expressed approval of the IRB's work by directly equating the deterrence of "unfounded" claims with the IRB's success in diminishing the number of claims from countries such as Trinidad: "[The IRB] reduced significantly the number of manifestly unfounded claims; that is, we have reduced to a trickle individuals (such as Turks, Portuguese, Trinidadians, etc.) who are not refugees but who used to arrive in large numbers under the old system."[28] Jamaican and Trinidadian claimants were supposedly only poor migrants who had unduly overwhelmed the Canadian system for years. Thus, by rejecting them, the IRB showcased its capability in handling the work of refugee protection. Mass rejection of Jamaicans and Trinidadians only solidified the status of the board.

Of course, country conditions were not used solely against claims from Jamaica and Trinidad. National groupings provided an exceptionally adaptive method for systemic rejections. Organizing claim processing around claimants' nationality allowed administrators to produce and isolate target groups in accordance with situated institutional needs, including those of various regional offices. For instance, in the IRB's office in British Columbia, where a large proportion of claims came from China, Chinese claimants were rejected at considerably higher rates.[29] In 1990, full hearings of Chinese claims in Quebec produced 277 positive and 241 negative decisions, a relative acceptance rate of 53 percent.[30] The same hearings in British Columbia produced 81 positive and 167 negative decisions, a considerably lower relative rate of 33 percent. Nationally, 485 Chinese claimants received a positive decision at full hearings, while 600 claimants were declined, constituting a relative acceptance rate of 45 percent. In other words, Chinese claimants had a far smaller chance of receiving protection in British Columbia than in other jurisdictions. Needless to say, given that Chinese claims constituted over one-quarter of caseloads in British Columbia,[31] their high rejection rates were consequential to managing the workload of that office. The scale of these rejections was so large that it accounted for the disparities in acceptance rates across the IRB offices: while acceptance rates were 81 percent and 86 percent in Ontario and the Prairies, respectively, they were only 55 percent in British Columbia, thanks primarily to the low acceptance rates of Chinese claimants in this region.[32]

Furthermore, using claimants' nationality to manufacture excludable subjects allowed the IRB to dynamically produce target groups in response to changing patterns of incoming claims. The volume of claims that entered the IRB proceedings fluctuated based on international circumstances that produced displacement. Controlling this unpredictable caseload required timely and targeted responses to sudden changes in numbers. Thus, the IRB administrators monitored international developments as well as the numbers of incoming claims from various source countries. Although refugee law was precisely meant for the protection of displaced persecuted populations, an uncontrolled flow of the persecuted to Canada was not compatible with the administrative needs of the board. Hence, IRB officials had every incentive to prevent and contain unexpected hikes in the number of incoming cases, despite the *de jure* right of the displaced to seek refugee protection.

From the administrators' perspective, managing the fluctuating volume of workloads required, above all, restricting the access of claimants from regions and countries that sent large numbers of claims to Canada. In the early 1990s, the most concerning of these regions was Eastern Europe. Following the dissolution of the Soviet Union, the number of refugee claimants from Eastern European countries was on a steep rise. Although the IRB (1991, 13) positively characterized the fall of the Soviet Union as "democratization," it initially recognized the inevitable displacement produced by political and economic instability and ethnic and nationalist tensions. However, the sympathy for Eastern Europeans was quickly dampened by the arrival of large numbers of refugees in Gander, Newfoundland. The so-called Gander situation pushed the IRB's caseloads to unprecedented highs: the IRB received forty-two hundred claims in January, thirty-three hundred claims in February, and thirty-eight hundred claims in March 1990.[33] These numbers presented a major administrative crisis. Hence, Canadian officials urgently implemented a comprehensive array of strategies to contain and reduce the number of Eastern Europeans who could access the Canadian regime.[34]

The strategies implemented against Eastern Europeans were multifaceted and multi-departmental. First, Eastern Europeans, particularly those from Czechoslovakia and Poland, began to be rejected at higher rates at both stages of the adjudication process: referral rates of Polish claimants dropped from 83 percent in 1989 to 64 percent in the first half of 1990. The referral rates of Czechoslovakian claimants were reduced from 98 percent to 58 percent in the same period. At the full hearing stage, acceptance rates dropped even more sharply: Polish claimants were accepted at a rate of only 18 percent in the first half of 1990, compared to 73 percent in 1989. Czechoslovakians saw their rates drop from 75 percent to only 12 percent.[35]

Moreover, the Department of Immigration began to challenge the positive decisions of Eastern European claims regularly. While positive initial decisions on claims from countries such as Sri Lanka, Somalia, and Iran were almost never contested, in the first quarter of 1990, positive initial decisions of Czechoslovakian and Polish claimants were contested at rates of 41 percent and 64 percent respectively. Moreover, ministerial challenges against these claims were likely to reverse the positive initial decision: in the first quarter of 1990, 75 percent of contested claims from Czechoslovakia and half of the contested claims of Polish claimants overturned the positive initial decision.[36] With these concerted measures in place, Eastern Europeans' chances of receiving refugee protection in Canada dropped dramatically. As a result, large numbers of claimants, particularly those from Poland, withdrew or abandoned their claims. Additionally, the Department of Immigration imposed visa restrictions against Eastern Europeans to curb their access to the inland system. Visa restrictions proved highly effective in driving down the numbers. In a matter of months, the number of Eastern Europeans who entered the Canadian case-processing proceedings dropped considerably.[37] With these claimants successfully kept away from the Canadian regime, the IRB began to see noticeable drops in the number of its incoming cases by March 1991.[38] Bureaucratic control had been achieved at the cost of blocking the supposedly universal right of the displaced to protection.

In sum, despite the exceptional legal expansions that had produced the new regime, the first years of systematic refugee protection in Canada involved significant measures of restrictionism. These measures, which were often delivered through administrative means, actively curtailed the impact of legal expansions. Importantly, bureaucratic restrictionism was a matter of structural necessity; soon after the IRB began its work, managing the administrative realities of neoliberal state-controlled refugee protection was predicated on restricting access to the inland system. To achieve this goal, the claim-processing bureaucracy devised and advanced systemic methods of mass rejection, often by using national groupings. As a result, the work of refugee protection quickly devolved to an institutionalized battle against dynamically manufactured groups of "fraudulent" claimants. Although strategies of mass rejection were instrumental to guarding the struggling bureaucracy from collapse, they undermined the humanitarian principles of refugee law. In effect, the supposedly "universal" right of the displaced to seek refuge was undermined to ensure bureaucratic survival.

In the earliest years of its operation, the contemporary regime of refugee protection in Canada managed the conflictual demands of state-controlled refugee protection through articulated arrangements that allowed their simultaneous and negotiated advancement. While the law acted as a force of expansionism, the bureaucracy enforced restrictions. Further, legal expansions and bureaucratic restrictions were articulated around supposedly distinct categories of claimants. Hence, while convention refugees became rightful subjects, "economic migrants," who were often delineated by classed and racialized categories of nationalities, were placed outside of the expanding bounds of right. Thus, despite legal expansions, the bureaucracy operationalized restrictionism. The dynamic interplay between the fields of law and bureaucracy allowed the new regime to be, in principle, humanitarian, and yet administratively calculating. In short, the Canadian regime persisted in and through its paradoxes.

Part 2

The Middle Trenches, 1993–2006

A Nice Symbolic Gesture 3
The Making of the Gender Guidelines

> I remember the pride and hope I felt for our country when the Gender Guidelines were made public in 1993 … I thought Canada was at the cutting edge of social policy, that we were contributing to an important shift in the international refugee paradigm.
>
> – Greta Hofmann Nemsiroff, president of Sisterhood Is Global Institute (CCR 2003)

In March 1993, the Immigration and Refugee Board of Canada (IRB) issued its much-anticipated Guidelines on *Women Refugee Claimants Fearing Gender-related Persecution* (*Gender Guidelines*) and made Canada the first country in the world that formally recognized gender-based violence as a ground for refugee protection.[1] The IRB's *Gender Guidelines* pushed the boundaries of refugee jurisprudence to new and unprecedented limits; not only did the *Guidelines* make refugee law more relevant to women's experiences of gendered harm, but they also opened the door to recognizing other previously unacknowledged forms of violence, such as those experienced on accounts of sexual orientation and gender identity.[2] In short, the *Gender Guidelines* changed the course of refugee jurisprudence in significant and irreversible ways.

Yet jurisprudence is only one piece in the much larger machinery of state-controlled refugee protection. As we saw in Part 1, state-regulated refugee protection is not determined exclusively by the directions of legal forces, such as those of legislation and jurisprudence. Rather, ultimately, protection is the outcome of complex and dynamic interactions between legislative and jurisprudential developments and the bureaucratic and administrative strategies that mediate legal effects. As such, gender-based jurisprudential expansions are only one part of the story of Canadian refugee protection in the 1990s and early 2000s.

This chapter provides a contextualized account of the development of the *Gender Guidelines* in Canada to make two interrelated points. First, the desire to expand refugee protection to gender-based claims was internal to the Canadian régime and originated organically from the work of systematic refugee protection. In fact, the IRB's top administrators were among the strongest proponents of gender-based refugee protection since the earliest days of the board's operations. This interest in expanding refugee rights for women, nonetheless, coincided with an unmistakable rise of restrictionism in Canadian migration control: while refugee jurisprudence was stretched to account for gender-based violence, procedural regulations were tweaked via legislation to restrict access to the Canadian regime. In other words, humanitarian expansions emerged alongside statist restrictions.

Second, the IRB's *Gender Guidelines* were the negotiated outcome of considerable political mobilization in the face of strong political opposition. These pragmatic negotiations ultimately formulated Canada's gender-based refugee policy in a relatively modest administrative format that ensured its minimal practical efficacy. As a result, the hard-earned jurisprudential expansions remained largely inaccessible to the women who could stand to benefit from them. Unsurprisingly, thus, these expansions did not increase access to refugee protection in any substantial measure. In effect, the articulation of the conflictual interests of state-controlled refugee protection in the fields of jurisprudence (for expansions) and administration (for restrictions) enabled their simultaneous and negotiated fulfillment: refugee rights were expanded, yet access to them remained limited. The Canadian regime persisted despite and through its paradoxes.

Rights and Restrictions: The Restrictive Context of Gender Expansions

In the 1990s, the IRB issued the *Gender Guidelines* and broke ground in interpreting refugee law in exceptionally gender-sensitive and expansive ways. The *Guidelines* acknowledged formerly unrecognized forms of violence, such as sexual assault and domestic abuse, and, in doing so, redefined the bounds of refugee protection. The IRB's voluntary norm setting produced a ripple effect that set refugee jurisprudence on a path of global expansion; soon, other countries came under pressure to follow the Canadian model[3] and also recognize gender-based violence as a legitimate ground for refugee protection.

Notwithstanding its expansive effects, the IRB's *Gender Guidelines* emerged, somewhat ironically, within an increasingly restrictionist context. In fact, as Canadian refugee jurisprudence expanded to better accommodate gender-based refugees, Canada's border and migration control systems underwent significant transformations to reduce access to the inland refugee protection regime. In effect, the expansions introduced by the *Gender Guidelines* were enveloped in an otherwise restrictionist momentum. This momentum was, above all, spearheaded by Bill C-86.

Bill C-86, *An Act to Amend the Immigration Act and Other Acts in Consequence Thereof*, which came into effect in February 1993, significantly reconfigured the procedural roadmap to refugee protection.[4] For instance, Bill C-86 eliminated the initial stage of refugee status determinations. In the brief period of its existence, the initial stage was a joint operation by immigration officers and IRB (1990, 13) adjudicators to determine the eligibility and basic credibility of claims before they entered full hearings. Given that the vast majority of applicants were eligible[5] for refugee protection and that the initial stage only used a low-threshold test to determine basic credibility, acceptance rates at this stage were extremely high (see IRB 1990, 14; 1991, 18; 1992, 21). As a result, the initial stage was considered somewhat superfluous to the adjudication process. By eliminating the initial stage of adjudications, Bill C-86 separated the two functions of eligibility and credibility assessments and assigned them to different bodies: credibility assessments were placed under the exclusive jurisdiction of the IRB (1994, 9), and eligibility screenings were assigned to the Department of Immigration (see also Dench, n.d.). This allowed the department to amass greater unilateral control over the incoming flow of claims: claimants' ability to enter refugee status determination proceedings was now exclusively controlled by immigration officials.

Although the elimination of the initial stage eradicated the IRB's (1993, 11) control over eligibility screenings, IRB officials welcomed the change wholeheartedly. From these administrators' perspective, the elimination of the initial stage gave the IRB more flexibility in managing and optimizing the use of its resources: without the need to schedule and run multiple rounds of determinations, the IRB could now concentrate all of its adjudicators on finalizing claims. In effect, giving up control over who could enter the claim-processing proceedings was likely to amount to higher rates of output. Already stretched by unforgiving workloads, the IRB was keen to trade pockets of authority in exchange for improved productivity.

In addition to eliminating the initial stage of adjudications, Bill C-86 implemented a host of other restrictive measures in Canadian border and migration control. While widely protested by advocacy organizations, these measures were squarely in line with the emerging international developments in border control and security across the global North (Kelley and Trebilcock 1998). In the early 1990s, Western European and North American countries were adopting increasingly restrictive provisions that narrowed the access of displaced persons to asylum and international mobility. Canadian officials observed these trends and believed that failing to replicate similar provisions would lead to an influx of claims in Canada (IRB 1991, 14; 1993, 17). The world of migration control was bolting toward increased restrictionism, and Canada was to also join the race to the bottom of refugee protection.

Taking these geopolitical considerations to heart, Bill C-86 introduced unprecedented levels of securitization and control to the Canadian regime of refugee protection (Kelley and Trebilcock 1998).[6] In this new era, not only were refugee claimants fingerprinted and photographed as a matter of routine protocol, but they could also be searched by immigration officers if they were suspected of possessing undeclared identity documents and other evidence.[7] Any document discovered through these searches could be used against the claimants in refugee proceedings. Bill C-86 also instated harsher detention provisions (Kelley and Trebilcock 1998; Dench, n.d.). Moreover, the Bill facilitated the discretionary exclusion of prospective claimants from the inland refugee determination process. Under Bill C-86, immigration and medical officials had greater latitude in determining whether those wishing to enter Canada constituted a risk to public health and safety. As a result, potentially large numbers of migrants could now be refused entry to Canada at the whim of administrative officials. Similarly, the Bill extended criminal inadmissibility provisions, enabling Canadian immigration officials to deny entry on grounds of criminality. Importantly, migrants did not even need to have been convicted of a crime to be made inadmissible; officers' discretionary judgment about migrants' past and future criminality were sufficient to deny entry to Canada. Once rendered inadmissible, migrants had very limited opportunity for appeal. This made inadmissibility provisions an easy method for restricting access to the inland refugee system: those blocked from entering Canada were automatically blocked from making inland refugee claims.

Furthermore, Bill C-86 restricted the access of prospective claimants to Canadian refugee protection by reintroducing the safe third country provisions.[8] These provisions, which purportedly intended to stop the so-called practice of asylum shopping, denied claimants the choice of where they filed their claims. Refugees were now required to make their claims in the first "safe" country in which they arrived after fleeing the country of persecution. This meant that claimants had to travel directly to Canada without stopping in a safe third country on their route to qualify for Canadian protection. Needless to say, given Canada's geographical remoteness from the most turbulent regions of the world, the safe third country provisions cut access to refugee protection considerably: no travellers arriving by land and only those embarking on the most arduous sea journeys were now eligible for Canadian protection;[9] in effect, access to the Canadian regime became largely limited to those stepping off direct, continuous flights.[10] To make matters worse, the Department of Immigration was afforded the authority to determine which countries were "safe." As a result, immigration ministers and officials held great latitude in potentially blocking large numbers of prospective claimants by way of "safety" designations.[11]

Additionally, Bill C-86 hindered access to refugee status by raising the threshold of adjudication for some groups of claimants. Whereas, at the time, most refugee decisions required only one positive evaluation from a two-person adjudicating panel, Bill C-86 created three classes of claimants who could only be accepted by a unanimous positive assessment: claimants who were believed to have destroyed or disposed of their identity documents without valid reason; claimants who had visited the country of persecution after making a claim in Canada; and those from supposedly "safe" countries were subject to higher adjudicative standards. Importantly, none of these conditions legally disqualifies an asylum seeker from protection in and of itself.[12] In other words, Bill C-86 obstructed the access of claimants who were otherwise entitled to rights in refugee law.

Lastly, to make Canada less attractive as a refugee destination, Bill C-86 instituted punishing conditions for those who made refugee claims. Most notably, the Bill disallowed refugee claimants to receive work permits while they awaited the finalization of their cases. Withholding work permits had devastating consequences: without the right to work lawfully, claimants were forced into poverty, exploitative unauthorized employment, and reliance on social assistance. Eventually, the increased strain on provincial welfare systems forced the federal government to restart issuing work permits to claimants.[13] Notably, the legal right to work was regranted not to relieve claimants from the harsh conditions of forced poverty but, rather, to protect welfare systems from those who needed assistance.

It was in this increasingly restrictionist context that the IRB issued its *Gender Guidelines* to formally recognize gendered forms of persecution. While the larger immigration and border control apparatus was implementing an array of restrictionist measures, the IRB was looking to expand the reach of refugee protection to previously unacknowledged groups of claimants. Importantly, the desire for a gender-conscious refugee policy had emerged organically from systematic refugee protection in Canada. Since the earliest days of their work, IRB administrators had noticed women's distinct patterns of displacement and persecution and had taken steps to respond to these gendered needs (IRB 1991, 30; 1992, 32; 1993, 12, 32). These early internal conversations and policy developments laid the groundwork for the *Gender Guidelines,* which were issued by the second chairperson of the IRB, Nurjehan Mawani. Ever since taking office, Mawani had been fiercely committed to producing a formal instrument for recognizing gendered forms of persecution. Significantly, she was not the only IRB chairperson to vocally support this development. The first chairperson of the IRB, Gordon Fairweather, had also championed a gender-conscious refugee protection framework. Even after his retirement in 1992, Fairweather openly spoke in favour of recognizing gender as a ground for refugee protection (Broadbent 1992). Indeed, the first two chairpersons of the IRB were among the earliest and most outspoken advocates of gender-based protection, well before the policy had found any popular momentum. In other words, the impetus to expand protection for gender-based claims grew from within the Canadian regime of refugee protection itself; the work of systematic refugee protection had revealed the need for, and sparked an interest in, protecting women as a distinct category.

Despite this internal interest, recognizing gender-based claims was a complex legal undertaking. Given that gender is not enumerated as a ground for refugee protection in international or Canadian law,[14] recognizing gender-based persecution required some creative jurisprudential reasoning. The IRB's *Gender Guidelines* provided this basis: first, the *Guidelines* argued that gender may be reasonably understood as a form of membership in a "particular social group," a ground that already warranted protection under refugee law. Second, the *Gender Guidelines* proposed that the distinct forms of violence experienced by women amounted to persecution. These jurisprudential interventions made women a protected group within the existing provisions of the 1951 *Refugee Convention;* as a result, refugee protection became immediately applicable to women fleeing gender-based violence without the need to alter or amend the law.

Although instrumental in revisioning Canadian refugee protection, the IRB's *Gender Guidelines* are not law; as such, they are neither binding nor legally enforceable.[15] Nonetheless, the *Guidelines* are an important tool for improving the quality and consistency of decision-making for women refugee claimants. The *Gender Guidelines,* for instance, indicate the preferred position of the IRB's leadership on gender-based claims and provide guidance on how to interpret and assess gender-based persecution.[16] Further, the *Guidelines* incentivize recognition of gender-based claims: while decision makers are not obligated to follow the *Guidelines,* they are required to provide explanations if they choose to diverge from them.[17] Thus, the *Guidelines* provide a mechanism for unifying the decisions of hundreds of independent adjudicators across Canada and enhance the consistency, and, ultimately, the legitimacy of the IRB's humanitarian work.

Although integral to fair and meaningful refugee protection, the emerging gender-based expansions were not an uncontested state agenda. In the increasingly restrictionist context of the 1990s, recognizing gender-based claims required navigating an expansive proposal through the overwhelmingly restrictive webs of border and migration control. The Canadian regime of refugee protection once again needed to strike a difficult balance between its desire to expand refugee rights and its impetus to limit access to refugee protection.

Gender Guidelines: The Politics of "Doing Exactly Nothing"

Today, the IRB's *Gender Guidelines* are a well-established instrument and a key source of fame and pride for Canada. The secure and celebrated position of these *Guidelines,* however, obscures two important points about the history of their development. First, the *Gender Guidelines* were the result of a prolonged struggle against considerable political opposition. It was only because of sustained feminist and pro-refugee mobilization that the opposition to the *Guidelines* was eventually overcome; in fact, until only one month before the *Guidelines* were issued, the immigration minister continued to reject them as a viable option. Second, the *Guidelines* were only one method among a range of competing proposals for addressing the need for gender-based refugee protection. Other proposals, some of which were markedly further reaching, were ultimately cast aside in favour of the more modest contribution of the *Guidelines*. Indeed, the *Gender Guidelines* triumphed over other proposals in part because of the built-in concessions that made them palatable to political and administrative considerations. In short, the *Guidelines* were neither the necessary nor the most imaginably expansive format for Canada's gender-based refugee policy; rather, they were the outcome of dynamic forces that came to articulate Canadian gender-based refugee protection.

The interest in recognizing gender-based claims in Canada followed budding international conversations on the topic. As early as the mid-1980s, the United Nations High Commissioner for Refugees (UNHCR) had considered gender as a basis for refugee protection. In 1985, the UNHCR's member states, including Canada, adopted and endorsed a Conclusion on gender-based claims.[18] This instrument argued that although absent from the text of the *Refugee Convention*, gender can be interpreted as a ground for refugee status (Oziewicz 1993; Valpy 1993). Despite this endorsement, the member states did little to formally include gender-based claims in their national frameworks. Canada was not an exception in this regard.

While mostly sidestepped by member states, the expansive jurisprudence introduced in the UNHCR's Conclusion was not without impact. Following the Conclusion, gender-conscious interpretations of refugee law began to seep into some refugee decisions in Canada. For instance, a 1987 decision drew on the UNHCR's Conclusion, to grant refugee status to a Turkish woman survivor of sexual violence (Oziewicz 1993; Valpy 1993). Although significant in their own rights, these early instances of gender-based protection reflected, above all, the commitment of individual decision makers to gender-conscious refugee jurisprudence. These decisions, however, lacked any force in shaping refugee adjudications beyond the individual claims they assessed.

Systematic recognition of gender-based persecution eventually broke the heavy ice of ambivalence and resistance following a few high-profile cases. These cases brought the topic of gender-based protection to the public and made the issue a matter of mobilization and demand. Most famous among these instances was the case of a highly outspoken woman known as "Nada." Nada was a young Saudi Arabian woman who actively defied gender norms and socio-political sanctions against women in her country. A self-professed feminist, Nada particularly opposed compulsory veiling.[19] She also objected to gender-based discrimination in education and employment as well as restrictions on women's freedom of movement and travel (Broadbent 1992). Nada's refusal to comply with gender norms, particularly in wearing a full veil in public, had exposed her to street and police harassment and violence; she had been ridiculed, threatened, spat at, and beaten for appearing in public unveiled and without proper male company (Neuwirth 1992; Oziewicz 1993; Ulbrich 1993). Adamant in her feminist beliefs and fearing physical violence and arrest, Nada eventually fled to Canada in 1991 (*Hamilton Spectator* 1993b; Oziewicz 1993). To her surprise, when she explained her reasons for making a refugee claim, Canadian immigration officers laughed.

The trouble with Nada's case was that it did not readily fit with the dominant readings of the refugee definition. To decide her claim, adjudicators had to consider novel questions. For example, since Nada explicitly framed her claim as a case of persecution based on feminist beliefs, adjudicators had to decide whether feminism constituted a legitimate form of political opinion and, as such, whether it would warrant refugee protection. Moreover, adjudicators had to determine whether street harassment and gendered forms of regulation amounted to persecution. As the minister's spokesperson later explained apologetically, "normal cases of persecution involve physical abuse of a horrible sort" (*Hamilton Spectator* 1993a, A5). Put differently, Nada's experiences of everyday harassment and chronic restraint seemed to fall short of the level of atrocity commonly associated with persecution. Lastly, adjudicators had to decide whether Nada's punitive interactions with the police in Saudi Arabia constituted the legitimate right of a sovereign state to prosecute a citizen who defies the law or a matter of violation of basic human rights. In sum, Nada's experiences of gendered violence diverged from the established masculinized and state-centred notions of rights.

Unsurprisingly, given these complications, the IRB adjudicators who heard Nada's claim refused to grant her refugee status. The two adjudicators ruled that Nada did not meet the standards of refugee protection. As they perceived the case, Nada's defiance of gendered norms in Saudi Arabia could not be taken as a matter of legitimate political opinion, nor did her troubles amount to persecution. In fact, the two decision makers suggested that Nada could simply avoid these troubles by complying with the laws of Saudi Arabia. They even advised her to "show consideration for the feelings of her father" (Broadbent 1992, A17). Once Nada's claim was rejected, she was ordered to be deported. Determined not to return to Saudi Arabia, Nada disregarded the deportation order and went into hiding (Broadbent 1992). Soon, a warrant for her arrest was issued (Neuwirth 1992). Despite this, Nada remained in hiding and made connections with refugee lawyers and human rights, refugee, women, and feminist organizations. With the support of these advocates, Nada's case broke in the media and became a large and sensational public spectacle. Sympathetic media coverage of her case and speculations about the prospects of her forced return to Saudi Arabia raised considerable momentum in her support. Outraged by the negative and patronizing decision, Nada's supporters called for women's rights to be acknowledged as human rights. They insisted that Nada's troubles amounted to persecution and that her defiance ought to be recognized as feminist political dissent. Large mobilizations led to strong campaigns that called on the Department of Immigration to cancel Nada's deportation and grant her permanent residence in Canada (Broadbent 1992).

Nada's case became a rallying point for several groups and organizations that were invested in instituting an expansive gender-based refugee protection framework. But Nada was not the only refugee who sparked public discussion on the topic. Several other failed cases also soon found their way to the media. These cases, involving women from Trinidad, Bangladesh, and Iran, introduced a wide range of topics to the conversation. Issues of spousal abuse, unauthorized abortion, and sexual violence became points of public debate in refugee rights (Landsberg 1992; J. Miller 1993b; Trueheart 1993; Wheelwright 1993; York 1993a). The topics of domestic abuse and spousal violence ignited particularly nuanced discussions about the scope of refugee protection. These discussions considered whether seemingly private forms of violence, such as domestic abuse, could be understood as persecution (see Macklin 1995).[20] Alongside these ongoing jurisprudential debates, heart-wrenching and, at times, graphic accounts of domestic abuse cases regularly hit the media. Reports of the violence and abuse that these women had endured mustered strong public support for recognizing gendered persecution. Feminist lawyers, refugee advocates, legal scholars, and women and human-rights organizations kept these cases on the public's consciousness and called for blanket deportation relief for the rejected women (Cardozo 1993; Ulbrich 1993; York 1993a).

While the rejected gender-based claims were widely cited in the media, not all gender-based claims, of course, were denied by the IRB adjudicators. In fact, several claims with comparable circumstances received positive decisions from the IRB adjudicators in the same period (J. Miller 1993a; Oziewicz 1993). In effect, in the absence of a unifying policy, it was largely up to the discretion of individual decision makers to determine whether gender-based claims were compatible with the provisions of refugee law. Consequently, as lawyers and advocates rightly noted, gender-based decisions were highly inconsistent (Scanlan 1993). Perhaps even more importantly, negative decisions were made largely against the more expansive vision of the senior IRB administrators. Clearly, the Canadian regime was in need of a cohesive policy on gender-based cases.

While advocates pressed for the establishment of a gender-based refugee policy in Canada, they also vigorously debated the various forms that such policy should take. In these discussions, the *Gender Guidelines* were only one relatively modest alternative among a range of proposals. In fact, some of the proposals envisioned much more substantial forms of recognition than the *Gender Guidelines* could ever offer. For instance, women's groups, refugee advocates, lawyers, some politicians, and even the retired chairperson of the IRB called for amending Canadian immigration law to recognize gender as a basis for refugee protection (Broadbent 1992; A. Thompson 1993d; York 1993a). From the perspective of these advocates, the *Guidelines* lacked sufficient legal authority in shaping consistent decisions (Ulbrich 1993); gender-based protection, in other words, had to be enshrined in the law and afforded full legal authority. Other advocates took the issue even further and called on the Canadian government to take the question to the United Nations and lead international conversation on amending the *Refugee Convention* itself to include gender as a *Convention* ground (Scanlan 1993; Wheelwright 1993).

Yet state actors, including Mawani, were largely in support of more modest formulations that instituted a gender-based refugee policy without amending the *Immigration Act*.[21] In these officials' views, the existing legal definitions allowed sufficient room for recognizing gender-based claims (A. Thompson 1993c). Indeed, the existing legislation had been used in several cases to recognize gender-based cases without much difficulty (A. Thompson 1993a). Hence, these officials believed that the arduous work of undertaking legislative change was not necessary. Rather, decision makers could be trained, guided, and encouraged to interpret the existing definitions in more gender-sensitive ways. Moreover, for some advocates, the *Gender Guidelines* were the most plausible proposal given the restrictionist climate of the time. From these advocates' perspective, expanding the *Refugee Convention*'s definition at a time when the UNHCR's member states wished to minimize access to refugee protection as much as possible was unrealistic and even possibly dangerous (Oziewicz 1993; Trueheart 1993). Further, some legal scholars rightly pointed out that gender was not the only important omission in the *Refugee Convention;* amending the *Convention* to include gender but neglect other issues, such as sexual orientation and socio-economic status, was considered problematic (Oziewicz 1993).

The debate over the appropriate form and scope of Canada's gender-based refugee protection was further complicated by serious political opposition to the policy: although the IRB's leadership was largely in support of an expansive, albeit pragmatic, protection framework, other state actors, particularly Bernard Valcourt, the Progressive Conservative immigration minister, solidly opposed the idea. Speaking from what soon became the wrong side of history, Valcourt refused the calls to expand refugee protection to gender-based claims for two reasons. First, he argued that altering the refugee definition to include gender constituted an imperialist imposition of Canadian values on the world; Canada, the minister suggested, had no right to amend the internationally recognized definition of refugees (A. Thompson 1993a). Second, Valcourt argued that expanding refugee rights to gender-based claims would open Canada to an overwhelmingly large number of cases (J. Miller 1993a; Ulbrich 1993; York 1993b). With millions of people on the move around the world, the cost of expanding the refugee definition was simply too high. The proposed expansions were particularly counterintuitive at a time when Canadian border control and immigration policy, like in much of the Western world, was by and large focused on curbing the flow of refugee claims (Scanlan 1993; A. Thompson 1993a).[22]

Proponents of gender-based refugee policy rejected both of Valcourt's arguments. Against the first argument, advocates insisted that protection against gender-based violence was no more imperialistic than protection against racial or religious persecution (Broadbent 1992; Neuwirth 1992). Advocates also refused the notion that recognizing gender-based claims opened Canada to large numbers of refugees. Several advocates explained to the media why establishing a gender-based refugee policy would not create a surge in refugee numbers (Broadbent 1992; Scanlan 1993; York 1993a). As these advocates correctly noted, the policy only applied to women who made inland refugee claims. In other words, women had to flee their home countries and successfully travel to Canada before they could be recognized. Of course, women's gendered struggles, including their lack of access to financial resources, largely prohibited their international mobility (Scanlan 1993; York 1993a). Hence, since the vast majority of the women who could potentially benefit from the policy simply could not travel to Canada to access it, the policy was not likely to lead to a flood of claims. As Edward Broadbent, the director of the International Centre for Human Rights and Democratic Development and a key supporter of gender-based refugee policy, remarked: "A large majority of women ... would never hear about it and others would have no opportunity of getting here" (quoted in Todd 1992, C5).

Broadbent's remark was a rightly modest estimation of the impact of Canada's gender-based refugee policy. Indeed, recognizing gender in Canadian refugee jurisprudence was not likely to revolutionize women's access to refugee protection. Encouraging decision makers to adopt gender-sensitive interpretations of refugee law did little to change the broader circumstances that systematically undermined women's ability to secure protection against violence and abuse. The policy had a very limited reach and, thus, no serious bearing on the number of incoming claims. Despite the well-placed accuracy and humility of this reasoning, Broadbent's remark is striking as a logic of protection: in effect, Broadbent and several other advocates defended gender-based refugee policy against restrictionist concerns by emphasizing its inaccessibility to the women who could benefit from it.[23] The policy was defensible precisely because it was ineffectual: the expansions were neither to disrupt the rise of restrictionism in Canadian immigration and border control nor to greatly facilitate women's access to protection. In striking irony, gender-based refugee protection was expected not to protect very many women at all.

At last, sustained mobilization and overwhelming public support forced Valcourt to change his position on gender-based refugee claims. Suspected of wishing to appeal to the public (Cardozo 1993) and in what came to be pejoratively described as a "policy flip-flop" (York 1993b, A4), Valcourt intervened to stop the deportation of several high-profile rejected women, including Nada (Oziewicz 1993). He further signalled his approval by announcing the imminent release of the IRB's *Gender Guidelines* (A. Thompson 1993c).

Valcourt's announcement brought an end to the ongoing discussions on Canada's gender-based refugee policy. With the minister's change of position, the *Gender Guidelines* became an immediately achievable goal. The other more expansive proposals were still facing considerable political resistance; the minister had already refused to work toward legislative change or lead international dialogue on gender-based claims (A. Thompson 1993a). Moreover, the IRB was well prepared to issue its *Guidelines* on gender-based persecution.[24] Since the *Guidelines* were to directly inform the IRB's decisions, they were likely to produce a quick and practical impact. In short, the *Guidelines* were the most viable middle ground between the more substantial demands of advocates and the practical and political considerations of government and political authorities. Hence, the *Guidelines* prevailed over other proposals and, within a month, were published as the first gender-based refugee protection instrument issued by a state (*Arizona Daily Star* 1993; J. Miller 1993a).

The IRB's *Gender Guidelines* were the result of the tireless work of lawyers, advocates, and feminist and refugee organizations, and they represented a major expansion in refugee jurisprudence. However, the jurisprudential expansions offered by the *Guidelines* had minimal impact in increasing actual access to refugee protection. As anticipated, in the years following the publication of the *Guidelines,* the number of women who benefited from Canada's gender-based refugee policy remained very small (IRB 1995): in 1994, only 650 claims were classified as gender-based. By 1995, only 2 percent of the total number of claims referred to the IRB were based on gender.[25] Despite the expansive jurisprudence that had made gender a relevant ground in refugee law, gender-based refugee policy proved to be, to borrow from Lauren Edelman (1992, 1535), "minimally disruptive to the status quo." In its transition from the field of jurisprudence to the field of administration, the meanings, aspirations, and implications of gender-based protection were severely tamed and modified. Forced through the highly narrow administrative scope of inland refugee protection, the policy became a way to demonstrate Canada's (symbolic) commitment to gender equality to an admiring international audience (Neuwirth 1992; Cardozo 1993), more so than an effective device for protecting women refugees from gendered violence. In an ironic turn of events, the gender-based refugee policy became a tool for benefiting Canada.

In sum, the IRB's *Gender Guidelines* offered substantial jurisprudential and symbolic value without engendering noticeable practical change. The *Guidelines* were, in effect, a negotiated settlement that did not, and were not meant to, increase women's access to refugee protection. Instead, the *Guidelines* provided a compromise between the conflictual demands of Canadian refugee protection in the early 1990s: the desire to expand refugee rights for women and, yet, restrict access to protection. These paradoxical agendas made Canada's gender-based refugee protection limited by design: its well-intentioned jurisprudential expansions were delivered in a narrow administrative straitjacket that ensured their practical inefficacy. Put differently, the potentially expansive impact of feminist jurisprudential developments was undermined by the force of administrative logics, forms, and actors that formulated Canadian gender-based refugee protection. Hence, beyond a small level of well-celebrated relief, the *Guidelines* offered little actual change. In the words of the noted refugee law scholar James Hathaway, by agreeing to the *Guidelines*, "my understanding is that the government has done exactly nothing" (quoted in Oziewicz 1993, A13).

4 The Losing Game of Protection

Administrative Failure and Restrictionist Salvage

In the 1990s, Canadian refugee protection was, by any standard, a package of mixed content: while Canada was praised globally for its exceptional initiative in expanding refugee rights for women, the Immigration and Refugee Board of Canada (IRB) was receiving scathing domestic reviews for its poor humanitarian conduct. To be sure, neither the praise nor the reproach was unjustified; over the course of the period that the IRB produced and consolidated the *Guidelines on Women Refugee Claimants Fearing Gender-related Persecution (Gender Guidelines),* it also devoted considerable energy to administering unprecedented measures of restrictionism.[1] In effect, the Canadian regime opened the door of refugee protection for some while simultaneously closing it on others. This simultaneous opening and closing were made possible by the supposed distinction in law and administrative logics between subjects of expansion and those of restriction.

This chapter provides a close view of the operations of the IRB in the 1990s and early 2000s. This discussion will further my overarching contention that the contrasting drives of the Canadian regime to open and close the reach of refugee rights are inherent to state-controlled refugee protection. The Canadian regime took up both initiatives voluntarily and with great resolve and, when necessary, in savvy collaboration with a wide range of allies. For instance, in the struggle over gender-based refugee policy, the IRB joined forces with refugee advocates and supportive media against the Department of Immigration. Yet, in a span of only a few years, the IRB formed critical alliances with immigration officials to further the cause of restrictionist control. In both instances, the bureaucracy exhibited great agency in strategically pursuing its own situated interests.

This chapter consists of two sections. The first section considers the dilemmas of the IRB as it matured beyond its early years. I examine the IRB's struggles in striking an acceptable balance between the quality of its work and the quantity of its output. I demonstrate that the impossibility of fulfilling the paradoxical demands of humanitarianism, border control, and administrative efficiency regularly placed the IRB in positions of unavoidable failure: criticized either for rejecting too many claims or accepting too many refugees, the IRB failed to perform the work of refugee claim adjudication to the satisfaction of its many contradictory constituents. Further, the unceasing trouble with workloads kept the bureaucracy perpetually, and often unsuccessfully, striving for administrative control. Given these challenges, restrictionism remained central to how the IRB envisioned and operationalized the work of refugee claim processing.

The second section explores the restrictionist strategies that were developed and implemented by the IRB in the late 1990s and early 2000s. I show that over time, the board's methods of systemic rejection became increasingly complex and multilayered and began to involve interdepartmental collaborations. These evolving strategies helped mitigate the administrative challenges of the Canadian regime by practically diminishing access to refugee rights for groups who became their targets. While undoubtedly consequential to managing the bureaucratic work of claim processing, the IRB's strategies of mass rejection came at the cost of the ability of the displaced to seek refuge and the legal standards that were meant to regulate access to this supposedly universal right. In short, in its quest for administrative control, the bureaucracy violated the protection that had been promised by the law.

No Way to Win: The IRB in the 1990s

As the IRB administrators learned over the course of the 1990s, bureaucratic refugee protection is an act of impossible juggling. Throughout the 1990s, the structural paradoxes of state-controlled refugee protection continuously pulled the IRB (2000, 2) between the humanitarian desire to produce consistent and high-quality refugee decisions and the administrative demand to "work smarter" and increase productivity. The IRB worked hard to find an acceptable balance between quality of decisions and quantity of output. However, achieving these goals often proved impractical. Irrespective of how the IRB conducted its operations, it regularly came under harsh public and political scrutiny. In effect, the impossibility of fulfilling the paradoxical demands of state-controlled refugee protection made the IRB's work a never-ending rehearsal of failure.

In the early 1990s, the IRB led the world in recognizing gendered forms of persecution. Despite this well-celebrated achievement, the board immediately found itself at the centre of a series of public crises. The emerging issues shook public trust in the integrity of the IRB, both as a workplace and as an agency in charge of processing refugee claims. The criticisms against the IRB were raging and relentless and even included attacks on the character of the chairperson (for example, see Nolan 1992). The accusations followed one another seamlessly, painting a troubling picture of the board. First, Sam Ifejika (1993) resigned from his position as a refugee status adjudicator in 1992 to protest racism, favouritism, and tokenism in the appointments and reappointments of decision makers as well as bureaucratic interference in adjudications (see also Vincent 1992a, 1992c, 1993). Ifejika accused the IRB of incentivizing negative decisions.[2] He further publicized details of a conversation with a federal bureaucrat who had pressured him to decide against a claimant. Although the IRB and the Department of Immigration rejected Ifejika's accusations, the charges were evidently not without substance: at least one accused IRB official, Anna Ker, was removed from her post for pressuring adjudicators to reject claims (Vincent 1992a, 1992b).

While Ifejika's scathing review of the IRB was circulating publicly, a few other disturbing reports of misconduct at the board also surfaced in the media. In one case, Lisa Rosenblatt, a Toronto lawyer, accused two IRB decision makers of passing sexist notes about her during a hearing and denying her client a fair adjudication (*Globe and Mail* 1992; Small and Vincent 1992). Two other adjudicators, Naomi Goldie and Ralph Snow, also came under scrutiny for mocking a torture victim in notes that they passed to one another during a hearing; apparently, the torture method described by the Iranian claimant, which involved placing boiled eggs under the survivor's armpits, had proven too amusing for the decision makers (Small and Vincent 1992; Vincent 1993). The IRB permanently removed Goldie and Snow and issued an apology to Rosenblatt. Despite these actions, refugee advocates and lawyers continued to call for an independent probe into the operations of the board (Vincent 1992a). The public had lost confidence in the integrity of the IRB's humanitarian agenda.

The IRB moved quickly to repair its public image. The newly appointed chairperson, Nurjehan Mawani, created a code of conduct for adjudicators, commissioned an independent study of the board, and appointed a new assistant deputy chairperson to exclusively manage trainings (IRB 1993, 11; 1994, 4; 1995, 4). Training adjudicators in cross-cultural communication and sensitivity became a particularly key focus (IRB 1993, 11). Moreover, the IRB began a rigorous process of "house-cleaning" (M. Green 1993, A12). In addition to assessing, removing, and training existing personnel, the board recruited several well-respected refugee lawyers and advocates. The new appointees were given the latitude to shape training and plan educational seminars.[3] The scale of these personnel changes was substantial: in 1994–95, approximately half of the experienced adjudicators in the Refugee Division were replaced (IRB 1996, 9).

While somewhat effective in restoring the IRB's humanitarian reputation, these efforts soon produced a conservative backlash. The board had barely recovered from the earlier waves of critique when a series of new accusations relaunched public scrutiny. This time, two former decision makers, Bill Bauer and Gary Carsen, accused the IRB of accepting too many claims and under-reporting acceptance rates (*Winnipeg Free Press* 1995). Bauer and Carsen charged that adjudicators who rejected claims faced hostility at the board. Calgary Conservative Member of

Parliament Art Hanger stirred more controversy by alleging that the IRB's expedited processes offered easy entry to terrorists, prostitutes, and homosexuals (Cernetig 1994; Rinehart 1994; A. Thompson 1994). Importantly, in this new round of public outrage, the IRB came under fire for supposedly accepting too many refugees; too much of an investment in humanitarian protection, it seemed, had undermined the IRB's role in migration control.

Put simply, the IRB was in an impossible position. No matter how the board conducted its work, it was bound to come under attack. By having succumbed to the pressure to reject and deter claimants in the previous years, the IRB, of course, had undermined the principles of humanitarian protection and, thus, sparked outrage in refugee advocates. The board's subsequent attempts to rectify the state of refugee protection, in turn, had made for poor immigration control and, therefore, angered conservative critics. As the IRB was quickly learning, satisfying these oppositional constituents was not simply a matter of competence or hard work; the two camps could never be simultaneously pleased. Indeed, the task itself was contradictory: it was impossible to both protect refugees with generosity and exercise stringent migration control. In short, the IRB was set up for inevitable failure. Bureaucratic refugee protection was nothing but a losing game.

In addition to these public crises, the IRB was in serious administrative trouble. In the 1990s, the board was struggling with colossal caseloads. Following the elimination of the initial stage of adjudications, seventeen thousand transitional cases were transferred to the IRB for processing. Consequently, processing times almost doubled in a matter of months from about four months in 1992 (IRB 1993) to seven-and-a-half months in 1993 (IRB 1994). Moreover, organizational changes, extensive training, and high rates of turnover had begun to take a toll on the IRB's (1994, 1995, 1996) rates of output: productivity was low, adjudication costs per claim had risen, and the number of claims awaiting review was mounting. Despite the fact that the number of incoming claims only modestly increased or even decreased in the mid-1990s, processing times were growing by the year. In 1994, claims were processed in an average of nine months (IRB 1995, 10). By 1996, average processing times had reached thirteen months (IRB 1997, 15).

The IRB scrambled to deal with its unsatisfactory productivity levels. Although the election of the Liberal government in 1993 had incited the IRB's humanitarian revival, it had not displaced the impetus or the necessity for bureaucratic efficiency in refugee claim processing. Throughout the 1990s, the Canadian government was increasingly remodelling itself after the private sector. Neoliberal logics of economic viability were in full force. Departmental reports were soon transported to formats that emphasized quantifiable outputs, encouraged business-sector language, and required detailed cost analyses (for examples of these changes, see IRB 1996, 1997, 1998).[4] This shift in the culture of public administration placed even more pressure on the IRB to improve its output and report more flattering numbers. Surviving as a state entity in the age of neoliberalism required prioritizing productivity. Bureaucratic efficiency was a necessary administrative compulsion.

The IRB's (1997, 6, 14) struggles for improved outputs were set against a budget cut as well as an understaffed adjudicator capacity. However, low productivity rates made it difficult to secure resources and exposed the IRB to paternalistic control and attention from the Department of Immigration. For instance, the IRB's request for the appointment of two additional decision makers to the Immigration Appeal Division in 1995 was met with conditional and controlling responses:[5] the department only approved a temporary addition of staff and expressed the expectation that the IRB would "be able to fund the positions through savings or reallocation from other areas of the program" after the temporary period ended. The Department of Immigration further took this moment as an opportunity to voice concern about the IRB's productivity levels and announce that it would monitor the division's performance.[6]

The IRB employed multiple strategies to improve its rates of output. First, the board began to develop new case management practices, particularly to deal with unexpected surges of claims (IRB 1996, 9; 1997, 12; 1998, 19; 1999, 25–26). Second, it extended the application of expedited processes beyond the narrow limits of their original design. Soon, claims from all countries could be expedited, and 35–40 percent of cases were diverted to expedited procedures (IRB 1993, 21). Third, the IRB (1997, 15) began to rely more heavily on single-person panels: in 1996, 21 percent of hearings were conducted by only one adjudicator, compared to 9 percent in 1995.[7] Fourth, the IRB encouraged decision makers to issue oral decisions from the bench. Oral decisions increased the efficiency of claim processing by eclipsing the time spent forming decisions and crafting written reasons following a hearing. However, this mode of decision-making at times sacrificed rigour for efficiency: oral decisions prioritized quick decision-making over thoughtful consideration of complex sets of evidence.[8] Despite this glaring flaw, the IRB (1998, 8; 1999, 16) strove to make oral decisions the norm: by 1997, 40 percent of the IRB decisions were rendered orally. Evidently, bureaucratic efficiency was to be achieved even at the expense of attenuating adjudicative rigour. Indeed, the bureaucratic compulsion for efficiency operated in partial defiance of strict and demanding legal considerations.

The IRB's efforts were fruitful, and productivity levels began a slow upward trend in 1996. After much hard work, the IRB (2000, 8) was finally on its way toward reducing processing times to the target goal of eight months. Yet, to the utter dismay of the administrators, an unexpected and dramatic increase in the number of incoming claims disrupted all projections: in 1999, the number of incoming claims suddenly rose by 23 percent (IRB 2000, 6). This unexpected increase undid the IRB's hard-earned achievements. Despite increased productivity, the average cost per claim increased by 10 percent and the number of claims awaiting review rose by thirty-three hundred (IRB 2000, 6–7). In addition, the IRB administrators were under pressure to prepare for the substantial legislative changes that were to be imminently imposed by the *Immigration and Refugee Protection Act* (IRB 2000, 3).[9] There was no likely relief in sight for the IRB.

The IRB closed the 1990s with considerable outstanding challenges and in a tenuous and perpetual chase for administrative control. Nonetheless, in the impossible task of juggling humanitarian protection, restrictive migration control, and bureaucratic efficiency, the IRB had yet another tool at its disposal: using claimants' nationality to isolate large groups of claimants for quick rejection. As the IRB moved through the 1990s, national groupings continued to provide the board with ready subjects of exclusion and adaptive forms of administrative strategy.

Renewed Restrictionism: Advancing Methods of Bureaucratic Rejection

The administrative necessities of bureaucratic refugee claim processing had engrained the young IRB with an investment in restricting access to Canadian protection since its creation in 1989. Using claimants' nationality to identify blocks of excludable claimants became a favoured method for handling the challenging volumes of caseloads. Although these practices diverged from legal requirements of individual and equal assessment, they were used extensively throughout the Canadian regime. Excluding claimants based on national groups allowed the IRB to process large portions of its caseload quickly and with few resources. Moreover, this strategy made for highly flexible methods of case processing that accommodated shifting administrative needs. In short, bureaucratic refugee protection quickly turned into a work of curated exclusion.

Throughout the 1990s and early 2000s, the Canadian regime of refugee protection continued to use claimants' nationality to isolate and reject large numbers of claims. As the IRB became more established, its restrictionist strategies took increasingly involved, innovative, and collaborative shapes. Despite their earlier troubled relations, the IRB and the Department of Immigration soon found a common and unifying interest in controlling access to Canadian protection, and they began to engage in progressively coordinated projects. These projects focused largely on managing the flow of incoming claims.

For the IRB administrators, the most agonizing (and recurring) obstacle in the way of controlled bureaucratic operation was sudden and unpredicted hikes in the number of incoming claims. Unforeseen surges in claim numbers compounded the IRB's chronic struggle with caseloads and turned administrative goals into moving and evasive targets. While orderly bureaucratic conduct required controlling the volume of its workload, managing the patterns of international displacement was well beyond the IRB's ability. However, as Canadian officials learned through trial and error, displacement abroad did not necessarily need to equate to placement in Canada: although every displaced person had the nominal right to seek refuge, their actual ability to find protection in Canada could be substantially mediated through bureaucratic procedures and border control protocols. Indeed, for the board to survive the inhospitable political landscape of the neoliberal era, it could not afford to act simply as a subservient or even neutral vehicle for the universal right to refuge. To the contrary, the IRB was, as it had to be, an active and influential player in shaping access to rights in accordance with its own restrictionist needs.

The IRB's active involvement in controlling case levels thoroughly redefined the meanings associated with surges in the number of claims. In the world of Canadian bureaucrats, a rise in the number of claims was, first and foremost, a matter of administrative trouble rather than, for instance, an indication of increased need for protection in the face of human tragedy. As a result, in dealing with these surges, the IRB officials were minimally concerned with how to best serve a potentially disenfranchised population or apply principles of refugee law to a given geographical region. Rather, for these officials, the most pressing question was how to best shield the board from the impact of increased numbers. In other words, the work of bureaucratic refugee protection revolved around protecting the bureaucracy itself.

To protect the board against unexpected increases in caseloads, the IRB began to develop involved case-processing systems. Thanks to a sharp rise in their numbers, Chileans were among the first groups to become targets of the IRB's evolving case management techniques. The Chilean "problem" had a simple geopolitical root: in 1995, the Canadian government lifted visa requirements for Chile to promote tourism and trade between the two countries. As travel to Canada became more accessible to Chilean nationals, the number of their inland refugee claims quickly multiplied: from only eighty-eight in 1994, the number of Chilean claims rose to 1,637 in 1995 and to 2,625 in 1996 (Da 2002).

The growing number of Chilean claims produced several administrative and geopolitical difficulties in Canada. These numbers, of course, troubled the IRB administrators because they increased workloads. Moreover, Chilean claims posed a political dilemma for immigration officials. Given the cordial and improving relations between the governments of Canada and Chile, Canadian officials were not inclined to accept Chileans as victims of political persecution. In fact, Canadian immigration officials considered Chile to have no major political or human-rights crisis and, as such, did not expect Chileans to be in need of refugee protection (Sarick 1995). Therefore, the IRB and immigration authorities shared an interest in rejecting and deterring claims from Chile. The fact that most of the incoming Chilean claimants originated from the economically deprived city of Valparaiso provided the basis for mass rejections: regarded to be simply in search of better economic conditions, Chileans were swiftly relegated to the disfavoured class of economic migrants (see *Reuters* 1996). Since economic deprivation is not recognized as a ground for asylum in refugee law, Chileans became excludable from protection.

The IRB acted quickly to contain the unwelcome increase of Chilean claims. To ensure a timely response, the board abandoned its usual practice of adjudicating claims on a first-come, first-served basis and instead prioritized processing Chilean cases over older claims (IRB 1997, 15). By processing (and rejecting) these claims faster, the IRB meant to deter prospective Chileans from filing more claims in Canada. While key to reducing workloads to more manageable levels, deterrence made an irony of the supposed universality of the right to seek refuge: a universal right that nonetheless Chileans were to be dissuaded from exercising. More troublingly, the IRB's deterrence strategies established a two-tiered adjudication process that primed Chileans for rejection even before their claims were formally evaluated; the hearings of Chileans were expedited not simply to resolve their cases faster but also to reject them more quickly. In other words, administrative deterrence took precedence over legal adjudication.

Despite these issues, the IRB was committed to lowering the number of Chileans who entered the Canadian system. Soon, Chileans began to be rejected in large numbers: their acceptance rates dropped from 26 percent in 1995, to only 1.7 percent and 2.7 percent in 1996 and 1997 respectively. As a result, over two thousand Chileans were rejected, and another fifteen hundred abandoned or withdrew their claims, in these two years alone.[10] Once the Department of Immigration reinstated visa requirements in 1996, the number of incoming Chilean claims dropped dramatically (IRB 1997, 15): in 1997, only fifty-three Chileans claimed refugee status in Canada (Da 2002). All in all, the rise in the number of Chilean claims was managed through layered strategies that involved both the IRB and the Department of Immigration. The case of Chile, however, was only the tip of the increasingly involved and coordinated multi-departmental strategies of mass rejection.

The most extensive instance of restrictionist strategies in the 1990s was developed in relation to Romani claimants from Eastern Europe. In the case of Roma claimants from Hungary, in particular, the Canadian regime of refugee protection went to unprecedented lengths to reject and deter claimants. The creative and questionable strategies deployed against Roma claimants are well documented and critiqued (*Hungarian Free Press* 2017[11]; Arhin 2013; Macklin 2013; Levine-Rasky, Beaudoin, and St. Clair 2014; Beaudoin, Danch, and Rehaag 2015; Levine-Rasky 2016). Here, I only highlight aspects of these strategies that illustrate the active and autonomous role of the claim-processing bureaucracy in restricting access to refugee protection.

In the late 1990s, the number of Roma claims from Hungary and the Czech Republic went through a steep hike, making the Roma a population of high concern for the IRB and the Department of Immigration alike (Levine-Rasky, Beaudoin, and St. Clair 2014). The department managed to control the number of incoming Roma claimants from the Czech Republic through visa requirements in 1998 (Levine-Rasky 2016). However, political considerations impeded the imposition of similar restrictions on Hungarian nationals for several years.[12] As a result, the number of claims from Hungary remained high: between 1997 and 2002, about twenty-five thousand Roma Hungarians made refugee claims in Canada (*Hungarian Free Press* 2017).

The issue came to a head in 1998, when Canadian officials received information that fifteen thousand Romani claimants were to arrive from Hungary. Although unverified, this information prompted Canadian officials to search for lasting and effective solutions for controlling the rising number of Roma claims (Macklin 2013). Importantly, the problem with Roma Hungarians was not that they did not fit the definition of a refugee. To the contrary, Roma Hungarian claimants were regularly recognized as refugees in status determination proceedings. However, Canadian officials believed that both the volume and the acceptance rates of these claims were too high.[13] In other words, Roma Hungarians had to be rejected not because they were not refugees but, rather, because there were too many of them in the case-processing system (*Hungarian Free Press* 2017).

To reject and deter Roma Hungarians, the IRB developed the soon to be infamous Lead case. The Lead case was a device for increasing the efficiency and consistency of refugee adjudications. The case was meant to serve as a well-researched and well-crafted "model" decision that could be used as a template in deciding claims of comparable circumstances; thus, by following the example of the Lead case, other claims could be adjudicated more efficiently. In theory, the Lead case was an administrative tool of general applicability.[14] However, in practice, the Lead case was only ever applied to the Hungarian Roma before its notoriety made it virtually unusable in any other instance.[15]

The Lead case was produced in 1998 on the refugee claims of two Roma Hungarian families.[16] The case used the two claims as an opportunity to examine conditions of life for Romani people in Hungary. The adjudicating panel was given exceptional resources to study the cases in depth. The panel, for instance, heard testimonies from four expert witnesses that were flown in from Hungary.[17] In the end, the adjudicators ruled that although the Roma faced discrimination in Hungary, their experiences did not amount to persecution. Furthermore, the adjudicators suggested that the conditions of life for Hungarian Roma populations were rapidly improving. As a result, the two families' claims were rejected.

The Lead case soon became highly controversial and was challenged in court for its blatant disregard for principles of administrative impartiality. As the court uncovered, the IRB administrators who had developed the case were neither impartial to its outcome nor keen on ensuring that the adjudication process was conducted with impartiality. For instance, a key official in charge of administering the case, Vladimir Bubrin, had regularly rejected Roma claimants in his role as an adjudicator. The same administrator had then gone on to serve as one of the two adjudicating members on the panel (*Hungarian Free Press* 2017). In other words, not only was the case designed by administrative authorities who were inclined against Roma claimants, but the decision-making process also lacked adequate separation between administrative and adjudicative roles. As such, the case violated the legislated independence of refugee decisions: the Lead case had clearly prioritized the administrative interest in rejecting Roma Hungarians over the legal requirements of independent and impartial adjudication.

In addition, the selection of experts who had testified on the conditions of Roma populations in Hungary was cause for serious critique. In an evident breach of basic standards of impartiality, all but one of the expert witnesses had direct connections with the Hungarian government; hence, the witnesses were partial to favouring socio-political conditions in Hungary. Moreover, the adjudicating panel had refused to hear conflicting testimonies from other experts (*Hungarian Free Press* 2017). Therefore, the corpus of examined testimonies was of dubious calibre.

Lastly, the Lead case was challenged for involving problematic instances of political interference. As appeal proceedings revealed, the IRB and the Department of Immigration had collaborated in both developing the case and disseminating its outcome. For instance, in a coordinated move with the department, the IRB had leaked the outcome of the case to Hungarian media to discourage prospective Roma claimants.[18] By actively advancing the goal of immigration officials to curb the number of Roma Hungarian claims, the IRB had undermined its own legislated independence from political authority and interest. As the Federal Court ruled in 2006, the IRB's practices had created reasonable apprehension of bias; put differently, Roma claimants' confidence in the political and administrative impartiality of the IRB was reasonably eroded. Hence, the Lead case was overturned.

The successful repeal of the Lead case was a significant victory for Hungarian Roma claimants and their advocates. However, the appeal did little for the thousands of Roma Hungarians who were turned away from Canada between 1998 and 2006 (*Hungarian Free Press* 2017). During the eight years that it was in place, the Lead case had devastating consequences for Hungarian Roma refugees. Not only did the case signal the preferred position of the IRB administrators on Roma claims, but it also incentivized negative decisions by making rejections quicker and less labour intensive. At times, the adjudicators were even pressured to comply with the conclusions of the case. In one extreme instance, an adjudicator who refused to change his positive decision was sabotaged and eventually suspended from the board.[19] As a result of these concerted efforts, immediately following the release of the Lead case, acceptance rates of Hungarian Roma claimants dropped from 71 percent in 1998 to 16 percent in 1999 (Levine-Rasky 2016, 115). Although the rates improved in some of the subsequent years, they remained relatively low, ranging between 11 percent to 30 percent in the following five years. Once the Lead case was overturned, acceptance rates of Roma Hungarians improved substantially: in 2006, 62 percent of Hungarian claimants received refugee protection.

Although legally problematic, the bureaucratic measures against Chilean and Hungarian Roma claimants were highly effective in hindering access to the Canadian regime of refugee protection and, consequently, reducing caseloads. In devising and implementing these measures, the claim-processing bureaucracy actively pursued its own interest in thwarting the rising number of claims, even if it came at the cost of undermining legal requirements of impartial, independent, and individual assessment; indeed, the justice promised by refugee law was retracted by the bureaucracy. The maturing IRB continued to be stretched between conflictual demands of humanitarianism, border control, and administrative efficiency. The impossibility of fulfilling these paradoxical demands made the work of refugee protection a juggling act of many failures: regardless of how the IRB chose to conduct its work, it never managed to stay clear of criticism. In this fraught context of perpetual struggle, the IRB developed increasingly convoluted restrictionist methods to manage the administrative task of refugee claim processing. However troubling from a humanitarian and legal perspective, these strategies were only adaptive responses to the unforgiving demands of bureaucratic work. State-controlled refugee protection continued to necessitate ingenious methods of mass rejection.

Ultimately, throughout the 1990s and early 2000s the Canadian regime of refugee protection remained an articulation of expansionist and restrictionist impulses. As we have seen, the Canadian regime actively worked to expand refugee rights on the basis of gender and yet carefully designed and implemented restrictive measures against new sets of national groups. Further, whereas expansions were pursued in the field of jurisprudence, restrictions were largely achieved through the bureaucracy and via procedural measures. These articulated arrangements allowed refugee rights to expand in Canada, without becoming accessible to those who needed refuge. As a result, the Canadian regime maintained, even if only tenuously, its legitimacy both as a humanitarian agency and as a part of Canada's larger migration regulation apparatus. Thus, Canadian refugee protection persisted despite its internal paradoxes and, ironically, through perpetual failure.

Part 3

Recent Times, 2007–17

Pivoting on Gay 5
Sexual Rights and Migration Restriction

In September 2017, Chrystia Freeland, then minister of foreign affairs, found herself in a quickly deteriorating position with Russia for having led a clandestine mission of spiriting away persecuted Chechen gays and bisexuals to Canada (Murphy 2017). The political displeasure was multifold: not only were Chechen authorities incensed by the suggestion that LGBT people existed in the republic, but Russian officials were also offended by the insinuation that they had failed to protect their own nationals. Meanwhile, third party spectators insisted that while unusual, Canadian involvement in resettling persecuted Chechens was not in violation of international law. Nonetheless, Russia threatened consequences against Canada were this involvement proved to be true (Ibbitson 2017b). A diplomatic crisis was at the verge of eruption over the fate of thirty-one young queer refugees.

Although tolerating this level of diplomatic risk for the sake of foreign nationals is remarkable, the Canadian operation was not out of line with the growing support for sexual orientation and gender identity and expression (SOGIE) refugees in Canada. In the new millennium, Canada entered, arguably, a golden age of LGBT rights and inclusion. Since the mid-2010s, Canada has featured a government that openly supports non-heteronormative communities within Canada, and an immigration system that is favoured by gender and sexual non-conforming expats wishing to live open queer lives in relative safety (see, for example, Fernandez 2021).[1] Yet the status of Canada as an unfaltering protector of LGBT persons is only a recent aberration from an otherwise violently homo and transphobic history. In fact, the current Canadian stance on sexual inclusion is a sharp turn from the criminalization and legalized exclusion of sexual and gender non-conformity that ensued as European settlers accumulated political power over the lands that were confederated into the dominion of Canada.

This chapter takes a close look at the emergence of SOGIE refugee protection in Canada to argue that the conflictual interests of state-controlled refugee protection continued to mark the operations of the Canadian regime in the recent era of gay inclusivity. The first section traces the paradoxical developments in refugee rights in the new millennium. By exploring the simultaneous legislative expansions and procedural restrictions since 2001, I show that the Canadian regime of refugee protection continued as an internally conflictual articulation that ultimately produced a contradictory backdrop for the development of SOGIE refugee rights in Canada. The second section historicizes Canadian SOGIE refugee protection by situating it within the recent history of expanding sexual rights in Canada. The interest in SOGIE refugee rights arose from the humanitarian impulse to push the boundaries of refugee law along the seams produced by gender-based expansions. The jurisprudential logic was simple: if gender-based violence could be considered persecution, so could the violence experienced on the basis of sexual orientation and gender identity. The concurrence of this jurisprudential intervention with the rapidly transforming landscape of sexual rights in Canada turned homosexuals from subjects of immigration exclusion to recipients of proactive protection, all within the span of a few decades. However, as we will see, the articulation of these well-meaning jurisprudential expansions within the larger restrictionist impulses of migration control made SOGIE protection expansive in law but largely ineffectual in practice.

Expansive Protection, Restrictive Protocol

The new millennium changed much in the Canadian regime of refugee protection without undoing its long-standing impetus to simultaneously expand and restrict access to refugee rights. At its core, Canadian refugee protection remained an articulation of expansionist and restrictionist forces that pursued incongruent interests. This is perhaps most evident in the first major immigration legislation of the era, the *Immigration and Refugee Protection Act* (*IRPA*).[2] The *IRPA* made several contradictory changes to the state of refugee protection in Canada. On the one hand, the *Act* extended the legislated reach of refugee rights beyond the terms of the 1951 *Convention Relating to the Status of Refugees (Refugee Convention);* in the new *Act,* forms of violence outlined in the *Convention against Torture and Other Cruel, Inhuman or Degrading Treatment or Punishment* were also warranted refugee protection.[3] As a result, the Immigration and Refugee Board of Canada's (IRB) scope of work broadened considerably: the legal definition of the refugee was no longer reserved exclusively for those persecuted based only on the five grounds of race, religion, political opinion, nationality, and membership in a particular social group. Rather, anyone at the risk of cruel or degrading treatment, even if for reasons other than the five *Refugee Convention* grounds, became entitled to refuge. Thereby, those left out of the *Convention* now had a stronger case for protection, and new groups of persecuted persons could be recognized as legitimate refugees. The *IRPA,* in other words, had extended the reach of refugee rights substantially.

On the other hand, the *IRPA* introduced a number of restrictive procedural measures to the Canadian regime of refugee protection. For instance, the *Act* transitioned the IRB's adjudications from two-person panels to adjudications conducted by one decision maker only. Importantly, single-person adjudications were not a legislative invention or imposition; to the contrary, the IRB had used single-person panels to process uncomplicated cases with the claimants' consent for several years. Indeed, by regularizing single-person adjudications, the *Act* only followed the interest and initiative of the claim-processing bureaucracy in optimizing the use of resources. Single-person panels, of course, were an easy method of increasing the productivity of refugee claim processing. However, the gain in bureaucratic output was not without cost to claimants' chances of securing protection: in two-person adjudications, only one positive decision was sufficient to grant refugee status. In other words, a single negative decision by one of the adjudicators did not disqualify claimants from protection. Conversely, in single-person hearings, every negative decision carried the entire weight of the determination. Thus, the newly defunct two-person model of refugee status determination provided a modest level of protection against unilateral rejections.[4]

To compensate for this increased risk, the *IRPA* legislated the creation of the Refugee Appeal Division (RAD). A new addition to the IRB's existing divisions, the RAD was to provide a mechanism for internal appeal within the board itself. The claimants rejected in single-person hearings were to be granted recourse to a second hearing presided over by a more experienced IRB adjudicator.[5] The RAD adjudicators had the authority to consider the claim with fresh eyes and, if need be, reverse the initial negative outcome without requiring the claimant to reinitiate their claim, unlike the case of successful appeals to the Federal Court. Therefore, the RAD constituted a far more accessible, transparent, and affordable process than the one available through the judicial system. While establishing an additional layer of protection for claimants, the RAD was also expected to reduce the inconsistencies in decision-making across the various IRB offices and correct adjudication errors before they reached the courts (IRB 2002, 10). As such, the internal appeal division was both to protect claimants and improve the quality and consistency of the IRB's decisions.[6] In effect, the RAD was a legislative offering in the way of ensuring and improving the IRB's humanitarian agenda. Importantly, this offering was also key to procuring the consent of refugee advocates to the transition to single-person panels.[7]

Despite its many anticipated benefits, the creation of the internal appeal division was delayed for several years after the *IRPA* came into effect. Soon after the *IRPA* passed, the Liberal government announced that it planned to postpone the implementation of the RAD due to budgetary constraints (IRB 2002, 10).[8] While the RAD was placed on hold, however, the IRB was quickly transitioned to single-person panels. In other words, the provisions that increased bureaucratic productivity took full force, while those that were meant to ensure comparable levels of protection for refugees were deferred; the selective implementation of the *IRPA* prioritized administrative interests over the intricacies of humanitarian protection: the justice promised by the law, yet again, was retracted due to administrative and economic calculations.

The RAD was eventually established in 2012, a decade after it had been legislated. Even then, instituting the RAD took significant political manoeuvring against opposing conservative members of parliament (Keung 2009). The instituted RAD, moreover, was a far cry from what had been originally promised. First, when the RAD was finally established, not all rejected claimants were allowed access to an internal appeal.[9] Second, unlike originally promised, the RAD did not provide a second round of full review to rejected claims; rather, appellants were only allowed to present "new" evidence. Of course, this process automatically disqualified those who simply required their existing claims to be reconsidered by a different decision maker. Third, rejected claimants had only fifteen days to submit their notice of appeal and thirty days to file their appellant's record.[10] These short timelines made gathering and preparing new evidence extremely difficult, further narrowing access to appeals. As a result of these procedural constraints, the RAD veered away from its promise of comparable protection against the increased risk of rejections in single-person panels. The legislative promise of protection, in short, was thwarted through procedural manipulations of the appeal system.

To be sure, the narrowing of access to Canadian refugee protection in this period was facilitated by measures well beyond the *IRPA*, or its selective implementation. In the early 2000s, the administrative landscape of Canadian refugee protection was being rapidly securitized. The arrival of hundreds of unauthorized travellers on boats on the west coast of Canada in 1999 and 2000 and the 9/11 attacks made border security and enforcement top national priorities (Mountz 2010). Soon, an entirely new department was created to handle the task of border security; the Canada Border Services Agency (CBSA), created in 2003, further complicated the interdepartmental relationships within the Canadian regime of refugee protection.[11] As the agency guarding Canadian borders, the CBSA amassed considerable authority over the flow of incoming refugee claims to Canada. Security became top concern, placed well above humanitarian obligations. The primacy of security considerations refuelled the impetus for administrative control. Indeed, national security and bureaucratic control became mutually interlinked. Both interests, for instance, were considered to be improved by streamlined determination processes and up-front security checks (IRB 2002, 5).

The rising prominence of border security in the administration of refugee protection was a global and collaborative phenomenon in the early 2000s. Across North America and Europe, wealthy countries had begun to more systematically share information and technologies to achieve stricter control over borders (Mountz 2010). Increased inter-state cooperation and securitization of migration restricted international mobility and access to refugee systems. As a result, the number of refugee claims began to drop considerably in the advanced industrial world (IRB 2004, 6). In North America, the harmonization of border enforcement strategies was associated with significant declines in refugee acceptance rates (Hyndman and Mountz 2010). The 2004 *Safe Third Country Agreement* between Canada and the United States was particularly impactful in limiting access to refugee rights in Canada and, arguably, in North America.[12] This *Agreement,* which remains in place today,[13] stipulated that refugee claimants must make their claims in the first "safe" country in which they arrive. Although seemingly bilateral, the *Safe Third Country Agreement* was primarily initiated and pursued by the Canadian government, which had much to gain from curbing access to its inland refugee regime by those arriving from the United States: while thousands of claimants routinely travelled from the United States to make their claims in Canada, only a few hundred chose the reverse route each year.[14]

The *Safe Third Country Agreement* was highly effective in making the Canadian regime inaccessible to large numbers of prospective claimants. Following the *Agreement,* the number of refugee claims in Canada dropped to the second lowest level in the IRB's (2006, 25) history. The largest impact was on claims made at Canadian borders (CCR 2005): within one year from the enactment of the *Agreement,* the number of these claims was cut almost in half (IRB 2006, 17). This *Agreement* was perhaps particularly detrimental to claimants whose cases involved persecution based on gender and sexuality (Hyndman and Mountz 2007; Haynes 2018); given that refugee jurisprudence on these forms of persecution is considerably stronger in Canada, requiring gender-based and

SOGIE claimants to make their claims in the United States, rather than in Canada, likely reduces the claimants' chances of securing protection. In other words, inter-state collaborative strategies pushed women and sexual minorities out of Canada and its relatively progressive refugee jurisprudence.

The subsequent legislation of this era, including the 2010 *Balanced Refugee Reform Act*[15] and the 2012 *Protecting Canada's Immigration System Act*,[16] imposed an array of other restrictive procedural changes on the Canadian regime. These changes diminished some claimants' chances of receiving refugee status and increased ministers' power in regulating access to refugee claim proceedings.[17] By widening the criminal scope of human smuggling and imposing stronger sanctions against this offence, the two *Acts* hampered and penalized assisted unauthorized travel. Clamping down on unauthorized travel ensured that prospective claimants were kept at an arm's length from the rights available in Canada. Thus, access to refugee rights became increasingly elusive: migration and border control procedures were carefully designed to keep rights and claimants at a distance: rights existed inside Canada, but claimants were kept to the outside of the Canadian borders.

The combination of these border control and procedural measures drastically reduced the number of displaced persons who managed to find secure status in Canada: the number of refugees admitted by the IRB dropped from 18,188 in 2003–04 to only 6,141 in 2007–08, a reduction of over 60 percent (M. Scott 2009). While the number of refugees declined to 8.8 percent of all newcomers in 2008 (from 11.8 percent in 2007), the number of investor immigrants and live-in caregivers climbed from 55 percent in 2007 to 60 percent in 2008. Put differently, the inflow of capital and care labour was facilitated, while the entry of refugees was hindered. Ironically, even though Canadian law had expanded to recognize wider ranges of persecution beyond those enumerated in the *Refugee Convention*, procedural tinkering with the refugee regime severely limited actual access to protection. The Canadian regime of refugee protection remained a contradictory amalgamation of expansive legal change and restrictive procedural and administrative interests. The conflictual impulses to expand and restrict continued to articulate Canadian refugee protection well into the new millennium.

SOGIE Claimants and Canadian Protection: From Banned to Rescued

In May 2017, the IRB issued its *Guidelines on Sexual Orientation and Gender Identity and Expression Claims (SOGIE Guidelines).*[18] To be sure, these *Guidelines* were not the first step Canada had taken in the way of SOGIE protection. Far from it, Canadian refugee status adjudicators had been recognizing persecution based on sexual orientation and gender identity since the early 1990s. Nonetheless, the IRB's *SOGIE Guidelines* represented a serious attempt at enforcing LGBT-friendly interpretations of refugee law, refining the emerging jurisprudential corpus on SOGIE cases and promoting nuanced adjudication practices.

The growing recognition of SOGIE claims at the IRB has been part of the broader, albeit recent, history of expanding sexual rights in Canada. In the last few decades, Canada has emerged as one of the global leaders in sexual inclusivity. Thanks to a series of court rulings and legislative developments, Canada now shares the spotlight with countries such as Sweden in topping the indexes of sexual equality: discrimination based on sexual orientation became explicitly prohibited via an amendment to the *Canadian Human Rights Act* in 1996, same-sex common law partners were granted equal social and tax benefits through Bill C-23 in 2000, and the *Civil Marriage Act* made legal marriage accessible to same-sex couples in 2005.[19] Today, in almost all areas regulated by the law, Canadian lesbian and gay citizens stand on par with heterosexuals.[20] Importantly, however, the same cannot be claimed for transgender Canadians for whom both legal recognition and protection lag far behind gay men and lesbians; a case in point is that gender identity only became specified as a prohibited ground of discrimination and hate crime in 2017, after significant controversy and debate. Thus, while Canada may be gay friendly, it remains far from being trans-inclusive.

The drive to include non-normative genders and sexualities under the equal protection of Canadian law is of very recent history. For most of its time, settler colonial Canada criminalized and persecuted non-heteronormative sex, lives, and relationships. Those who strayed from the norms of heteronormative gender and sexual conduct, including rules of heteropatriarchal monogamy, were often treated harshly by the law and state agents (see, for example, Hoy 2018). The legal sanctions that Canada inherited as a British colony categorized same-sex intercourse, particularly between men, as a serious offence well before Canada formed into a confederation in 1867. Indeed, until Canadian criminal law was reformed in 1869, "buggery" was punishable by death.[21] Following the introduction of "gross indecency" amendments to the *Criminal Code* of Canada in 1890, same-sex contact between men became a less severely punished, yet far broader, target of legal sanction; although, in the reformed law, anal intercourse was no longer subject to capital punishment, all same-sex activities, including proposals to engage in sex, became punishable offences (Dick 2009). As a result, in the ensuing eighty years before decriminalization in 1969, same-sex sex in private between consenting adults constituted illegal activity (Rau 2018). Of course, the mistreatment of sexually non-conforming persons by legal and state actors transcended far beyond the regulation of sexual relations. For instance, during the Cold War, Canadian gay men and lesbians were subject to systematic security surveillance due to homophobic presumptions about their supposed propensity for treason (Robinson and Kimmel 1994; Kinsman and Gentile 2010). All in all, for the majority of Canadian history, gender and sexual non-normativity was placed not only outside of the protective bounds of the law but also in direct opposition to the law itself.

Unsurprisingly, thus, legal animosity toward sexual and gender non-normativity also featured in Canadian immigration. In fact, up until 1977, those who engaged in same-sex relations were banned from immigration to Canada (Rau 2018). As the Canadian state assumed exclusive authority over migration control in the late nineteenth century, homosexuality emerged as a ground for exclusion in immigration law. The 1927 *Immigration Act* barred sexually non-conforming individuals from immigrating to Canada under the relatively obscure label of "persons of constitutional psychopathic inferiority" (R. Green 1987).[22] In 1952, "homosexuality" was enshrined as an explicit ground for denial of entry (LaViolette 2004). Those who engaged in same-sex sex were not even allowed to enter Canada as tourists; non-citizens who were discovered to take part in sexual encounters with people of their assigned sex were subject to deportation. The homophobic sentiments of Canadian migration and border control were beyond doubt: Canada did not want queers and certainly did not wish to receive them from abroad.

As Canadian law began to be challenged and reformed on account of sexual inclusion and equality by gay and queer liberation movements, expansive notions of sexual rights slowly trickled from Canadian nationals to non-citizens and immigration matters.[23] Almost a decade after the decriminalization of anal intercourse between consenting adults, the 1976 *Immigration Act* removed homosexuality as a basis of immigration exclusion.[24] In the emerging post-1976 vision of liberal Canada, refugees were a legal category, race was not a criterion of exclusion, and homosexuals were valid candidates for immigration. Nonetheless, Canadian immigration law was yet far from equal to sexually non-conforming folks. For instance, until 2001, when same-sex partners were fully incorporated into the streams of family reunification applications, spousal sponsorships were an exclusive heterosexual privilege.[25]

SOGIE refugee rights emerged from within this quickly shifting landscape of gay rights in Canada. The jurisprudence on SOGIE refugees derived much from the earlier feminist interventions on gender-based claims; like gender-based claimants, SOGIE refugees were proposed as members of a "particular social group," a ground that allowed their inclusion under the protected categories of refugee law.[26] Although the global development of SOGIE jurisprudence was not decidedly led by Canada, the Canadian regime of refugee protection was one of the first in the world to accept claims based on sexual orientation; the first known case was accepted by the IRB in 1991 (Molnar 2018).

Canadian SOGIE refugee jurisprudence developed in an expansive legal environment that included, most notably, the landmark Supreme Court of Canada 1993 decision *Canada (Attorney General) v Ward*.[27] In *Ward*, a decision on the seemingly unrelated refugee case of an Irish political dissident, the Supreme Court made a point of naming sexual orientation as a form of membership in a particular social group. This small contribution, in fact, was highly consequential to the course of SOGIE protection in Canada; as a result of *Ward*, SOGIE claimants' eligibility for protection was no longer a matter to be decided by individual decision makers but one that was mandated by Canada's highest court. By naming sexual orientation as a form of membership in a particular social group within the terms of the *Refugee Convention*, the Supreme Court of Canada removed the question of SOGIE eligibility out of the hands of adjudicators and placed these claims firmly within the bounds of refugee law. Henceforth, SOGIE claimants became entitled to protection pending only a positive evaluation of their credibility. The violence experienced based on sexual orientation, or gender identity and expression, as the Court demanded, was now legally recognizable as a form of persecution.

The expanding SOGIE jurisprudence and growing openness to sexual diversity in Canada created a relatively positive adjudication culture for SOGIE claims. As a result, SOGIE cases have been commonly accepted at rates higher than average. For instance, between 2013 and 2015, SOGIE claims were accepted at an average rate of 70.5 percent, compared to the overall rate of 62.5 percent for all claims (Molnar 2018). Despite the impossibility of providing indisputable proof of sexual orientation, SOGIE claims are not considered particularly difficult to adjudicate by the IRB decision makers.[28] Adjudicators' intuition[29] or observations of hearing room dynamics, such as moments of flirtation or demonstrations of jealousy,[30] routinely help Canadian decision makers make credibility assessments on these cases. SOGIE claims, as one former adjudicator argued, are personal and relatable and, hence, supposedly easier to decide:

> I found the sexual orientation cases easier, because they were more personal ... You're not talking about the political environment, you're talking about what happened to you ... And you see the country conditions are very straightforward ... Proving sexual orientation is no more difficult in terms of evidence than proving, um, religion. And in fact, I find, for me it was easier. Because you could talk about your own very personal circumstances.[31]

Notwithstanding these perspectives, credibility assessments in SOGIE cases are a highly contentious area in refugee jurisprudence. Deciding whether a claimant is "truly" gay, for instance, is not an uncomplicated task. As a large and insightful scholarship on SOGIE refugee adjudication has established, SOGIE credibility assessments often rely on stereotypical assumptions about "gay" behaviour and expression or invoke ethnocentric expectations of gay identity formation, sexual experience, and community connections (Millbank 2003; Fadi 2005; A. Miller 2005; O'Leary 2008; Rehaag 2008; Berg and Millbank 2009; Jordan 2009; Lee and Brotman 2011; Murray 2011). In short, it is very difficult, in fact, to establish the "truth" of SOGIE claims.

The most significant contribution of the IRB's *SOGIE Guidelines* is perhaps their critical engagement with the recurring problems in SOGIE credibility assessments. The *Guidelines* establish a high standard of treatment in credibility adjudications. Not only do the *Guidelines* advise adjudicators on appropriate use of language, but they also provide guidance on handling sensitive and personal information. The *Guidelines*, further, prohibit relying on stereotypical assumptions in determining the veracity of cases. For example, adjudicators are urged not to take claimants' appearance or mannerisms, their participation in religious or cultural traditions, or even past heterosexual relationships as the basis of their decisions. Moreover, the *Guidelines* acknowledge the impact of trauma on claimants' memories and ability to report harsh experiences coherently. All in all, the *SOGIE Guidelines* are a nuanced jurisprudential and policy intervention that in the words of an IRB spokesperson, "[are] intended to promote a greater understanding of the diversity and complexity of the situation of sexual and gender minority individuals" (as reported in Bielski 2017).

The accomplishments of the IRB's *SOGIE Guidelines* are not incidental: the *Guidelines* were produced through several consultations with community and advocacy groups, researchers, lawyers, and social workers. Through these consultations, 2SLGBTQ+ activists, community groups, and advocates shaped the content of the *Guidelines* and, at times, radically expanded bureaucrats' visions of sexuality, gender, and SOGIE protection. For instance, during a consultation in the fall of 2016 in which I was a participant observer, advocates suggested that the *Guidelines* should account for the fluidity of gender and sexuality, a notion that is, admittedly, deeply testing to the categorical epistemologies of bureaucratic operation. Faced with advocates' calls for "queering" refugee protection, the IRB representatives exchanged confused glances, took notes, and thanked the audience for offering novel and complex concepts to consider.[32] When the *SOGIE Guidelines* were released six months later, gender and sexual fluidity was incorporated in the text of the *Guidelines;* for instance, under section 2 on terminology, the *Guidelines* define the term "gender" by emphasizing that "an individual's gender includes gender identity and expression, both of which can be *fluid* and *flexible*."[33] While it would be imprudent to draw a direct causal link between the specific interaction that I observed and the final form of the *Guidelines,* the consultation process displayed the IRB's openness to community and advocacy input, even if these posed challenging moments. Given the largely positive collaborations between the IRB and community and advocacy groups in developing Canada's SOGIE protection framework, the *Guidelines* have been generally received well by lawyers and advocates (Keung 2017).

While the IRB's *SOGIE Guidelines* have been an important component in the expansive vision of protection for sexual and gender nonconforming folks, Canada's interest in protecting gay and lesbian refugees has gone far beyond producing a nuanced jurisprudential and policy instrument. Indeed, since the early 2000s, Canada has taken a highly active role in resettling SOGIE refugees and, at times, has prioritized resettling particularly vulnerable SOGIE groups – for example, those displaced due to the war in Syria (Molnar 2018).[34] Furthermore, Canada has gone above and beyond its international obligations by rescuing some SOGIE groups from within their countries of nationality, despite the fact that according to the terms of the *Refugee Convention,* the signatory states are not obliged to recognize or protect persecuted individuals who have not yet deserted their countries of habitual residence.[35] The Canadian government's involvement in the clandestine SOGIE refugee resettlement program discussed in the introduction to this chapter is an example of such extraordinarily proactive protection.[36] In this exceptional case, Canada committed to resettling as many qualified gay Chechens as available and willing, even at the risk of a diplomatic breakdown with Russia.

Despite these remarkable practices, much remains to be desired in the treatment of SOGIE refugees in Canada. For instance, bisexual refugees often struggle to establish the credibility of their claims and are commonly rejected at much higher rates than other SOGIE groups (see, for example, Rehaag 2008). Further, SOGIE claims have emerged as an area of high skepticism in recent years; bureaucrats become particularly suspicious of SOGIE credibility when claim numbers suddenly increase from a source country.[37] Perhaps most importantly, the efficacy of Canadian SOGIE protection suffers from the very limitations that also fetter its gender-based refugee policy: the expansive protection offered by the *SOGIE Guidelines* is only applicable to claimants who manage to access Canada's inland refugee protection regime. Given the restrictionist border and migration control measures implemented in recent decades, this access is increasingly difficult to achieve, which means that notwithstanding Canada's strong SOGIE jurisprudence, the number of persons who can avail themselves of Canadian protection against homophobic and transphobic violence remains very low: between 2011 and 2015, SOGIE claims constituted only 4.8 percent of the total number of claims finalized by the IRB. As a result, despite SOGIE claimants' relatively high rates of acceptance, only about 7.3 percent of accepted claims in these five years were based on SOGIE persecution.[38]

The fact that Canada's expansive SOGIE jurisprudence is administered within an overwhelmingly restrictionist system of migration control has significant gendered implications. While Canada's SOGIE jurisprudence is, in theory, gender neutral, the ability to make use of this progressive jurisprudence to secure protection is blatantly gendered. Women, whose international mobility is drastically hampered by broader systems of gender inequality, are far less likely to appear in Canada's inland refugee protection regime. Hence, men consistently make up the bulk of SOGIE claims that are processed in Canada; between 2011 and 2015, gay men constituted 54.8 percent of the total number of SOGIE claims finalized by the IRB. Lesbian claims, conversely, stood at nearly one-third of that proportion, at only 19.3 percent.[39] Sadly, the state of trans protection is even more disastrous; categorized under the catch-all and obscure label "Varied/Other," trans claimants are virtually invisible in the Canadian system. In the five-year period between 2011 and 2015, those individuals categorized as "Varied/Other" were a mere 2.8 percent of the total number of SOGIE claims processed in Canada. In short, not only does Canada's expansive interpretation of refugee law provide a very small window of protection against heterosexist violence, but the respite offered by the Canadian regime is also, by and large, operational only for a subgroup of those within the SOGIE category.

Lastly, while laudable in many respects, the IRB's *SOGIE Guidelines* do not undo the fundamental limitations of refugee law in conceptualizing persecution exclusively as a break-down in citizen-state relations. Indeed, the *Guidelines* re-enforce the understanding that persecution on the basis of SOGIE can, and should, be understood as a violation of civil rights rather than, for instance, as a larger question of gender and sexual violence or a legacy of colonization.[40] By tunnelling expansive SOGIE protection through the narrow frame of civil and political rights, the *Guidelines* ultimately isolate homophobia and transphobia from the broader imperial histories and geopolitical relations that reproduce heteropatriarchal violence and, instead, present these as unfortunate divergences from the otherwise "civilized" rules of liberal governance. Consequently, claimants become poised for protection on the basis of the supposedly individualized violation of their sexual rights, even if larger issues, such as economic deprivation, political instability, and sexual imperialism substantially contribute to both their displacement and vulnerability to transphobic and heterosexist violence. This narrow vision of protection leaves the Canadian regime in a state of remarkable paradox: the praiseworthy era of SOGIE protection has come to produce some of the darkest moments in the contemporary history of Canadian refugee protection. Put differently, the expansion of SOGIE rights, ironically, has been highly restricted and restrictive.

As the Canadian regime moved into the new millennium, the state of refugee protection remained deeply paradoxical: while refugee rights were expanded through legislation and jurisprudence, they were at once made less accessible through restrictionist migration regulation and case processing provisions. The Canadian regime of refugee protection, in other words, was simultaneously expanded and made more restrictive. Canadian SOGIE protection emerged from within these contradictions, and in a rapidly transforming landscape of sexual rights. Given the shifting status of homosexuality in Canadian law, sexually non-conforming persons quickly turned from subjects of criminalization and exclusion to deserving recipients of proactive protection. With these changes,

Canada soon attracted global acclaim for its progressive LGBT-friendly refugee framework. Yet, the expansion of SOGIE refugee rights in Canada did little to impede the overarching restrictionist impulses of state-controlled migration regulation. SOGIE expansions operated within the limiting boundaries of liberal rights and migration control. Hence, while SOGIE rights expanded in the law, refugee protection grew to be increasingly difficult to secure in practice.

Protection on Life Support

6

Bureaucracy, Intersectionality, and SOGIE Protection

In the early 2010s, I was told by the head of the Toronto-based Iranian Queer Organization that the office of Jason Kenney, then minister of immigration, was always enthusiastically responsive when it came to resettling gay Iranian refugees. The ultra-conservative Kenney, who had consistently voted against 2SLGBTQ+ rights and protection as a member of the Canadian Parliament, was surprisingly a formidable supporter of gay Iranians.[1] Indeed, during his tenure as the minister of immigration (2008–15), sexual orientation and gender identity and expression (SOGIE) refugees did very well in Canada: between 2011 and 2015, a total of 3,668 inland SOGIE refugees were accepted at remarkable rates ranging from 56 percent in 2013 to 69 percent in 2015.[2] To be sure, the good fate of SOGIE claimants continued passed the days of Kenney; with the 2017 release of the Immigration and Refugee Board of Canada's (IRB) *Guidelines on Sexual Orientation and Gender Identity and Expression Claims (SOGIE Guidelines)*, sexual rights were formally established in Canada's refugee protection framework.[3] In the broad sketch of things, the Canadian regime of refugee protection has been exceptionally inclusive of SOGIE cases. The devil, however, is only in the details.

This chapter tells the story of the bureaucracy in the age of SOGIE protection. My close examination of the struggles of bureaucratic refugee claim processing in the new millennium uncovers restrictionist cracks in the otherwise expansive momentum of SOGIE rights. In the first section of this chapter, I explore the administrative and political challenges of the IRB in order to understand and contextualize the board's unwavering attachment to restrictionist control. As we will see, budget cuts, interdepartmental tensions, and shrinking human resources made the 2000s a difficult time for refugee claim processing. These difficulties ultimately came at a cost to both those who sought refuge and those who adjudicated refugee claims: to survive its institutional challenges, the IRB had to simultaneously press more out of adjudicators and dodge refugee claims where possible. The second section of this chapter offers an under-explored intersectional view of inland SOGIE refugee protection in Canada. By considering the unlikely recipients of Canadian SOGIE protection, I complicate Canada's narrative of exceptional sexual inclusivity. As we will see, in this period, the bureaucratic drive for restrictionism coalesced with strong anti-refugee political will to produce some of the harshest episodes in the history of systematic refugee protection in Canada. Indeed, restrictionism advanced at full speed despite the expansions in SOGIE rights. The culmination of restrictionist interests ensured that not all SOGIE claimants were treated with generosity: those subject to systematic bureaucratic and political exclusion were in no place to benefit from progressive SOGIE or gender-based jurisprudence.

Of course, this critique is not meant to undermine the significance of Canada's SOGIE protection framework. There is no doubt that expansive SOGIE jurisprudence has made an unmistakable difference to the lives of many non-normative persons. Nonetheless, while a broad view of the Canadian regime tells a familiar story of exceptionalism and inclusion, a more meticulous intersectional approach excavates the conflictual make-up of SOGIE rights; considering those who were systematically cast out of the realm of protection helps delineate the limits of refugee law in delivering meaningful protection in a context rife with restrictionism. The bureaucracy remains an influential and autonomous force in advancing the restrictionist interests of state-controlled refugee protection.

Running on Empty: Bureaucratic Refugee Protection in the New Millennium

Throughout the 2000s, the Canadian refugee claim-processing bureaucracy was continuously adopting, lamenting, or resisting an unending array of procedural changes that aimed to make it leaner, faster, and more efficient. After almost twenty-five years of relative legislative stability, the Canadian regime was reformed three times in the span of twelve years. These changes diverted much of the IRB's resources to adapting to new regulations, at the same time that the board was struggling with heavy workloads under conditions of political neglect and austerity.[4] The IRB was receiving less and expected to achieve more.

Doing more with less required offloading pressure onto various actors throughout the claim-processing regime. If budgetary constraints did not allow the operation of routine procedures, processing routines had to be modified to absorb the financial shortfalls. The gains in productivity made by the transition to single-person panels in the early 2000s are a case in point: single-person panels improved output rates by pressing more out of each adjudicator.[5] The change was particularly consequential for new and inexperienced decision makers, who were now expected to hit the ground running. After only a few observation sessions, new adjudicators were left to handle the high-stakes task of refugee status determination without collegial support. As one former adjudicator, who had begun her career before the transition, wondered: "When they [transitioned to single-person panels] I thought to myself 'oh my God, I do not know how these people [new adjudicators] do it!' … I had two-[person] panels for maybe a year before I started [on my own] … I felt like I needed that time to learn from my co-[adjudicator]."[6]

Yet the IRB had no time to be concerned with the erosion of institutional support for decision makers. The need for improved productivity was undeniable as the board was hit with another major surge: in 2000–01, the IRB (2001, 3) received thirty-five thousand new claims, 40 percent more than the previous year. The number of incoming claims grew even larger the following year, reaching 45,100 (IRB 2002, 5). Despite high productivity, caseloads drastically outsized existing capacities (IRB 2003, 22, 24). Hence, the volume of claims awaiting review grew exponentially: by the end of the 2001–02 fiscal year, the IRB (2002, 5) had already accumulated a record number of forty-nine thousand backlogged claims, an increase of 57 percent in just one year. Backlogs reached an unprecedented high of 52,600 by March 2003 (IRB 2003, 22). The age of cases awaiting review, average processing times, and costs per claim were also on the rise (IRB 2002, 17–18; 2003, 30). The IRB was once again in deep administrative trouble.

By 2003–04, the IRB's foremost priority was to reduce the number of backlogged cases. New times called for new strategies. Soon, maximizing the time value of hearings became a key administrative goal: hearings were made shorter and more focused, and new case management systems ensured claims received the minimum amount of hearing time possible (see IRB 2003, 24; 2004, 33).[7] Even the conventional course of inquiries was tweaked to optimize the use of hearing time. For instance, in the mid-2000s, the IRB began to prohibit the customary practice of allowing counsel to open hearings with introductory remarks. Counsels' remarks, the IRB administrators believed, lacked the brevity and focus needed for efficient hearings.[8] Eliminating these remarks increased adjudicators' control over hearings: decision makers could now limit the inquiry only to the areas they saw fit. Increasing adjudicators' control, in turn, enhanced administrative goals; after all, adjudicators' practices could be shaped through trainings, management techniques, and evaluation metrices designed by administrators. In short, increasing adjudicators' authority could make hearings faster and more productive.

The increasing control of adjudicators over the hearing process was not received well by refugee lawyers, who found the new system too interventionist and even adversarial.[9] As counsel rightly noticed, the power dynamics in hearing rooms were shifting away from claimants and their legal representatives. This growing imbalance displaced the relatively egalitarian standing of counsel vis-à-vis decision makers in the legislated non-adversarial model of refugee status determination. Yet egalitarianism was too inefficient and costly. Increased output required greater concentration of power. Thus, the intricacies of non-adversarial refugee protection had to be sacrificed for the sake of bureaucratic productivity.

To the IRB's relief, by the middle of the first decade of the new millennium, some respite was in sight. The implementation of stricter border and travel control strategies had made gaining access to the Canadian regime far more difficult (IRB 2004, 6).[10] Although the dropping numbers of incoming claims were an insult to the supposedly universal right to seek refuge, they were a blessing to the board: with new claims aggressively held away, the IRB was finally making significant headway in tackling its backlogged cases. By the end of 2004–05, the number of pending claims was down to 24,889 (IRB 2005, 25).

As the backlogs were coming under control, a more insidious problem began to cast its inauspicious shadow over the IRB. Electoral cycles, partisan considerations, and the transition of governments had led to persistent delays in appointments and reappointments of the IRB adjudicators. While the mandates of existing adjudicators expired, new decision makers were not appointed to the board. Hence, a growing shortage of adjudicators was beginning to debilitate the IRB. The board was desperate for new appointments. Reminding the Parliament of the number of vacancies and their implications for rates of output became a regular theme in the IRB's (2002, 16; 2003, 25; 2005, 26; 2006, 4) annual reports. Despite the board's frequent requests, the Conservative government continued to stall appointing new adjudicators. Although a large pool of qualified candidates had been independently vetted and prepared under the previous government, new decision makers were not forthcoming (Keung 2007). News of the IRB's disastrous understaffing soon reached the media, and opposition members of parliament, advocates, and lawyers openly criticized the delays.[11] In spite of the public outrage, the IRB's struggles with vacancies grew steadily. In 2000–01, the IRB (2001, 6) operated with a 3 percent vacancy in its adjudicator complement. Toward the end of that decade, the staffing shortfall had reached alarming levels: in 2007–08, the IRB's (2008, 29) Refugee Protection Division operated with an average of seventy-nine decision makers out of a 127-adjudicator complement, a vacancy rate of almost 40 percent. Even the Auditor General's report noted the high vacancy rates and warned about their implications (Keung 2009). Of course, no level of administrative creativity could compensate for the damaging effects of these significant shortfalls.

The persisting delays in appointments caused great friction between the IRB and the government. When Diane Finley, the Conservative minister of immigration, announced intentions to increase political control over the appointment process, the tension reached its peak (Keung 2007). The minister's announcement reversed years of reform that had curbed political involvement in appointments[12] and had provided the IRB (2004, 33) with considerable authority in selecting and managing its adjudicators.[13] The attempt to reintroduce political control in the appointment process was too big of a setback for the IRB to bear, and its administrators were outraged. Indeed, following the announcement, Jean-Guy Fleury, the IRB's chairperson, resigned from his post (Jimenez 2007).[14] Fleury's resignation came shortly after the departure of several other senior IRB officials from the board (Mayeda 2007).[15] The IRB was suddenly both without a sufficient complement of adjudicators and missing key administrators. To make matters worse, a new surge in the number of incoming claims was on its way. Interdepartmental tensions and human resource deficits had left the IRB ill-prepared to handle yet another colossal challenge. The board's performance began to decline, and the volume of backlogs once again climbed: by the end of 2007–08, forty-two thousand refugee claims were awaiting review, sixteen thousand more than the previous year (IRB 2007, 27; 2008, 3, 29).

Eventually, new adjudicators began to be appointed to the IRB. Yet filling the large number of vacancies was a time-consuming process, and, thus, the rate of appointments continued to lag behind the IRB's needs (IRB 2008, 5). On the twentieth anniversary of its establishment, the IRB (2009, 1) was still struggling with a shortage of adjudicators. The accumulated deficit caused by years of understaffed operation had become so severe that even a full complement of adjudicators could no longer stop backlogs from growing. In addition, the volume of incoming claims continued to surpass the IRB's funded capacity.[16] By the end of 2008–09, the number of claims pending review stood at fifty-eight thousand, and the average processing time was expected to grow to 16.4 months (IRB 2009, 2). Desperate times called for desperate measures. The IRB (2009, 16) even began to process simple claims that shared the same counsel in groups despite the legislated requirement of individual assessment. Yet no strategy, however creative and unique, was to save the IRB. The board had to ask for additional funding (IRB 2009, 2).

The chronic shortage of adjudicators made for difficult working conditions at the IRB. The need for increased productivity translated to growing pressure on adjudicators to finalize larger numbers of claims. As one former adjudicator who served from the early 2000s to the end of that decade reflected, "at the beginning [of the decade] it wouldn't be unusual for [adjudicators] to do, like, two, two and a half hearings, like, cases a week. And over the years that was increased to, like, four. So almost doubling it."[17] While adjudicators' workloads doubled, the institutional support they received declined substantially. The elimination of refugee hearing officers (RHO) was particularly consequential to adjudicators' workloads: without RHOs, whose role was to assist decision makers in preparing for and conducting hearings, adjudicators had to shoulder larger volumes of work.[18] As a result, the entire determination process had to be radically re-envisioned. For instance, in the absence of RHO support, conducting thorough background research or gathering substantial volumes of documentation was no longer practical. Instead, adjudicators were encouraged to compensate for gaps in pre-hearing investigations through interviewing techniques: "And now people don't even have the time to do [the thorough research] ... So, you had to do the questioning yourself. So, there was much bigger emphasis on questioning techniques and questioning methods." Even the general administrative assistance offered to adjudicators gradually shrunk:

> Initially you would have one administrative assistant who would be assigned for the [adjudicators] to help them ... that soon changed, and their job became more like an editor ... but they would have many more people to do that for, so you didn't really have as much support. So, you had to do a lot more of your own admin-type work.[19]

With diminishing pre- and post-hearing support, claim adjudications came to primarily rely on real-time oral inquiries by solo adjudicators. Refugee status determinations now happened largely in hearing rooms, arguably, to the detriment of traumatized claimants who have difficulty performing as coherent narrators under stressful conditions.[20]

The pressure to do more with less transformed the culture of adjudications at the IRB. The emphasis on adjudicative rigour and administrative justice was displaced by the need to finalize larger numbers of claims. In the increasingly austere administrative culture of the IRB, adjudicators' work became much more narrowly focused on finalizing claims rather than on safeguarding the integrity of the adjudication process. For instance, adjudicators began to be discouraged from adjourning and postponing hearings, a practice commonly used to allow a fuller presentation of evidence at a later date.[21] To reduce the inefficiencies caused by adjournments and postponements, administrators took the authority to determine hearing preparedness into their own hands.[22] Even though adjudicators, in practice, had the legislated latitude to delay hearings to ensure a thorough determination process, their ability to exercise this right was limited by the normative expectations imposed by administrative authorities. The compulsion for productivity pushed the IRB to unprecedented levels of micro-managing adjudicators. Decision makers were now encouraged to hold shorter hearings, issue more oral decisions, and produce shorter written reasons.[23] Regular performance reports and comparative statistics on productivity levels kept decision makers aware of administrators' goals and expectations. Quantifiable output rates were set and discussed openly in the IRB offices. The administration of Canadian refugee protection was becoming increasingly managerial and, consequently, removed from its humanitarian and judicial agenda.[24]

By the end of the first decade of the new millennium, the IRB (2010, 1, 8) was finally operating with a near full complement of adjudicators and a controlled workload.[25] As the board began to recuperate from years of starved operation, however, a succession of new immigration legislation supplied new challenges. The 2012 *Protecting Canada's Refugee System Act (PCRSA)*, in particular, created long-lasting troubles by dramatically reducing the timelines for making and processing refugee claims.[26] The IRB was now obliged to schedule hearings within three or six months after receiving a new claim. Meeting these timelines was a monumental struggle (IRB 2014, 7).[27] Not only did these timelines undermine the IRB's control over its scheduling practices, but they also sidelined some of the board's well-honed case management techniques. For instance, the requirement to schedule new claims within the legislated timelines meant that the IRB could no longer optimize the use of its geographically specialized adjudication teams: new claims had to be assigned to adjudicators quickly, regardless of whether they fit with the regional expertise of the decision maker (see IRB 2014, 15). Of course, sidestepping the wealth of specialized knowledge accumulated by geographical teams was detrimental both to the quality of the decisions and the efficiency of the claim processing. Even more troublingly, the new timelines did not account for the 30,300 claims that were already in the system when the *PCRSA* came into force (IRB 2013, 8). In fact, no formal capacity was allotted to resolving these older claims, making their processing largely a matter of administrative creativity (IRB 2013, 8; 2014, 15; 2016, 19).[28] As a result, processing older claims became slow and difficult (IRB 2014, 15; 2016, 19–20). Quick hearings proved not to be fair, efficient, or of optimal quality.

Unfortunately, handling the strenuous requirements of the new legislation was not the only major challenge faced by the IRB. In the early 2010s, government funding was becoming increasingly scarce. A cut of 13 million dollars (or 10 percent) from the IRB's (2014, 1–2) budget turned systematic refugee protection into a work of resource patchwork. Even the board's routine procedures now required creative manoeuvring of an unyielding budget. Not only was the processing of older claims practically funded without additional resources, but any fluctuation in the volume of caseloads also had to be absorbed within the reduced budget (IRB 2015, 2). Thus, to handle an increase in intake, the IRB (2016, 1) had to reallocate more than 3 million dollars internally to hire additional decision makers.[29]

The election of the Liberal Party to government in 2015 at the height of the Syrian civil war changed the political discourse on refugee protection across Canada. The revival of liberal humanitarianism provided the IRB with some relief; under the new government, for instance, the IRB began to defy legislated timelines and prioritize the resolution of older cases. The revitalization of humanitarian interest, however, did little to alleviate the IRB's (2017, 1, 2) chronic troubles with insufficient funding and growing intake. Bureaucratic refugee protection remained in the grasp of structural challenges that fuelled a need for restrictionist control.

The Era of "Palliative Care": Intersections of Bureaucratic Restrictionism

The challenges of fitting the IRB's sizable portfolio into a skinny budget kept restrictionism high on the bureaucratic agenda well into the 2000s. The board continued to monitor the number of incoming claims in order to manage its caseloads. It was through this tracking that IRB officials first became concerned with the rising number of Mexican claims (IRB 2003, 23). Mexico soon came to rank as the top source country of refugee claims in Canada for several consecutive years (IRB 2008, 28). The numbers were rising steadily: in 2005, thirty-four hundred Mexicans filed refugee claims in Canada; in 2008, that number reached a peak of ninety-four hundred (O'Neil 2009). In the 2007–08 fiscal year, Mexicans accounted for nearly 25 percent of all new claims (IRB 2008, 14–15). Claims from Mexico were clearly the most significant contributor to the IRB's caseloads.

In addition to pushing the bureaucratic workload to unmanageable levels, Mexican claims were also cause for political headache. Accepting large numbers of Mexican nationals as refugees was a difficult pill for Canada to swallow. After all, Mexico was Canada's *North American Free Trade Agreement* trade partner, a close ally, a democratic country, and, in former Prime Minister Jean Chrétien's words, Canada's "amigo" (Simpson 2009).[30] After the election of conservative governments in both countries in 2006, Canada's relations with Mexico were even further strengthened; in fact, neither country required entry visas for nationals of the other. In short, Canadian political authorities did not consider Mexico to be a refugee-producing country and did not wish to sour the good relations by accepting large numbers of Mexican refugees (*Globe and Mail* 2008; Jimenez 2008; Ivanyi 2009). Yet the provisions of refugee law required Canada to adjudicate Mexican claims without account for geopolitical considerations.

Notwithstanding these mounting political and administrative difficulties, Mexican claimants were undoubtedly fleeing unsafe conditions. In the 2000s, Mexico was in the grip of rampant and indiscriminate violence: an open war between drug cartels and the Mexican government, police corruption, and human-rights abuses by the national army had threatened and taken thousands of lives.[31] In 2008, more than thirteen hundred people had been killed in Ciudad Juàrez alone, a city of 1.3 million (Valpy 2009). Across Mexico, the number of the dead tallied well over three thousand in just one year (Jimenez 2008). Violence was pervasive and easily caught innocent bystanders and civilians. Extortion, kidnapping, rape, decapitation, asphyxiation, and shootouts had become everyday occurrences (Jimenez 2008; Taylor 2008). The Mexican state was at the cusp of losing control over the country (Valpy 2009).

Despite these alarming conditions, Canadian officials were adamant that Mexicans did not constitute legitimate candidates for refugee protection. Multiple departments across the Canadian migration control regime were keen to reject and deter refugee claims from Mexico. At the IRB, Mexican claimants rarely received a positive decision. In 2008, a year of considerable violence in Mexico, acceptance rates of Mexican claimants were only 11 percent, well below the overall average of 34 percent (Jimenez 2008). The low rates were particularly surprisingly given that Mexican claims often involved forms of persecution that from lawyers' points of view, normally produced high rates of acceptance in other national groups (Day 2009).

The Department of Immigration was also quickly turning against Mexican refugees. Mexicans soon became direct targets of restrictionism. In fact, the Department of Immigration reimposed visa restrictions on Mexican nationals in 2008 to cut their access to Canada's inland refugee protection regime.[32] Even more troublingly, Kenney, the Conservative immigration minister, began an open campaign against Mexicans: exceptionally blunt in expressing his views, Kenney spoke publicly and frequently against Mexican claimants, calling them "bogus" (Keung 2009), "queue jumpers" (Fekete 2009), and "systematic abusers of the Canadian system" (Edwards 2009). Not only were Mexican nationals excluded from Canadian protection, but they were also demonized for attempting to practise their supposedly universal right to seek refuge. To be sure, Kenney's active campaign against Mexicans was problematic from a judicial, and not just a humanitarian, perspective: in a system whose adjudicators were ultimately appointed and reappointed by the minister, Kenney's outspoken stance against Mexican claimants arguably created a reasonable apprehension of bias (Showler 2009). Put differently, Mexican claimants could no longer be confident in adjudicators' ability to decide cases independently and without concern for the prospects of their own careers if they were not to comply with the minister's position. Hence, Kenney's open anti-Mexican statements undermined the legislated independence of refugee adjudications from political interference.

Nonetheless, in his attempts to exclude Mexicans from Canadian protection, Kenney had a strong ally in the refugee claim-processing bureaucracy. Although not nearly as explicit as the minister in its intentions, the IRB was equally eager to drop the number of Mexican claims. Indeed, IRB officials relied on the distinctive devices at their disposal to impede Mexicans' access to refugee status. For instance, in May 2008, the board adopted a Persuasive decision that largely invalidated Mexicans' claims to refuge (Jimenez 2008).[33] While acknowledging the pervasive violence in Mexico, the decision suggested that the Mexican government was able and willing to protect its citizens. As a result, Mexicans' fate in the Canadian regime hinged on their ability to convince adjudicators that they had not, despite significant effort, managed to secure protection in Mexico.[34] Consequently, refugee decisions began to rely more heavily on adjudicators' subjective assessments of the protective capacities of the Mexican state than on the credibility of the claims (Zabjek 2009; Keung 2010). In fact, IRB adjudicators regularly rejected claimants that even in their own estimations had endured serious forms of violence. Tragically, the preoccupation with the role of the Mexican state had displaced the focus on the more central question of persecution.

To make matters worse, not all adjudicators believed that the level of violence in Mexico amounted to persecution. Unfortunately, experiences of gender-based violence by many Mexican women were regularly considered insufficiently grave. In one particularly disturbing example, an adjudicator described the case of a seventeen-year-old woman who had been kidnapped and raped by a drug gang as "horrific" but not "atrocious and appalling" enough to warrant refugee protection (Taylor 2008, A1). Even though the IRB's much-celebrated *Guidelines on Women Refugee Claimants Fearing Gender-related Persecution* had long established sexual violence as a form of persecution, this expansive definition was not applied to several Mexican women.[35] This made Mexicans exceptionally, and problematically, excludable. Indeed, when the negative decisions on six gender-based Mexican claims were successfully challenged in the Federal Court of Canada in 2008, the Court reproached the IRB for its gross insensitivity to Mexican women (Taylor 2008). In its haste to reject and deter Mexicans, the IRB had lost touch with the humanitarian and judicial principles of protection, even the ones it had itself worked to institute.

Although surprising, Mexicans' low rates of approval were not an accidental outcome of adjudication proceedings. Rather, the IRB administrators had a strong hand in curating rejections: the IRB had concentrated adjudicators with anti-refugee attitudes and low acceptance rates in the regional team that heard Mexican claims.[36] Therefore, Mexicans were commonly heard by decision makers who were far less inclined to accept refugees, which made the IRB an intensely hostile environment for Mexican claimants. Refugee lawyers who represented Mexicans in these years paint a disturbingly grim picture of the state of affairs: refugee adjudications had turned into openly adversarial encounters, regularly involving confrontations between adjudicators and counsel. One lawyer described the increasingly antagonistic hearings of this period:

> Going into these hearings, it was, it was palliative care, right? The only way that we could, I think many of us [refugee lawyers], could get through ... was to think okay, you know, I have to radically re-adjust my expectations of this process. I'm not going in to try to get someone refugee status. I'm going in to try to make this the most dignified process it can be. I'm going to provide moral support, you know. I'm going to provide emotional support. I'm essentially gonna try to defend this person, I'm gonna try to protect her from having this person [the adjudicator] brutalize her for three hours, before giving her the negative decision, right? So, let's just give the goddamn negative decision. But don't kick my client in the face for three hours before you do it, right? Like that's now my role.[37]

In the face of overwhelmingly unfavourable odds, lawyers' understanding of their own work had to be thoroughly redefined: "successful" legal representation was no longer about securing claimants refugee status. Negative decisions, after all, had become virtually inevitable. Thus, lawyers simply aimed to shield claimants from degradation and abuse in a process that now guaranteed a cruel encounter. The practice of refugee law was reduced to providing palliative care to a dying promise of protection. Legal representation was only a very sombre joke.

Still, the Canadian regime had not exhausted its strategies against Mexican claimants. In 2012, the Conservative government introduced an innovative fast-tracking system, which unlike earlier expedited processes, was externally controlled and decidedly skewed toward rejections.[38] The designated countries of origin (DCO) was an explicit strategy of deterrence: it was meant to cut the supposedly large number of "unfounded" claims that clogged Canada's refugee protection system by allowing the minister to create a list of countries that in his estimation were unlikely producers of refugees (see Citizenship and Immigration Canada 2013, 2017). Claims from these "safe" countries were then diverted to procedures that ensured their minimal chances of approval. For instance, DCO claims were heard within only thirty or forty-five days, compared to sixty days for other claims (Citizenship and Immigration Canada 2013).[39] These truncated timelines gave claimants little time to secure legal representation, prepare for hearings, and gather necessary supporting documents and evidence. Hence, it became practically impossible for DCO claimants to put forth strong cases. Furthermore, DCO claims were excluded from the right to appeal negative decisions to the IRB's new Refugee Appeal Division (RAD). This made appeals to federal courts the only possible avenue for challenging negative outcomes. Yet the time, cost, and procedural and judicial limitations of federal appeals made them highly inaccessible, particularly as the Department of Immigration began to expedite the deportation of rejected claimants (Citizenship and Immigration Canada 2013; Levine-Rasky, Beaudoin, and St. Clair 2014).[40] In short, the DCO made negative decisions easy to make and difficult to reverse.[41] Mexico was swiftly placed on the DCO list, despite its well-documented records of human-rights crises (see Government of Canada 2019b).

Importantly, although the DCO was externally imposed on the IRB, it was not wholly out of line with the board's administrative goals. To the contrary, the DCO represented a coalescence of political and administrative interests in increasing the speed and productivity of bureaucratic refugee claim processing. The DCO's restrictionist provisions helped the IRB process masses of claims out of its caseloads (Citizenship and Immigration Canada 2017). Speed and productivity, however, came at the cost of the legal standards of adjudication; the quick processing of DCO claims undermined the requirements of political independence, individual assessment, and procedural fairness in adjudications. In effect, the DCO restricted access to the full range of rights envisioned by refugee law via a combination of procedural measures imposed by political authorities.

The alliance of political and bureaucratic authorities against Mexican claimants diminished their chances of receiving refugee protection in Canada. By the early 2010s, very few Mexicans managed to enter the Canadian regime and very few exited it with refugee status. In 2014, for example, Mexican claimants were accepted at a rate of 29 percent, compared to the overall average of 50 percent. Mexicans, further, numbered only 328 of the 19,954 adjudicated claims. Unfortunately, being of Mexican nationality markedly reduced a claimant's chance of receiving protection, even for those who were otherwise accepted at high rates. For instance, claims that involved persecution based on sexual orientation and gender identity and expression generally did well in Canadian refugee adjudications. In 2011 and 2012, 64 percent and 60 percent of SOGIE claims received positive decisions, which were well above the overall acceptance rates of 38 percent and 35 percent respectively.[42] Yet Mexican SOGIE claims were not treated with equal measures of generosity: in 2011, only twenty out of a total of 112 Mexican SOGIE claims (18 percent) were accepted. In the years preceding the release of the IRB's celebrated *SOGIE Guidelines*, Mexican SOGIE claimants faired considerably worse than other SOGIE cases.[43] Even their ability to enter refugee adjudication proceedings had drastically declined. In 2014, only one of nine Mexican SOGIE claimants (11 percent) received a positive decision; in 2015, no Mexican cases were among the 1,286 SOGIE claims that the IRB adjudicated. In some years, the acceptance rates of Mexican SOGIE claims were even lower than other Mexican cases. For instance, Mexican SOGIE claims were accepted at a rate of only 11 percent in 2014, while the acceptance rates of all Mexicans averaged 29 percent.

Figure 3 Acceptance Rates of SOGIE, Mexican, and Mexican SOGIE Claims

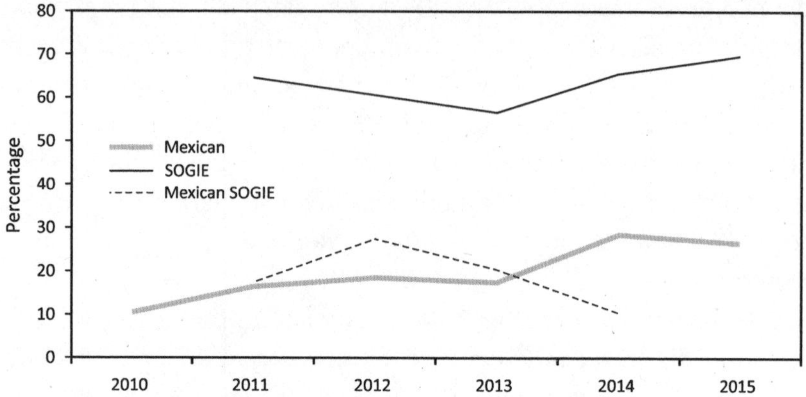

Thus, the efficacy of SOGIE refugee rights in Canada was, in practice, mediated by the intersectional filter of national origin. SOGIE claims from Mexico were impeded by procedural measures that took force well before these claims were in any position to benefit from the expansion of SOGIE rights. Visa restrictions, curated teams of hostile adjudicators, insufficient case preparation timelines, and lack of access to appeal proceedings restricted the access of all Mexican claimants, irrespective of the nature of their claims. In effect, in the Canadian regime, Mexican SOGIE claimants were Mexican first and SOGIE second. As a result, their acceptance rates aligned more closely with those of Mexican, rather than SOGIE, refugees (see Figure 3). In short, the coalition of restrictionist strategies by political and bureaucratic authorities overrode the expansive effects of SOGIE rights for Mexican refugees. Mexican SOGIE claimants were subject to systematic rejection based on their nationality in ways that made it unlikely for them to benefit from the expansion of SOGIE rights. As the dismal acceptance rates of these claims suggest, the convergence of political and bureaucratic disadvantage may easily undermine any advantage offered by expansive jurisprudence. SOGIE rights, in a word, were made ineffectual by political and bureaucratic manoeuvres.

However ingeniously achieved, effective restrictionism in the refugee protection context is of tragic consequence. A case in point is Grise, a twenty-four-year-old pregnant woman who was abducted and murdered by drug traffickers, as she had feared she would be, shortly after she was deported to Mexico by the Canadian government (Keung 2009; Greenaway 2009). Grise, along with her mother and sister, had attempted twice to secure protection in Canada. Her claim had been rejected both times by adjudicators who had decided that her family had not made enough effort to secure safety from Mexican authorities. Even the customary pre-removal risk assessment[44] had failed to properly recognize the danger of returning her to Mexico. When Grise's family was eventually granted re-entry to Canada as the result of mass activism in their support, her grieving mother lamented the price they had to pay for their safety: "My daughter had to be killed in order for Canada to believe in our story. The price is just too high" (Keung 2009, GT1).[45] Grise is perhaps only one of the unnumbered casualties of systematic restrictionism against Mexican refugees in this period. The price of increased administrative and political control has been, no doubt, too high.

This chapter has considered the struggles of bureaucratic refugee claim processing in the new millennium to understand the unceasing compulsion for restrictionist control. Heavy workloads, political neglect, and chronic understaffing meant that the IRB was operating under constant threat of collapse. In this structurally fraught context, restricting the number of incoming claims remained integral to institutional survival. Hence, the board continued resolutely invested in systematic rejection and deterrence. The bureaucratic interest in lowering claim numbers concurred with strong anti-refugee political sentiments to create a formidable restrictionist alliance. Claimants who became targets of systemic restrictions in this period were ruthlessly removed from the possibility of protection by multi-stage and multi-departmental strategies. While highly effective in producing a controlled regime of claim processing, restrictionist strategies undermined the judicial and humanitarian principles of refugee protection and came at a high cost to those in desperate need of safety. Restrictionist procedures even hindered the expansive effects of gender-based and SOGIE jurisprudence. Expanding rights were not applied evenly to all claimants. Rather, political and bureaucratic exclusion took effect first, undoing the possibilities offered by jurisprudential expansions. Indeed, those who were filtered out of the realm of rightfulness, albeit due to their nationality, tell the untold story of Canadian exceptional SOGIE protection: SOGIE rights are exceptional for some, yet virtually non-existent for others.

Ultimately, in recent years, the Canadian regime remained conflicted between an expansionist desire to extend protection, particularly to those fleeing persecution based on sexual orientation, gender identity and gender expression, and a restrictionist commitment to limit the access of those who arrived in large numbers, even if out of legitimate fear of harm. The expansion of refugee and SOGIE rights was achieved primarily through legislation and jurisprudence; conversely, restrictions were operationalized via procedural and administrative measures. The articulation of expansions in fields and in relation to subjects that were, supposedly, distinct from those of restrictions allowed the Canadian regime to, once again, accommodate paradoxical agendas simultaneously: the Canadian regime conferred more rights while becoming more restrictive than ever.

Conclusion
For Whose Protection?

Between May and October 1847, otherwise known as the "Black '47," 38,560 famished Irish migrants arrived at Toronto's waterfront, then a city of only twenty thousand residents. The migrants were sick and penniless. Their arrival brought disorder, death, and confusion. Some Torontonians received the migrants with sympathy; others objected to their presence with racist contempt.[1] Despite the initial shock, the city gradually absorbed and passed along a refugee population of almost double its size. Migrants came, died, resettled, or moved to other parts of Canada. And no major calamity or long-term damage ensued to life in Toronto.

Today, one hundred and seventy odd years after the Black '47, it is thoroughly inconceivable for a city like Toronto to play host to even a remotely comparable population of hungry and ill refugees. The cost and inconvenience of receiving that large of a volume of needy migrants is enough to rule the entire notion out of the realm of plausibility. To be sure, it was also massively costly and inconvenient to receive the famished Irish migrants. However, in 1847, concerns with cost and inconvenience were not as readily and capably accommodated by logics and technologies of governance. Thus, the famished migrants arrived, and the only possible response was to receive them, even if reluctantly so. Ironically, as refugee protection has become more formalized, it has become harder for displaced populations to find safety in relatively stable and prosperous regions of the world. The events of Black '47 are perhaps no longer conceivable precisely because of the advent of formalized, state-controlled, economically conscious regimes of refugee protection in the liberal democratic world. There is, of course, no shortage of refugees. Millions upon millions of people continue to be displaced by famine, war, and other tragedies comparable in scale to the Great Hunger in Ireland. But the displaced hardly ever reach Canada, nor are the famished even considered legitimate refugees. Contemporary regimes of refugee protection are now far more advanced and much more capable of minimizing the cost and chaos that displaced populations may produce in wealthy host countries. Black '47 is now an unimaginable mishap of the past because it would be completely irrational, economically unfeasible, and socio-politically disorderly for such an event to take place again.

Although liberal democratic countries led the development of international refugee law, the bulk of refugee protection has now primarily fallen onto the laps of far less wealthy and less "liberal" countries. Countries with fewer resources, less codified regimes of refugee protection, and slighter legal systems now host most of the refugees in the world. Turkey, for instance, is housing 3.8 million refugees, while Colombia and Pakistan host 1.8 and 1.5 million respectively.[2] Lebanon, a country of only 6.8 million with many recent economic and political calamities, houses over 1 million refugee residents, giving it the world's second highest ratio of refugees per capita.[3] Importantly, none of these top refugee-receiving countries are among the initial signatories of the 1951 Convention Relating to the Status of Refugees *(Refugee Convention).*[4] In fact, Lebanon and Pakistan have yet to sign the *Refugee Convention* and its 1967 *Protocol Relating to the Status of Refugees.*[5]

Lebanon, a country that has hosted Palestinian refugees since 1948, neither has signed the *Refugee Convention* nor has national legislation on refugees (Janmyr 2016). The ironic absence of refugee rights in Lebanon is the result of decades of geopolitical struggle with and against liberal notions of refugee protection: at the time of the drafting of the *Refugee Convention,* Palestinian refugees were already under the mandate of the United Nations Relief and Works Agency for Palestine Refugees in the Near East – hence, they were excluded from the protection of the *Convention*. Arab states supported this exclusion because they wished neither to erode the special legal status of Palestinian refugees nor to assume responsibility for their care (Knudsen 2009). Thus, Lebanon, and much of the Arab world, continued to host displaced Palestinians yet never became a party to the *Convention*. As a result, today, Palestinian refugees are not within the jurisdiction of any singular international body, and, consequently, they suffer from major gaps in protection (Suleiman 2006).[6] Needless to say, the absence of codified legal obligations to refugees in Lebanon has serious implications for Palestinians and other refugees in that country.[7]

In the case of Pakistan, the myopic Eurocentricity of the "international" refugee accord impeded the ratification of the *Refugee Convention*. As is well known, the *Refugee Convention* was originally concerned primarily with European displacement, making its protection framework rather irrelevant to the 14 million South Asians who had been forced into displacement as a result of the 1947 partition between India and Pakistan. Given that the displaced South Asians were not considered to have lost the protection of their nationality, they were not counted among the ranks of legitimate convention refugees (D. Robinson 2012). Both India and Pakistan strongly objected to this exclusion and, in protest, refused to become parties to the *Convention*. Meanwhile, the mass displacement in South Asia was addressed through regional refugee regimes that developed in parallel to the international system. In subsequent decades, refugee protection in Pakistan remained a makeshift project, and refugees' access to services were limited, at times, to the bare necessities. In some instances, the Pakistani state even actively obstructed refugees' access to basic rights, such as education and employment, to discourage their stay.[8]

These troubled histories of formalized refugee protection have created a scene in which most of the world's refugees live in countries whose refugee systems are less rigorously organized around international provisions or liberal notions of justice. By any honest estimation, refugee law has failed to protect refugees or to establish their universal human rights. The failure of human-rights law is a noteworthy, if not an astonishing, reality: over the course of the human-rights–focused twentieth century, arguably more human-rights violations have occurred than ever before (Douzinas 2000). Moreover, the equality of refugees' supposedly "universal" rights is regularly undermined in practical encounters between national governments and outsiders (Kapur 2006). As Denise Ferreira da Silva (2001, 424) suggests, (racist) inequality is not external to liberal justice; rather, exclusion "circumscribe[s] the zone of operation of [liberal] universality." Hence, it is perhaps not surprising that today, the vast majority of the world's refugee population is actively and systematically excluded from the territorial realm of liberal rule. Refugees quite literally remain on different continents than the liberal regimes of refugee protection.

Whom, then, do liberal regimes of refugee protection protect? In this book, I have proposed that refugee protection is, and has long been, a highly paradoxical state project in Canada. I have suggested that the Canadian paradox is only a reflection of the much larger problem of state-controlled refugee protection: the difficulty of instituting universal rights through the exclusionary mechanisms of the nation-state. Indeed, the paradox of refugee protection spans far beyond Canada and its refugee claim-processing system. The Canadian state is, after all, only a small part of a much larger regime that exerts exclusionary control over mobility and access to rights across the globe. In the global regime of nation-states, exclusion and inequality are not incidental; nation-states are meant to discriminate against and exclude non-citizens. Consequently, refugees have a highly tenuous claim to equality. And, yet, nation-states remain in charge of administering refugees' access to equality. The problem, in other words, is not singularly Canadian.

The paradox of refugee protection, moreover, is not just about refugees or the difficulties of protecting them. The astounding underperformance of regimes of state-controlled refugee protection is perhaps one rather humble example of the ironies of liberal equality and the functional failures of states that claim them. Refugee protection fails to protect refugees because, plainly speaking, universal equality is not set up to ever be fulfilled, certainly not via the economically motivated and efficiency-focused regimes that are designated to its administration. The larger problem, hence, concerns the paradoxically un-universal equality of "universal" rights.

This book has argued that the Canadian regime of refugee protection is a complex and dynamic articulation of an expansionist impetus for humanitarianism and a restrictionist compulsion for control. I have further argued that the paradoxical impulses of refugee protection are articulated in specific and systematic arrangements. The humanitarian impulse to expand the reach of rights has been primarily achieved in the field of law and in relation to tightly guarded legal categories. Chapter 1, for instance, explored the expansion of refugee rights through the legislation of the refugee category in the 1976 *Immigration Act*.[9] This legislative change and the emerging jurisprudential rulings dramatically increased refugee claimants' scope of rights. Chapters 3 and 5 followed the subsequent expansions of refugee rights through progressive jurisprudence. Feminist reinterpretations of the 1951 *Refugee Convention*, the changing legal status of sexual minorities in Canada, and a Supreme Court of Canada ruling made gender-based and sexual orientation and gender identity and expression (SOGIE) claimants unquestioned subjects of rights and protection. In all these instances, humanitarian expansions were led or heavily aided by forces within the field of law.

In contrast, the impulse to restrict access to protection has been largely applied in the field of bureaucracy and imposed against malleable and shifting target groups. Chapter 2 traced the administrative desire for restrictionism in the early years of the contemporary regime of refugee protection in Canada. We saw that keeping specific national groups away from refugee rights became a bureaucratic strategy of survival. Chapters 4 and 6 provided several examples of how the claim-processing bureaucracy manufactured, isolated, and excluded strategic groups of claimants in subsequent decades. Coordinating practices with political forces, accelerating the rejection of unwanted claims, and advancing "model" decisions against target groups constituted some of these restrictionist methods. Restrictionism was regularly implemented, advanced, and originated in the field of bureaucracy.

Of course, this is to suggest neither that the bureaucracy is exclusively restrictionist nor that the law is purely expansive. To the contrary, this book has noted the fundamental restrictions in refugee law and the occasional desire of the bureaucracy to expand the reach of rights. Indeed, it would be highly mistaken to take the law as the vanguard of universal inclusion. If anything, refugee law provides a highly qualified vision of protection. Most notably, by reproducing the liberal primacy of the political domain above all else, refugee law has narrowed the scope of refugee rights to only direct violations of individual citizens by sovereign states. Thereby, the existing legal provisions fail to recognize violations that concern other, supposedly distinct, domains. As a result, for instance, those individuals violated by economic dispossession, generalized violence, or ecological devastation remain unprotected. Unsurprisingly, then, most of the displaced population of the world is without access to systematic protection: 68 million displaced persons do not even fit within the protection mandate of the United Nations High Commission for Refugees.[10]

Nonetheless, in the past thirty years, the Canadian regime has articulated its expansionist impulses mostly in the field of law and much of its restrictionist desires in the field of bureaucracy. Further, I suggest that it is through these arrangements that the Canadian regime has managed to advance contradictory agendas and yet sustain itself over time. This observation may pertain to other realms of statecraft as well: the quandary of how it is that states regularly undertake contradictory projects may be explained, in part, by a closer view of the disparate sets of agents and institutions that operationalize distinct agendas.

Much of this book has been a testimony to the relative autonomy and independence of the bureaucracy in effectuating the laws that it supposedly "only" administers. The Canadian refugee claim-processing bureaucracy is an impactful, calculating, and relatively agentic actor in shaping and regulating access to refugee rights. Despite its seemingly neutral demeanour, the bureaucracy is highly biased toward specific interests. Above all, the bureaucracy is structurally disposed to rational, controlled, and efficient conduct (Weber [1922] 1978; Ritzer [1993] 2013). This disposition often places the bureaucracy on a track that is different from that of the law. For instance, while refugee law is principally concerned with the equal, fair, and individual assessment of claims, the bureaucracy is interested in quick and cheap procedures. While the law prioritizes principles of administrative justice over convenience, the bureaucracy pursues control and feasibility. While refugee law establishes the universal right to seek asylum, the bureaucracy is hard at work controlling and restricting the actual number of claimants who may file refugee claims. The law and bureaucracy are organized and motivated by different sets of logics and objectives; they are fields that operate in relative autonomy from one another (Bourdieu 1993a).

Although the law is undoubtedly a powerful actor, the bureaucracy is not without its own distinct devices. As several examples in this book have suggested, when the bureaucracy sees fit and is able, it actively manipulates, sidesteps, or even undermines the law in pursuit of its own interests. For example, in repeatedly promoting group-based processing of refugee claims, the Canadian refugee claim-processing bureaucracy has quietly undermined the legal standards of individual claim assessment. In its collaborations with political forces to curb the flow of incoming cases, the bureaucracy has violated principles of political independence and impartiality. In sum, the bureaucracy is an active and influential player that works with and, at times, against the law. Thus, the Immigration and Refugee Board of Canada's (IRB) (2019; emphasis added) professed mandate of "making well-reasoned decisions on immigration and refugee matters, efficiently, fairly and *in accordance with the law*" should be taken with a grain of salt.

Of course, the bureaucratic agenda is not always and necessarily in opposition to that of the law. Nor is the bureaucracy an unhampered agent that may autonomously advance its own agenda without regard for other powerful fields and forces. As an actor encapsulated in a tight network of laws and politics, the bureaucracy has only limited and relative autonomy. In fact, in numerous instances, the Canadian refugee claim-processing bureaucracy willingly cooperates with the objectives of the law or is otherwise forced to comply with legal requirements. For instance, the development of the *Guidelines on Women Refugee Claimants Fearing Gender-related Persecution* was in part the result of the bureaucracy's wilful cooperation with emerging feminist jurisprudence. In contrast, the imposition of unrealistically short processing timelines by the *Protecting Canada's Immigration System Act* presented a moment of disgruntled compliance by the bureaucracy.[11]

Importantly, the outcome of the battles between the law and bureaucracy is not predetermined by any singular factor. When legal and bureaucratic agendas clash, what transpires is contingent on the circumstantial alignments of other surrounding forces. If the law is supported by a well-mobilized community of advocates, for instance, bureaucratic practices can be challenged or overturned. The successful repeal of the Lead case is a case in point. Conversely, if political forces are squarely aligned with the objectives of bureaucrats, the results may turn in favour of the bureaucracy. The designated countries of origin policy are an example of such alignment: it was with the support of political forces that the bureaucracy operationalized legally questionable and procedurally unequal systems of mass rejection. In short, the law and the bureaucracy interact in a real-time game of strategic alliance; they lose, win, and continue playing. Thus, rather than proposing an inflexible dichotomy between the law and the bureaucracy, I suggest that the complex and dynamic attachments between the two constitute an articulation: a durable and un-predetermined formation that persists despite internal contradictions and inconsistencies.

This book has provided a detailed and relatively compassionate account of the restrictionist inclinations of the Canadian refugee claim-processing bureaucracy. Although the bureaucracy is a serious repeat offender of restrictionism, its penchant for reducing access to refugee rights is not a simple matter of ill will. As Akhil Gupta (2012) has argued in relation to the postcolonial state's failure to eradicate mass poverty in India, the goal of establishing equality is somewhat incongruent with the bureaucratic structure; the structural design and situated needs of the bureaucracy necessitate imposing weighty restrictions on the access to rights. Thus, a substantial portion of this book has been devoted to enumerating the significant hurdles that have constrained and overwhelmed the Canadian refugee claim-processing bureaucracy over the course of its existence. Unexpectedly large workloads, insufficient funds and human resources, and political threat and interdepartmental sabotage have placed the bureaucracy in a continuously tenuous position. Institutional survival was never guaranteed, but it was achieved through pragmatism, strategizing, and proactive and restrictionist planning.

The bureaucratic work of refugee protection in Canada has been further troubled by the growing weight of neoliberal logics in the past thirty years. Even the moralized work of humanitarianism has not escaped the austere force of neoliberal economic calculations. As a result, over the course of the past three decades, the Canadian claim-processing bureaucracy has become increasingly strained. Pressed by large workloads and insufficient resources, the bureaucracy has had no choice but to prioritize productivity over justice. Fast and cheap claim processing, in turn, has required restrictionist administrative control: economically viable refugee protection has necessitated deterrence and exclusion. Put differently, the strained, neoliberalized bureaucracy has been ill-fitted to the moral and humanitarian task of refugee protection; hence, refugee protection has been carried out with remarkable failure.

Ever since refugee rights became codified in Canadian law in 1976, Canada has administered refugee protection through systematic deterrence and rejection of those seeking refuge. Scapegoating unwanted claimants based on their nationality has become a routine and adaptable method of controlling workloads and rates of acceptance. In Chapters 2, 4, and 6, I have traced the various national groups that became subjects of exclusionary strategies during the thirty-year lifespan of the contemporary regime of refugee protection in Canada. Every era of refugee protection has produced its specific targets: claimants from poor Caribbean countries, particularly Jamaica and Trinidad, were the first scapegoats for the young bureaucracy. Eastern Europeans quickly became the new foci for administrative strategizing. Chileans and the Roma featured in the exclusionary projects of the 1990s. Mexicans were the main targets in the late 2000s. Importantly, the fall of these groups to the rank of excludability was intimately linked with the administrative needs of the bureaucracy and the political sensibilities of the time: only groups whose numbers disturbed the timely processing of refugee claims and whose exclusion was politically unproblematic became targets of restrictionism. In short, scapegoats were strategic administrative and political productions.

The empirical analysis in this book trailed off in the later parts of the 2010s. Yet strategic exclusion remains a key aspect of Canadian refugee protection. To this day, new configurations of excludable claimants periodically emerge in the public and administrative discourses of refugee protection. Irregular Haitian claimants of 2018, for instance, are among some of the more recent groups of excludables. The administrative panic with the irregular arrival of Haitians has been somewhat understandable: after Donald Trump was elected as the US president, more than thirty thousand people "irregularly" crossed into Canada to seek protection (Zilio 2018b). In comparison, in 2016, only two thousand asylum seekers entered Canada without going through an official port of entry (Samuel 2018). Many of these irregular border crossers were Haitians who had been living under temporary protected status in the United States since the 2010 earthquake in Haiti. Once the Trump administration threatened their temporary status in May 2017, thousands headed north in hopes of avoiding deportation or an undocumented life (Campbell 2017; Zilio 2018b). While troublesome for Canadian administrators and border control agents, irregular crossings were a creative, if not desperate, strategy on the part of migrants. Entering Canada irregularly allowed migrants to circumvent the restrictive provisions of the *Safe Third Country Agreement* between Canada and the United States: since the terms of the *Agreement* only apply to those who enter through official ports of entry, crossing the US-Canada border irregularly make it possible for asylum seekers to enter Canadian refugee claim proceedings without being returned to the United States.[12]

Nonetheless, the dramatic increase in the number of irregular arrivals has been highly cumbersome for the Canadian regime of refugee protection. The IRB has struggled with the large inflow of irregular claims. Between February and October 2017, 6,304 Haitian refugee claims were referred to the IRB, yet only 298 cases were concluded (Campbell 2017). By June 2018, the IRB had only managed to process 15 percent of the irregular arrivals (Zilio 2018b). As a result, claim-processing times rose to twenty months. The bloated backlogs made the IRB's work an effort in vain; if the backlogs were not effectively controlled, the IRB officials predicted that new claims could face a wait time of eleven years by 2021 (Campbell 2017). Unsurprisingly, thus, the strained board once again became keen on mass rejection. Acceptance rates at the Quebec regional office, where the bulk of irregular claims were processed, dropped considerably lower than other offices (Zilio 2018b). Across Canada, a smaller portion of irregular border crossers began to be accepted as refugees: in 2017, 53 percent of irregular border crossers received refugee status. In the first three months of 2018, their acceptance rates dropped to 40 percent. Haitians did particularly poorly: while 84 percent of Syrian and 34 percent of Nigerian irregular claims made between February 2017 and March 2018 were granted, only 9 percent of Haitians secured refugee status in Canada (Samuel 2018).

To make matters worse, rejected Haitian claimants became targets of concerted deportations (Zilio 2018b). Even though Canada closed its embassy in Haiti and began to advise Canadians against travel to that country, many Haitian refugee claimants, including children, were sent back to unsafe and unstable conditions (Canadian Broadcasting Corporation 2019).[13] In addition, new provisions were introduced by the Liberal government to curb the access of irregular border crossers to refugee rights in Canada (see Wright 2019). As a result, many claimants who were in serious need of safety were turned away from Canada. Systemic rejection remained central to how the Canadian state administers refugee protection. The administrative and economic pressures imposed by the COVID-19 global pandemic have likely only exacerbated the restrictionist drive of the Canadian regime.

My account of the Canadian regime of refugee protection suggests that the failure to protect refugees is an inevitable consequence of conducting the work of humanitarianism through the administrative device of the bureaucracy. Of course, this failure is not limited to Canada. The Canadian regime is perhaps one of the better models of state-controlled refugee protection. Not only do claimants often have comparatively high rates of acceptance in Canada, but Canadian refugee policy is far less politicized than those of countries such as the United States (see Hamlin 2014).[14] Most other post-industrial, English-speaking countries process refugee claims directly through their Departments of Immigration or their sub-departments. As a result, their refugee status determination systems are not independent from political authority. For instance, in the United States, refugee claimants are interviewed by asylum officers at Citizenship and Immigration Services,[15] while, in Australia, the Department of Immigration and Border Protection is tasked with the initial assessment of claims.[16] In the United Kingdom, the Home Office remains responsible for administering asylum cases. Initial assessments by the Home Office are poorly made and are appealed at high rates (Refugee Council, n.d.). Refugee proceedings in the Australian system have also come under great scrutiny following disturbing evidence of impetuous decision-making.[17] In short, the problem of refugee protection is not uniquely Canadian: across the liberal world, refugee protection regimes regularly fail to protect refugees.

In this book, I have used Stuart Hall's (1980, 1985) concept of articulation to suggest that contradiction and failure are structural and functional to inland refugee protection in Canada. The articulated regime of refugee protection is not accidentally paradoxical; rather, it is fundamentally made up of conflictual forces, logics, discourses, and operations. Hence, failure is not a "mistake" but, rather, a necessary part of how the regime is meant to (partially not) work. As a matter of fact, the failure to protect has perhaps helped sustain the Canadian regime by creating the conditions for its futurity: the unfulfilled promise of protection has necessitated further promising, and the cycle of promising and failing has upheld Canadian refugee protection.

This book has set out to uncover the systematic failures of state-controlled refugee protection in relation to refugees. Yet the analysis in this book has also pointed to the many failures of bureaucratic refugee protection as a state mechanism of migration control. State-controlled refugee protection, as it appears, is not much more adept at controlling migratory movements than it is at protecting refugees. Indeed, controlling migratory flows through the refugee protection regime has proven highly cumbersome for state officials.

The moment Canada signed the *Refugee Convention* in 1969, refugee protection became a "problem" that no level of creativity and dedication has been able to fix. When the refugee category was legislated into Canadian law through the 1976 *Immigration Act,* the practical implications of protection only became more complicated. As Canadian political scientist Gerald Dirks (1995) has noted, no other aspect of the *Act* has produced as much headache and embarrassment for Canadian state officials as inland refugee status determination. My account of the Canadian regime corroborates the ordeal of state-controlled refugee protection for the Canadian state: administering a regime of refugee protection that upholds constitutional rights to due process and administrative justice, and yet remains compatible with other state operations and economic and foreign interests, has been, without doubt, unrelentingly troublesome.

The tribulations of the Canadian regime are perhaps not surprising. After all, Canada's refugee protection regime is only a makeshift solution to the weighty problem of global inequality and the displacement and dispossession it creates. Inevitably, refugee protection has been the ongoing work of supplying temporary and surface-level solutions to systematic problems. As a result, the rather minuscule mandate of inland refugee protection has required disproportionately large amounts of attention, labour, and resources. Refugee protection has been a frustrating and frustrated state project.

Of course, Canada's inland refugee protection regime protects some refugees and benefits the Canadian state in some respects. For instance, the Canadian regime has helped promote an image of humanitarianism across the globe and provides some regulatory control over migration flows. Nonetheless, this regime has contributed to both functions of humanitarianism and migration control without excelling at either. Failure has been a constant feature of Canadian refugee protection on all fronts.

The systematic failure of the Canadian regime to be adequately humanitarian or fully amenable to migration control has perhaps been key to negotiating the paradoxical demands of refugee protection. As I showed in Chapter 4, for instance, the IRB's dedication to humanitarian protection in the early 1990s caused strong public and political backlash. Conversely, the board's attempts to facilitate restrictive migration control through strategies such as the Lead case led to public outcry and judicial reproach. As it appears, keeping the paradoxical requirements of state-controlled refugee protection in relative equilibrium calls for exacting levels of mediocrity. Thus, the Canadian regime has managed to stay afloat by holding its incongruent stakeholders in constant states of tolerable dissatisfaction: the Canadian regime has done just enough refugee protection to maintain a slight claim to humanitarianism, enough abidance by the law to be considered lawful, enough cost-cutting to be barely economically viable, and enough migration control to count as part of Canada's broader apparatus of migration and border control. By conducting all these tasks with minimal competence, the Canadian regime has survived thirty years of paradoxical demands.

The biggest achievement of the Canadian regime of refugee protection, hence, may be its own continued existence as a deeply paradoxical project. The systematic failure and mediocrity of the Canadian regime has surprising implications for who becomes the subject of its protection. I conclude this book with a series of anecdotes from my fieldwork that perhaps most tellingly convey the irony of "refugee protection" in Canada. In the early months of my fieldwork in the summer of 2016, I attempted to interview several IRB officials. Through public events and information sessions, I met and made connections with three IRB employees. Upon meeting each employee, I introduced myself and explained the purpose of my research. They all received me with great politeness; while some seemed more forthcoming and interested than others, none refused to give me their work email address. I then emailed these employees to invite them for an interview. In all the emails, I explained the academic nature of my research and the ethical standards of anonymity and confidentiality. One employee responded relatively quickly and in a highly formalized tone informed me that he did not have the authority to speak on behalf of the IRB. He then forwarded my email to his supervisor. His supervisor indicated some openness to speaking with me and asked for my phone number. I provided my phone number, explained that my research process required a signed consent form, and asked to meet in person. The supervisor did not respond.

A second IRB employee expressed unexpected openness to my research when we first met. He even offered to help before I asked. After a very friendly chat, he volunteered his work email and told me that I should feel free to email him my questions. He indicated that he might decide to answer my questions on the phone; communicating on the phone rather than in writing, it seemed, gave him fewer reservations about speaking freely. I agreed and followed up with an email. He responded with warmth but appeared considerably more hesitant about speaking to me during this second encounter. He asked me to further clarify my areas of interest and suggested that I may be better served by contacting the IRB's official communications department. In a later email, he told me that he would consult his manager about my request and that he did not have the authority to speak on behalf of the board. He again suggested that I direct my inquiries to the IRB's communications team. In response to my subsequent inquiries, he replied that he would get back to me shortly. My follow-up emails remained unanswered. I suspected that the supervisor had not agreed to our interview. Soon, the senior communication officer from Ottawa contacted me to see how she could answer my questions. She then assigned another officer to the task. As expected, the responses I received from the communications department were general and mostly unhelpful (see Appendix A).

The third IRB employee did not appear to have any reservations about speaking with me at our initial meeting and responded with openness to my email invitation. But once I attempted to plan a meeting, he stopped responding to my emails. I later ran into him at an information session. He told me that he had indeed received my email and had decided to ask for permission from his supervisor before speaking with me. The supervisor, seemingly, had not yet responded to his request. The employee, who clearly felt uncomfortable about not having responded to my email, suggested that he might be able to appease his supervisor by submitting his answers to her before releasing them to me. From our conversation, I gathered that the employee and his supervisor had been discussing my request and remained undecided about how to proceed. His careful probes about my research revealed untold anxiety about the potential risks that my inquiries posed. I found myself emphasizing again that I was not a journalist, that I was not in search of scandalous details about the board, or in any way intended to violate the ethical terms of academic research. Nonetheless, I left the interaction unsure of whether I had convinced the employee of my intentions.

Eventually this employee's supervisor contacted me and asked that I send my questions in advance of an interview. I did so and again reassured her that I was not intending to scandalize any employee or the IRB. We eventually decided to have a phone interview a few days later. She agreed to sign the consent from but did not agree to be audio-recorded. On the day of the scheduled phone interview, the supervisor emailed to ask if she may relay the information in text rather than on the phone. Sensing her great reservation about speaking to me and having no other options, I agreed. She emailed me her written responses. Her answers were astonishing. They were either literally copied and pasted from the IRB's website or were thoroughly formalistic and empty (see Appendix B). For example, to my inquiry about the training process for new adjudicators, the supervisor responded that "[the] IRB [adjudicators] are highly qualified and well-trained." She answered four questions on the outcome of adjudications by stating that "each [case] is decided by an independent decision maker on its own merits. Each case is unique." Upon receiving these responses, I finally realized that I had been completely misguided in assuming that I could gain any meaningful access to the world of the IRB bureaucrats.[18]

Over the course of five months of communication with IRB personnel, I was told numerous times that a manager will be consulted, that employees did not have the authority to speak on behalf of the IRB, that I should contact communications officers, and that my inquiries would be returned "shortly." The IRB bureaucrats were well versed in the art of avoiding conversation without verbalizing outright refusals. Lower-level bureaucrats quickly referred my inquiries to their supervisors or the official communications team, diverting unwanted responsibility from themselves while signifying institutional loyalty to their superiors. Supervisors controlled their employees' behaviour behind closed doors and responded with formalistic statements. My requests for interviews were repeatedly evaded, while I was continuously assured of the IRB's commitment to reasonable transparency. Despite my best efforts, no real information ever crossed the lips of these bureaucrats. The polite silence on the surface masked a host of anxious conversations about my intentions. Lower- and higher-level bureaucrats, and possibly persons I had never met, discussed my requests and strategized a course of action for minimizing the risk that I posed. To my utter shock and disbelief, I – then a young and eagerly inexperienced doctoral candidate – was perceived as a threat. In the world of bureaucrats who handled literal matters of life and death for refugees on a daily basis, the meanings of "risk," "harm," and "protection" were distorted in astonishingly self-serving and self-centric ways. The Canadian regime of refugee protection seemed simply most capable of, and most dedicated to, protecting itself.

Appendix A
Information Received from the IRB Communications Office in Ottawa

1 *How are RPD Members hired? How are RAD Members hired?*

The information regarding the hiring process for Governor in Council Appointed Members for the RAD can be found on the IRB external website. *http://www.irb-cisr.gc.ca/Eng/NewsNouv/NewNou/Pages/CampRecrut072016.aspx*. RPD members public servants [sic] and are hired through the same competitive hiring process as all public servants.

2 ***In what ways are the RAD and RPD Members independent of one another?***

On the IRB website, see the Chairperson's Instructions Governing Communications Between Related Divisions at the Immigration and Refugee Board of Canada (the Instructions): *http://www.irb-cisr.gc.ca/Eng/BoaCom/references/pol/instructions/Pages/InstructDivisions.aspx*.

The purpose of the Instructions is set out in s. 1.1 as follows:

They reaffirm the fundamental principles of institutional independence, whereby members are free from improper influence. The Instructions also set out a framework for the level of separation expected between first-level and appeal-level Divisions of the IRB; that is, between the Refugee Protection Division (RPD) and the Refugee Appeal Division (RAD); and between the Immigration Division (ID) and the Immigration Appeal Division (IAD).

3 *What are the most common grounds based on which claims are denied? What are the most common grounds based on which claims are approved?*

For the RPD, see the attached document Top 10 RPD. When the RAD finds that there is an error fact [sic], error of law or mixed fact and law in the RPD decision, the appeal is allowed.

4 *What are the most common grounds based on which appeals are allowed? What are the most common grounds based on which appeals are dismissed?*

When the RAD finds that there are no errors in the decision of the RPD, the appeal is dismissed.

5 *How are RAD and RPD Members trained? What materials do these trainings cover? How long are the trainings? Who provides the training? Do RAD and RPD Members go through different trainings? If yes, in what ways are these trainings different?*

RAD members are trained by the Legal Services of the IRB over a period of close to one month on legal principles and jurisprudence as it concerns the RPD and the RAD. Six months or so after the initial training, there is a Continued Education programme of approximately one week where the knowledge is consolidated. There are monthly Professional Development Sessions thereafter. Members attend various legal conferences during the course of their appointment.

RPD members undergo an initial training program of several weeks. This program covers all aspects of in-Canada refugee status determination, including the refugee definition and associated jurisprudence. It also covers procedural issues, including the principles of natural justice. Finally, the program also covers practice based aspects, such as presiding over a hearing and drafting reasons. Various materials are used, including PowerPoint presentations, practice exercises, and mock files. IRB Legal Services provides the training on the legal elements, while the Division leads the training on practice elements.

The initial program finishes with new members sitting on three-member panels with experienced members for the purpose of enhancing their hearing presiding skills. This aspect of the training program is set out in the RPD's policy on the Designation of three-member panels – Refugee Protection Division available on the IRB's website: *http://www.irb-cisr.gc.ca/Eng/BoaCom/references/pol/pol/Pages/PolRpdSpr3MemCom.aspx.*

RPD members receive ongoing professional development. One aspect is regular jurisprudence updates on important Court decisions, provided by IRB Legal Services. In addition, professional development sessions on specific topics are routinely organized by the Division.

6 *How are training priorities for Members decided? Who is responsible for deciding these? How do they make these decisions?*

The materials are prepared by the IRB Legal Services. They are very extensive. They cover the following:

- The Legal Framework: Law, Regulations, Rules
- Conduct and Ethics
- Grounds of Protection: Section 96
- Grounds of Protection: Section 97
- Exclusion Clauses Sections E and F of Article 1 of the Convention
- Natural Justice
- Chairperson's Guidelines
- RPD grounds for decisions
- 3 days of reading RPD decisions and attending RPD hearings
- RAD's Legal Framework
- Study of a simulated RAD file
- Scope of RAD appeal

- RAD rules
- Charter of Rights issues
- Assessing evidence and credibility
- Weighing evidence
- Specialized knowledge
- New Evidence at the RAD
- Hearing at the RAD
- Recourses at the RAD
- Official Languages and language of the appeal
- 3 days Writing reasons
- 2 days shadowing a RAD member

7 *How long are training sessions?*

The RAD training is 20 days. In the middle, between the RPD and the RAD training, there is a pause of 3 to 5 days to do reading. Approximately 6 months after their initial training, RAD members attend a one-week Continued Education Programme. Thereafter, there is a Professional Development day each month. In addition, members meet nationally (2 or 3 days) at least once a year to discuss broad RAD legal issues.

For the RPD, the initial new member training lasts several weeks. Ongoing professional development sessions are typically scheduled for half a day, but vary depending on the topic.

8 *Do RAD and RPD members go through different trainings? If yes, in what ways are the trainings different?*

RPD and RAD members are not trained together, in order to maintain the institutional independence of the two Divisions.

9 *How are training priorities for members decided? Who is responsible for deciding these? How do they make these decisions?*

Training priorities for the RAD, at PD days for example, are decided jointly by the Deputy Chairperson of the RAD in consultation with the PD committee and the Legal Services (for example, a decision of a higher court may require immediate training to make sure RAD members apply the higher court decision).

RPD Professional development priorities are determined by the RPD Divisional management. Typically, management consults RPD members and IRB Legal Services in determining professional development priorities.

10 *How does the IRB deal with inconsistent adjudications?*

There are a number of different tools that are available to the IRB to promote consistency, coherence and fairness in the treatment of cases at the Board. On the IRB website, there are several IRB policies which discuss adjudication strategy:

> *section 1.2 of the Policy on the Use of Jurisprudential Guides:* http://www.irb-cisr.gc.ca/Eng/BoaCom/references/pol/pol/Pages/PolJurisGuide.aspx; *section 1.2 of the Policy on the Use of Chairperson's Guidelines:* http://www.irb-cisr.gc.ca/Eng/BoaCom/references/pol/pol/Pages/PolGuideDir.aspx; *and section 1.1 of the Policy on Higher Court Interventions:* http://www.irb-cisr.gc.ca/Eng/BoaCom/references/pol/pol/Pages/PolIntervention.aspx.

Note that the Refugee Appeal Division (RAD) is not referred to in these policies as it was launched on December 15, 2012, after these policies were issued.

With respect to the use of three-member panels as an adjudication strategy tool, see the following policy instrument on the IRB website: Designation of Three-Member Panels – Refugee Appeal Division: *http://www.irb-cisr.gc.ca/Eng/BoaCom/references/pol/pol/Pages/PolRadSar3MemCom.aspx*. A decision of a three-member RAD panel is binding on the Refugee Protection Division (RPD) and on a single-member panel of the RAD. The criteria for designation are set out in section 3.1, which include: "The appeal raises an issue in an area in which there is significant divergence or inconsistency in decision-making at either the RAD or the RPD."

Also, a principal way that the RPD promotes consistency is by having standard disclosure packages. See the following policy on the IRB website: Policy on Country-of-Origin Information Packages in Refugee Protection Claims: *http://www.irb-cisr.gc.ca/Eng/BoaCom/references/pol/pol/Pages/PolOrigin.aspx.*

11 ***Has creation of the RAD impacted the work of RPD in any significant way?***

A decision of a RAD three-member panel is binding on the RPD and on a single-member panel of the RAD. Therefore, any decision issued by a RAD three-member panel would have a significant impact on the work of the RPD. Although there have not been any decisions issued by a RAD three-member panel to date, there is currently a pending appeal that is being conducted by a RAD three-member panel. See the following notice on the IRB website: *http://www.irb-cisr.gc.ca/Eng/RefApp/Pages/notice3mempan.aspx.*

12 ***Is the IRB concerned with (some) lawyer practices, for example, whether they heavily coach their clients/the claimants?***

Unless the counsel conduct amounts to a possible breach of professional or ethical obligations, the IRB does not have a position on counsel practices. With respect to IRB procedures for dealing with possible breaches of professional or ethical obligations, see the following policy on the IRB website: Policy on Disclosing Information Regarding the Conduct of Authorized Representatives to Regulatory Bodies (*http://www.irb-cisr.gc.ca/Eng/BoaCom/references/pol/pol/Pages/PolCondRep.aspx*).

13 ***How are interpreters hired? Are they trained? Do the same interpreters work across RAD and RPD?***

Please see the attached information sheet on interpreters.

Appendix B
Written Interview with an IRB Manager

About Your Job[1]

1 *What does your job at the IRB [unit] entail?*

I manage [the unit's] intake, resources and outreach for [the region] ... My primary duties are to manage the [unit's] decision makers, as well as [the unit's] analysts, and to report to the [unit's] Deputy Chairperson in IRB headquarters.

2 *How long have you been working at the IRB?*

I became a [unit's] member in [late 1990s] and have been [a manager at this unit] since [early 2010s].

About the [unit]

3 *Why was the [unit] created?*

...

4 ***What do you see as the main goal, aim or mission of the [unit]?***

The [unit] renders quality decisions and resolves cases in a timely manner.

...

5 ***Is there a noticeable difference in the [outcome of claims processed by the unit]?***

These statistics are not available.

6 ***Why are some groups, such as [group], excluded from [your unit]?***

I cannot provide any comment as this specific question relates to a policy decision. Such questions however can be addressed to the department of Immigration, Refugees and Citizenship.

7 ***In what ways does [your unit] improve the Canadian refugee system?***

I cannot provide any comment on this specific question.

8 ***Do you think that [your unit] benefits refugee claimants? In what ways?***

Although I cannot give an opinion on whether [this unit] benefits refugee claimants, I will say that the [unit] provides an opportunity for [fair and expeditious decisions].

About the Relationship between [the unit] and [other unit]

9 ***In what ways is [this unit] separate and independent from the [other unit]?***

I refer you to the *Instructions Governing Communications Between Related Divisions at the Immigration and Refugee Board of Canada* which is available on the IRB's website. These Instructions reaffirm the fundamental principles of institutional independence, whereby members are free from improper influence. The Instructions also set out a framework for the level of separation expected between first-level and appeal-level Divisions of the IRB ...

10 *What is the working relationship between [this unit] and [other unit]?*

See answer above.

11 *Has creation of [your unit] impacted the work of [the other unit] in any significant way?*

I decline to comment on behalf of the [other unit].

About the [unit's] Members

12 *In what ways are the [unit's] Members independent from the [other unit's] Members?*

13 *How are the [unit's] Members chosen? Do Members themselves decide which [unit] they would like to work in?*

14 *How are the [unit's] Members trained? Do they receive the same training as [other unit's] Members?*

My answer to question 13 – 15 is that IRB members are highly qualified and well-trained. They go through a rigorous selection process.

About Outcomes of the [unit's] Decisions

15 *What are the general rates of successful* [cases at this unit]?

16 *What are the most common grounds on which [claims are accepted]?*

17 *What are the most common grounds on which [claims are denied]?*

18 *How likely is it for [this unit] to grant refugee status [without involving other units]?*

My answer to questions 16–21 is that each [case] is decided by an independent decision maker on its own merits. Each case is unique.

19 *Are some [unit's] Members more/less likely than others to [accept or reject cases]?*

Statistics on acceptance rates provide an insufficient basis on which to draw conclusions concerning the quality and consistency of decision-making at the IRB.

20 *How does the [unit] deal with such individual differences between Members?*

[no response provided]

About Interpretation

21 *Do the [various units] use the same interpreters?*

22 *Are interpretation problems a common or relatively common reason for wrongfully denied [claims]?*

23 *What are the most common interpretation mistakes/problems that lead to negative … decisions (if any)?*

24 *How does [the unit] deal with interpretation problems in … decisions?*

25 *How does the [unit]/IRB ensure that interpreters are translating accurately?*

Members are reminded of the importance of ensuring that interpreters understand the requirement to provide consecutive interpretation, meaning that everything said in one language should be interpreted faithfully and accurately into the other language using the exact equivalent meaning and structure.

Should communication issues arise during a hearing (either due to lack of an interpreter or issues with the interpretation), members have the discretion to adjourn the hearing so that appropriate measures can be taken.

Just as a side note, interpretation refers to oral communication while translating refers to written communication.

Conclusion

26 Do you have any concluding remarks?

Thank you for your interest in the [unit].

Notes

Introduction

1 *Convention Relating to the Status of Refugees*, July 28, 1951, 189 UNTS 150 (entered into force April 22, 1954) [*Refugee Convention*].

2 Although emerging protection frameworks have made great advances in recognizing persecution based on sexual orientation and gender identity, these frameworks continue to struggle with complex nuances of gender and sexuality. The result is that those identifying with the categories "gay," and "lesbian," and to a lesser extent "trans" and "bisexual," are much more readily intelligible to current systems of refugee protection. To acknowledge this uneven recognition, I have opted to use the decidedly limited term "LGBT," rather than the more inclusive terminologies of "queer" or "2SLGBTQ+" in this discussion.

3 "Inland" refugee protection refers to the adjudication and processing of refugee claims that are made from within Canadian borders or at Canadian ports of entry, in contrast to, for instance, being made abroad at Canadian visa offices or through international agencies such as the United Nations High Commissioner for Refugees (UNHCR).

4 "Restrictionism" is a term used in refugee and immigration policy literature to refer to policies that favour limiting immigration (see, for example, Markowitz 1973; Simcox 1997; Zetter and Pearl 2000; Pedraza 2014).

5 This is particularly true for procedural law. As the body of rules and regulations that govern legal proceedings, procedural law is more closely aligned with administrative considerations. In contrast, substantive law, which establishes the ideal

principles of justice and equality, is less bound by practicalities of administering justice. For more on this, see McShane 2006a, 2006b.

6 In legal scholarship, human rights and refugee rights are distinguished in part by their diverging positions in relation to the role of the state: in human-rights law, the state remains the basis and guarantors of rights, while, in refugee law, recognized rights are beyond the domain of the (persecutory) state. For more on this distinction, see Goldenziel 2016. Both bodies of rights, nonetheless, presume the natural equality of rights.

7 For a more thorough discussion of how the global nation-state system disadvantages citizens of poor countries, see Hindess 2000.

8 *Refugee Convention,* article 1, paragraph 2.

9 *Ibid.*

10 *Ibid.*, emphasis added.

11 *Protocol Relating to the Status of Refugees,* January 31, 1967, 606 UNTS 267 (entered into force October 4, 1967).

12 For a fuller discussion of these rights, see Marshall ([1950] 2009).

13 For a detailed discussion of these inaccuracies, see Whelan and Donnelly 2007; Zeleza 2007.

14 See *Refugee Convention,* article 1, paragraph 2.

15 Uday Mehta (1990) and Carole Pateman (1988) have shown that for John Locke and other liberal thinkers, the "natural" equality of humans was conditioned on possession of adequate rational capacities; these rational capacities, rather conveniently, were deemed to be deficient in people who were treated most unequally in liberal and colonial regimes: women and the colonized were considered simply not rational enough to be capable of liberty.

16 Given the rising tide of neo-fascism and violent nationalism in the liberal democratic world, one may rightly wonder if the liberal promise of equality remains relevant in our time. Two points may be made in defence of the relevance of this promise in the context of this study. First, although eroding now, the promise of equality has been key to the establishment of liberal rule. Hence, at least from a historical and genealogical point of view, this promise is worth exploring. Second, the fact that liberal states continue to gesture to universal equality by providing some measure of refugee protection, however minimally and nominally, suggests that the promise of equality has not completely lost its relevance in legitimizing liberal statehood.

17 For more on the role of failure in statecraft, see J. Scott 1998.

18 For examples of similar analysis in the European context, see Silverstein 2005; Mayblin 2017.

19 For more examples of this approach, see Ong 2003; Sidhu and Taylor 2007; Broeders 2010; Biehl 2015; Carver 2016; Gargiulo 2017.

20 A notable exception is the study by Loren Landau and Roni Amit (2014), who highlight the considerable autonomy of bureaucracies in shaping, implementing, and

resisting expansive refugee policy. Landau and Amit show that bureaucracies may resist legal and policy expansions by, for example, quietly refusing to commit to adequate training or prioritizing quantifiable output rates.

21 *Protecting Canada's Immigration System Act*, SC 2012, c 17.

22 This is not to argue that various fields operate in complete isolation from one another. In fact, as Pierre Bourdieu (1996) himself shows, some fields, such as the economic field, may significantly impact the operation of other fields.

23 For an exceptionally illuminating example of the independence and autonomy of state agents, see Scalettaris 2020.

24 From 2019 to 2020, 8,825 persons were detained, including 136 minors, for an average of 13.9 days (CBSA 2022). Most detainees are not considered to pose a threat to Canadian society even by the estimation of the Canada Border Services Agency itself: in 2019–20, 85.1 percent of those in detention were detained simply because they were considered unlikely to appear for their immigration proceedings. See also CCR 2016.

25 Various Canadian governments have mounted public advertisement posters and billboards abroad (Mountz 2010; Keung 2013), changed visa requirements (Levine-Rasky, Beaudoin, and St. Clair 2014; Harris 2016), and publicized low approval rates (Hamlin 2014) to discourage Roma Hungarians, Fijians, and Mexicans from making refugee claims in Canada.

26 The increase in the Immigration and Refugee Board of Canada's (IRB) acceptance rates since 2012 corresponds with, and may be an unintended consequence of, a number of procedural changes made to refugee status determination procedures by the last Conservative government. These include, for example, the imposition of shorter adjudication timeliness and the transition to a civil servant (as opposed to politically appointed) complement of adjudicators. Some of these changes will be discussed more fully in Chapters 5 and 6.

27 The Liberal Party of Canada was elected on an explicitly refugee-friendly platform at the height of public support for those displaced by the war in Syria. For more on this subject, see Canadians for Justice and Peace in the Middle East, "2015 Election Guide: Syrian Refugee Crisis," https://www.cjpme.org/an_2015_10_15_election_guide_syrian_refugees_crisis.

28 Although linear trend lines helpfully sketch the overall tendency of data, they are poor indicators of fluctuations or cyclical and non-linear patterns. Thus, this trend line should not be taken as a nuanced representation of refugee acceptance rates in Canada.

29 The government department that has handled the work of immigration regulation for the Canadian state has changed names and mandates several times over the course of the period that this book explores. At times, aspects of migration regulation have even been shared between various government bodies. Since the period encompassing the Second World War, immigration matters have been under the mandate of the Department of Mines and Resources (1936–50); the

Department of Citizenship and Immigration (1950–66); the Department of Manpower and Immigration (1966–77); the Department of Employment and Immigration (1977–91); the Department of Multiculturalism and Citizenship (1991–94); the Department of Citizenship and Immigration Canada (1994–2015); and currently, the Department of Immigration, Refugees and Citizenship Canada. For ease of discussion and to avoid confusion, in this book I will employ the generic term "Department of Immigration" to refer to the primary government body in charge of immigration regulation across time in Canada.

Chapter 1: Forty Years of Beginnings

1 Most notably, Canada refused entry to 907 Jewish refugees onboard MS *St Louis* fleeing Nazism in 1939 (Girard 2019).
2 *Convention Relating to the Status of Refugees*, July 28, 1951, 189 UNTS 150 (entered into force April 22, 1954) [*Refugee Convention*].
3 *Immigration Act*, SC 1976–77, c 52, s 1 [*Immigration Act* 1976].
4 "Report of Canadian Representative to Conference of Plenipotentiaries on the Status of Refugees and Stateless Persons Held at Geneva July 2–25, 1951," September 20, 1951, RG 2-B-2, box 205, file U-40-22, United Nations – Refugee and Stateless Persons, Privy Council Office fonds, Library and Archives Canada (LAC).
5 "International Refugee Organization; Canadian Policy," October 15, 1946, RG 2-A-5-a, vol 2639, microfilm reel T-2364, item 7581, Privy Council Office fonds, LAC.
6 "International Refugee Organization," August 12, 1946, RG 2-A-5-a, vol 2638, microfilm reel T-2364, item 7334, Privy Council Office fonds, LAC.
7 For more on the history of the International Refugee Organization (IRO), see "Summary of AG-018–007 International Refugee Organization (IRO)," United Nations' Archives and Records Management Section, https://web.archive.org/web/20160330235321/https://archives.un.org/sites/archives.un.org/files/files/Finding%20Aids/2015_Finding_Aids/AG-018–007.pdf.
8 "Immigration Policy; Public Enquiry; Refugees," August 10, 1946, RG 2-A-5-a, vol 2638, microfilm reel T-2364, item 7428, Privy Council Office fonds, LAC.
9 "International Refugee Organization; Instructions to Canadian Delegation," June 16, 1949, RG 2-A-5-a, vol 2644, microfilm reel T-2366, item 9006, Privy Council Office fonds, LAC.
10 "Immigration Policy; International Refugee Organization," September 10, 1946, RG 2-A-5-a, vol 2638, microfilm reel T-2364, Item 7426, Privy Council Office fonds, LAC.
11 "Immigration; Admission of Political Refugees," May 14, 1948, 1, RG 2-A-5-a, vol 2642, microfilm reel T-2365, item 7040, Privy Council Office fonds, LAC.
12 "Report of Canadian Representative," September 20, 1951.
13 Letter from Brooke Claxton, Acting Secretary of State for External Affairs to the Executive Secretary, Conference of Plenipotentiaries on the Status of Refugees and Stateless Persons, Geneva, Switzerland, June 25, 1951, RG 26-A-1-c, box 110, file

3-24-12, Refugees and Stateless Persons – United Nations, Part 1, Department of Citizenship and Immigration (1950–1966) fonds, LAC.

14 "Convention on Refugees and Protocol on Stateless Persons," June 20, 1951, 3, RG 2-A-5-a, vol 2648, microfilm reel T-2367, item 11082, Privy Council Office fonds, LAC. One key area of reservation was the stipulated rights of refugees to services such as education and health care. While the spirit of these rights was not considered objectionable, the Cabinet considered it inappropriate to commit to rights that in the federal political system of Canada would fall within the jurisdictional authority of provinces.

15 "United Nations; Convention on Refugees and Protocol on Stateless Persons," June 26, 1951, 2, RG 2-A-5-a, vol 2648, microfilm reel T-2367, item 11096, Privy Council Office fonds, LAC.

16 "United Nations; Convention on Refugees and Protocol on Stateless Persons; Canadian Participation," June 29, 1951, 1, RG 2 A-5-a, vol 2648, microfilm reel T-2367, item 11112, Privy Council Office fonds, LAC.

17 Telegram from the Secretary of State for External Affairs, Canada to the Permanent Delegation of Canada to the European Office of the United Nations, Geneva, June 30, 1951, RG 26-A-1-c, box 110, file 3-24-12, Refugees and Stateless Persons – United Nations, Part 1, Department of Citizenship and Immigration (1950–1966) fonds, LAC.

18 "Report of Canadian Representative," September 20, 1951.

19 Telegram from the Permanent Representative of Canada, UNO, Geneva to the Secretary of State for External Affairs, Canada, July 13, 1951, RG 26-A-1-c, box 110, file 3-24-12, Refugees and Stateless Persons – United Nations, Part 1, Department of Citizenship and Immigration (1950–1966) fonds, LAC.

20 "United Nations; Convention on Refugees and Protocol on Stateless Persons," July 4, 1951, RG 2-A-5-a, vol 2648, microfilm reel T-2367, item 11117, Privy Council Office fonds, LAC.

21 Draft Telegram of Instructions to Mr. Chance in Geneva, July 1951, RG 26-A-1-c, box 110, file 3-24-12, Refugees and Stateless Persons – United Nations, Part 1, Department of Citizenship and Immigration (1950–1966) fonds, LAC.

22 "Report of Canadian Representative," September 20, 1951, 1.

23 "Convention on Refugees and Protocol on Stateless Persons," June 20, 1951, 3.

24 "United Nations; Convention on Refugees and Protocol on Stateless Persons," July 4, 1951, 2, RG 2-A-5-a, vol. 2648, microfilm reel T-2367, item 11117, Privy Council Office fonds, LAC [emphasis added].

25 Draft Telegram of Instructions to Mr. Chance in Geneva, July 1951, 1.

26 "Report of Canadian Representative," September 20, 1951.

27 "Draft Memorandum for Cabinet from the Secretary of State for External Affairs and the Minister of Citizenship and Immigration," December 1952, RG 76-I-B, vol 882, file 566-10, United Nations – Ad-Hoc Committee on Refugees and Stateless Persons, Part 1, Department of Employment and Immigration fonds, LAC.

28 In international law and treaty making, signing and ratifying treaties have significantly different legal meanings and implications. While signing a treaty, often performed by a delegate, is largely a gesture of support and interest, ratification constitutes formal approval of the treaty by the head of state and may require amending existing laws and procedures to ensure compliance with the terms of the agreement. Treaties only become legally binding upon ratification. Accession refers to ratifying (that is, becoming a party) to a treaty that has already been signed and/or ratified by other states. For a fuller discussion of these distinctions in the context of the Trans-Pacific Partnership trade agreement, see Geist 2015.

29 The *Refugee Convention* allowed states to enter formal reservations to several articles upon accession. This meant that states could become parties without accepting all provisions unconditionally. Reservations could only be made to provisions that were considered non-integral to refugee protection. Therefore, the refugee definition and the principle of non-refoulement were not open to reservations. See "Memorandum for the Deputy Minister of Citizenship and Immigration," December 18, 1952, RG 76-I-B, vol. 882, file 566-10, United Nations – Ad-Hoc Committee on Refugees and Stateless Persons, Part 1, Department of Employment and Immigration fonds, LAC.

30 Letter from the Deputy Minister of Citizenship and Immigration to the Under-Secretary of State for External Affairs, December 20, 1952, RG 76-I-B, vol 882, file 566-10, United Nations – Ad-Hoc Committee on Refugees and Stateless Persons, Part 1, Department of Employment and Immigration fonds, LAC.

31 Letter from the Under-Secretary of State for External Affairs to the Deputy Minister of Citizenship and Immigration, January 21, 1953, RG 76-I-B, vol 882, file 566-10, United Nations – Ad-Hoc Committee on Refugees and Stateless Persons, Part 1, Department of Employment and Immigration fonds, LAC.

32 See, for instance, "Memorandum for the Director of Immigration from the Deputy Minister of Citizenship and Immigration," January 20, 1953, RG 76-I-B, vol 882, file 566-10, United Nations – Ad-Hoc Committee on Refugees and Stateless Persons, Part 1, Department of Employment and Immigration fonds, LAC.

33 The other five countries included Belgium, Denmark, the German Federal Republic, Luxembourg, and Norway. UN Press Release, January 22, 1954, RG 76-I-B, vol 882, file 566-10, United Nations – Ad-Hoc Committee on Refugees and Stateless Persons, Part 2, Department of Employment and Immigration fonds, LAC.

34 See records throughout RG 76-I-B, vols 882 and 883, file 566-10, United Nations – Ad-Hoc Committee on Refugees and Stateless Persons, Parts 1–7, Department of Employment and Immigration fonds, LAC.

35 For an example of this following Australia's accession, see Letter from the Acting Under-Secretary of State for External Affairs to the Deputy Minister, Department of Citizenship and Immigration, February 18, 1954, RG 76-I-B, vol 882, file 566-10, United Nations – Ad-Hoc Committee on Refugees and Stateless Persons, Part 2, Department of Employment and Immigration fonds, LAC.

36 Officials of the Department of External Affairs, for instance, were concerned that the refusal to accede put Canada in the company of countries such as Colombia, Venezuela, and Iran, which had far poorer reputations of refugee protection. See, for instance, Letter from the Canadian Permanent Mission-Geneva to the Under-Secretary of State for External Affairs, September 25, 1957, RG 76-I-B, vol 882, file 566-10, United Nations – Ad-Hoc Committee on Refugees and Stateless Persons, Part 3, Department of Employment and Immigration fonds, LAC.

37 Letter from the Canadian Permanent Mission-Geneva to the Under-Secretary of State for External Affairs, September 25, 1957, 1.

38 "Memorandum for the Minister of Citizenship and Immigration," May 29, 1958, RG 76-I-B, vol 883, file 566-10, United Nations – Ad-Hoc Committee on Refugees and Stateless Persons, Part 4, Department of Employment and Immigration fonds, LAC.

39 Letter from the Canadian Permanent Mission-Geneva to the Under-Secretary of State for External Affairs, September 25, 1957, 1.

40 "Confirmation of the Decisions of Cabinet Committees – Canada's Adherence to International Instruments Relating to the Status of Refugees," January 30, 1969, RG 2-A-5-a, vol 6340, item 2764, Privy Council Office fonds, LAC.

41 *An Act Respecting Immigration*, 1952, sc 1 Elizabeth II, c. 42.

42 *An Act Respecting Chinese Immigration*, 1923, sc 13-14 George V, c. 38, blocked the vast majority of Chinese immigrants from entry to Canada. For more on the racist exclusions against Chinese migrants, see Chan 2017.

43 "Memorandum from the Director of Immigration to the Deputy Minister of Citizenship and Immigration," January 19, 1953, p. 1, RG 76-I-B, vol 882, file 566-10, United Nations – Ad-Hoc Committee on Refugees and Stateless Persons, Part 2, Department of Employment and Immigration fonds, LAC.

44 Unfortunately, minimal information exists on how the advisory committee applied provisions of the *Refugee Convention* to refugee claims. Despite my best attempts, I was not able to locate any relevant material on this matter in the archives.

45 For instance, Canada's slow response to Chilean refugees after the overthrow of Salvador Allende's government in 1973 has been attributed to political and ideological interests (CCR 2009).

46 *Immigration Act* 1976.

47 *Canadian Charter of Rights and Freedoms*, Part 1 of the *Constitution Act, 1982*, being Schedule B to the *Canada Act 1982* (UK), 1982, c 11.

48 *Singh v Minister of Employment and Immigration*, [1985] 1 SCR 177 [*Singh*]. The *Singh* decision was brought forth by seven refugee claimants whose cases had been refused between 1977 and 1981. For more on this case, see Foot 2006.

49 Documents are not strong tools for refugee claim adjudications. The transnational nature of refugee claims means that documentary evidence may not exist, may be exclusively in the possession of the persecutor, or may have been forged. In the absence of strong and comprehensive documentary evidence, refugee adjudicators

have to rely heavily on credibility assessments. These assessments, as the *Singh* decision argued, cannot be conducted fairly without direct contact between claimants and adjudicators. Of course, psychological studies suggest that credibility assessments are highly inaccurate even when adjudicators can examine subjects directly. Even professionals are bad at making accurate credibility assessments (for a fuller discussion of this, see Evans Cameron 2016). The question of procedural justice in a system that heavily relies on credibility assessments is, thus, a serious legal conundrum that the *Singh* decision left mostly untouched.

50 *Singh*, para 70.

51 Rabbi Gunther Plaut was an influential advocate for a non-adversarial model of refugee status determination. In his independent commissioned study, Plaut (1985) argued that unlike criminal or civil cases, refugee adjudication does not involve a conflict of interest (for example, between the Canadian state and refugees). Thus, refugee decisions should be made in a non-adversarial setting where all parties cooperate to establish the merit of cases without an active prosecutory agent. Of course, in practice, the aggressive interrogation styles of some adjudicators undermine the non-adversarial tone of the determination process. Thus, even the "non-adversarial" model can feel quite adversarial.

Chapter 2: With Rights Came the Rightless

Acknowledgment: Parts of this chapter were previously published in the Oñati Socio-Legal Series and arc reproduced here with the permission of the publisher. For the full article, see Masoumi 2020.

1 *Immigration Act*, SC 1976–77, c 52, s 1.

2 "Refugee Update Seminar for the Media," 1989, 1, RG 76-B-1, box 1993/1994, file 8620-19, vol 002, Refugee and Displaced Persons – General Immigration and Refugee Board, Department of Employment and Immigration fonds, Library and Archives Canada (LAC) [emphasis added].

3 To this date, the Immigration and Refugee Board of Canada (IRB) engages with international bodies that wish to consider the Canadian model. For instance, in 2017, the IRB was in communication with government officials from Scotland (observation at the Canadian Council for Refugees consultations in Fall 2017, Niagara Falls).

4 The IRB's struggles for survival continue to this date. In more recent times, threats of restructuring and dismantling the IRB's political independence have pushed the board to find allies in its long-time critics within the refugee advocacy groups (see Braganza 2018; Zilio 2018a).

5 The IRB's caseloads are in large part determined by overseas political crises and, hence, fluctuate based on factors that are well beyond the board's control. Although the IRB has always attempted to predict patterns of displacement by monitoring international events (see IRB 1991, 13–15; 1992, 13–17), it has never been able to

fully forecast or plan for incoming caseloads. Most often, IRB officials discover the volume of their workloads as claims are filed in Canada.

6 Letter from Nick Mulder to Paul Tellier, January 8, 1990, 2, RG 76-B-1, box 1993/1994, file 8620-19, vol 003, Refugee and Displaced Persons – General Immigration and Refugee Board, Department of Employment and Immigration fonds, LAC.

7 Numerous examples of these reports are available in the archived documents.

8 At the time, refugee hearings were conducted by two adjudicators. Only one adjudicator needed to accept a claim for the claimant to receive refugee status. Expedited and simplified processes were reserved only for claims that were considered "evidently well founded," often determined based on the supposedly well-established and unambiguous records of human-rights violations in countries of origin. In the early years of the IRB's work, claims from countries such as El Salvador, Iran, Lebanon, Somalia, and Sri Lanka were diverted to expedited procedures (IRB 1991, 19). Claimants from these countries already had extremely high acceptance rates, often ranging from 80 percent to over 90 percent.

9 Even procedural efficiency came to be understood as a means of deterring unwanted claims (see, for instance, IRB 1990, 11): the faster claims were processed, it was believed, the less likely prospective claimants were to seek protection in Canada without strong cause.

10 Letter from Mulder to Tellier, January 8, 1990.

11 At the time, the IRB officials suspected that the Department of Manpower and Immigration intentionally stalled immigration control functions in order to sabotage the effectiveness of the IRB's work (Hathaway 1993).

12 Acceptance rates in the early years of the IRB may be reported variously. For instance, acceptance rates in 1989 may be reported as 84 percent, 76 percent, or even 69 percent. These discrepancies are due to various methods of calculating acceptance rates (for instance, whether the numbers of withdrawn and abandoned claims are included in the calculations) as well as substantial procedural changes made to the claim adjudication process over the years. In the earlier years, the IRB followed a two-staged adjudication process. The first stage was conducted by officials from the IRB and the Department of Manpower and Immigration and focused on determining refugee eligibility using a low-threshold test. This stage was relatively quick and often produced very high acceptance rates (in the 90 percent). Claims approved at the first stage were then referred to the second stage. The second stage involved a full hearing with two IRB adjudicators and was much more time-consuming and rigorous. In 1989, the second stage produced an acceptance rate of 84 percent, while the two stages together produced an overall acceptance rate of 76 percent.

13 Letter from Mulder to Tellier, January 8, 1990, 2.

14 The overall acceptance rates reflect the acceptance rates of both initial and full hearing stages. The noted decline was owed in large part to noticeable drops in

the acceptance rates of a handful of countries (IRB 1991). For instance, overall acceptance rates of claimants from Czechoslovakia had dropped from 74 percent in 1989 to only 11 percent in 1990, and Polish claimants' rates dropped from 51 percent in 1989 to 12 percent (IRB 1991). Acceptance rates of Chinese claimants were quickly dropping as well: nationally, their acceptance rates at the full hearing stage had dropped from 74 percent in 1989, to 44 percent in 1990, and 37 percent in the last quarter of that year. "CRDD Statistical Report – December 1990," January 30, 1991, RG 76-B-1, box 1993/1994, file 8620-19, vol 003, Refugee and Displaced Persons – General Immigration and Refugee Board, Department of Employment and Immigration fonds, LAC.

15 In these early years, the first stage of adjudications was conducted by both the Department of Manpower and Immigration and IRB representatives, while the second stage was under the exclusive authority of the IRB.

16 "Review of Convention Refugee Determination Division Activities," July 1990, RG 76-B-1, box 1993/1994, file 8620-19, vol 003, Refugee and Displaced Persons – General Immigration and Refugee Board, Department of Employment and Immigration fonds, LAC.

17 Individual assessment is crucial to refugee protection because nationals of a country may experience country conditions vastly differently based on their specific positionality, characteristics, or circumstances.

18 "UNHCR Consultant's Visit," August 22, 1989, RG 76-B-1, box 1993/1994, file 8620-19, vol 002, Refugee and Displaced Persons – General Immigration and Refugee Board, Department of Employment and Immigration fonds, LAC.

19 "Refugee Update Seminar for the Media," 1989, RG 76-B-1, box 1993/1994, file 8620-19, vol 002, Refugee and Displaced Persons – General Immigration and Refugee Board, Department of Employment and Immigration fonds, LAC. See also IRB 1990, 15.

20 In Canada, refugee decisions are made by independent adjudicators who are not controlled by administrators. Hence, these low acceptance rates speak to the widespread disbelief of Jamaicans and Trinidadians by the IRB adjudicators. Although these acceptance rates cannot be directly attributed to the work of administrators, their explicit reporting in the annual report reflects administrators' preoccupation with (and approval of the rejection of) claimants from these two countries.

21 The initial stage was largely reserved for low-threshold assessments of eligibility and credibility (IRB 1990, 13) and generally did not exclude many claimants.

22 "Review of Convention Refugee Determination Division Activities," July 1990.

23 The eligibility of claimants for refugee status is determined based on factors such as claimants' history of criminality, past claims for refugee status in Canada, and access to citizenships or permanent residencies in safe third countries. These factors determine whether a claimant can be considered for refugee status. Credibility assessments, on the other hand, require examining the content of claims

to decide whether claimants are in need of protection. In the early years of the IRB, credibility assessments at the initial stage involved basic evaluations to determine if claims fit with the provisions of refugee law. Since comprehensive credibility assessments require in-depth engagement with the claims' content, thorough credibility evaluations were largely left to more substantial examinations in full hearings. Hence, claims were rarely rejected based on credibility at the initial stage.

24 "Statistical Summary," January 29, 1991, RG 76-B-1, box 1993/1994, file 8620-19, vol 003, Refugee and Displaced Persons – General Immigration and Refugee Board, Department of Employment and Immigration fonds, LAC.

25 In the non-adversarial model of refugee status determination, the minister remains a party in refugee decisions. This means that the minister has the right to contest refugee decisions that he or she finds problematic. By contesting decisions, the minister appeals the adjudication outcome and has a chance to provide reasoning and documentation against the decision. In the early years of the IRB, representatives of the minister had the right to contest positive evaluations of claims' credibility at the initial stage. Despite this right, the minister rarely contested initial decisions. The minister's decision not to contest a positive initial evaluation was called a concession. Concessions allowed claims to move to the second stage of adjudications for further examination.

26 "CRDD Statistical Report – December 1990," January 30, 1991.

27 "Review of Convention Refugee Determination Division Activities," July 1990, 8.

28 Letter from Mulder to Tellier, January 8, 1990, 1.

29 "CRDD Statistical Report – December 1990," January 30, 1991, 4.

30 The numbers reported in this discussion reflect the numbers of claims decided at full hearings and, hence, exclude the claims rejected at the initial stage of adjudication as well as abandoned and withdrawn claims.

31 "Statistical Summary," January 29, 1991.

32 "CRDD Statistical Report – December 1990," January 30, 1991.

33 "CRDD Statistical Report – First Quarter 1990," April 24, 1990, RG 76-B-1, box 1993/1994, file 8620-19, vol 003, Refugee and Displaced Persons – General Immigration and Refugee Board, Department of Employment and Immigration fonds, LAC.

34 These strategies were developed in consideration of the stricter border and refugee protection protocols against Eastern Europeans in Austria and the Federal Republic of Germany (IRB 1991).

35 "Review of Convention Refugee Determination Division Activities," July 1990.

36 "CRDD Statistical Report – First Quarter 1990," April 24, 1990.

37 "Review of Convention Refugee Determination Division Activities," July 1990.

38 "CRDD Statistical Report – March 1991," April 25, 1991, RG 76-B-1, box 1993/1994, file 8620–19, vol 004, Refugee and Displaced Persons – General Immigration and Refugee Board, Department of Employment and Immigration fonds, LAC.

Chapter 3: A Nice Symbolic Gesture

Acknowledgment: Parts of this chapter were previously published in *Feminist Legal Studies* and are reproduced here with the permission of the publisher, Springer Nature. For the full article, see Masoumi 2019.

1 *Guideline 4: Women Refugee Claimants Fearing Gender-related Persecution*, March 9, 1993 (*Gender Guidelines*). The IRB has recently revised and released this Guideline as *Chairperson's Guideline 4- Gender Considerations in Proceedings Before the Immigration and Refugee Board*, July 18, 2022, https://irb.gc.ca/en/legal-policy/policies/Pages/GuideDir04.aspx.

2 The jurisprudential reasoning used in the *Gender Guidelines* was later also applied to recognize claims based on sexual orientation, gender expression, and identity and intersexuality. See United Nations High Commissioner for Refugees (UNHCR), *Guidelines on International Protection no. 9: Claims to Refugee Status based on Sexual Orientation and/or Gender Identity within the context of Article 1A(2) of the 1951 Convention and/or Its 1967 Protocol Relating to the Status of Refugees*, HCR/GIP/06/07, October 23, 2012, http://www.unhcr.org/509136ca9.pdf.

3 Immediately after the publication of the Canadian *Gender Guidelines,* American and British advocates began to call on officials to follow Canada's example and formally recognize gender as a basis for refugee protection (see *Arizona Daily Star* 1993; Trueheart 1993; Wheelwright 1993).

4 Bill C-86, *An Act to Amend the Immigration Act and Other Acts in Consequence Thereof,* 3rd Sess., 34 Parl., 40–41 Elizabeth II, 1991–1992 came into effect in the final months of Brian Mulroney's Progressive Conservative government; however, the restrictionist effects of the Bill lived long past the Conservatives. In fact, the measures introduced by Bill C-86 were either upheld or intensified by the Liberals in the following years.

5 Eligibility for refugee protection is determined based on factors such as claimants' criminal record, their access to secure residence in a safe third country, and their history of failed previous claims in Canada.

6 The restrictive provisions of Bill C-86 concerned all persons who wished to enter Canada, including but not limited to prospective refugee claimants. In this discussion, I will only focus on the implications of the Bill for refugee claimants.

7 The search provisions were further intensified by Bill C-44, *An Act to Amend the Immigration Act and the Citizenship Act and to Make Consequential Amendments to the Customs Act,* 1st Sess., 35th Parl., 42–43–44 Elizabeth II, c. 15, 1994–1996, which was passed in 1995 (Kelley and Trebilcock 1998). Bill C-44 extended immigration officers' authority by allowing them to seize any documents discovered through searches.

8 These provisions had been crafted in Bill C-55, *An Act to Amend the Immigration Act, 1976 and to Amend Other Acts in Consequence Thereof,* 2nd Sess., 33rd Parl., 35–36 Elizabeth II, 1986–87, and passed in 1988.

9 As Audrey Macklin (2003) notes, safe third country provisions replicate the thinly veiled racist logic of an earlier immigration restriction in Canada. In the early twentieth century, Canada instated the "continuous journey" requirement, denying admission to migrants who arrived in Canada through a third country. Of course, this requirement conveniently disqualified much of the migration from Asia.

10 Of course, uninterrupted air travel is considerably more expensive than land, piecemeal, or mixed-transport travel. This means that safe third country provisions make Canadian refugee protection largely inaccessible to those with the least financial resources: poorer refugees are less likely to afford continuous journeys and, thus, may easily fail to qualify for protection in Canada.

11 Despite having been granted the authority, the Department of Immigration refrained from compiling a list of safe third countries (Kelley and Trebilcock 1998). Designating safe countries is a controversial practice that can provoke criticism and legal challenge, making the authority not always worth the trouble. For a recent case in point, see Canadian Council for Refugees (CCR) (n.d.) on the legal challenge against the Canadian government's designation of the United States as a safe third country for refugees.

12 Canadian refugee law recognizes that many refugees have no choice but to travel with fake documents (see Canadian Association of Refugee Lawyers 2018). Further, many refugees are instructed or choose to destroy their travel documents upon arriving in Canada. The Federal Court of Canada has ruled that claimants' choice to destroy their travel documents should have no bearing on refugee status decisions (see CCR 1996).

13 Sadly, similar attempts have followed in more recent years. In 2012, the Conservative immigration minister Jason Kenney reiterated similar logics of deterrence by diminishing the Federal Health Program, which provided health care to claimants while they awaited the outcome of their claims (see Chen and Liew 2017).

14 Following the *Convention Relating to the Status of Refugees*, July 28, 1951, 189 UNTS 150 (entered into force April 22, 1954) [*Refugee Convention*], and its *Protocol Relating to the Status of Refugees*, January 31, 1967, 606 UNTS 267 (entered into force October 4, 1967), Canadian law defines the refugee as a person who is outside of his or her country of nationality or habitual residence and is unable or unwilling to return to this country due to a well-founded fear of persecution. Importantly, persecution must be based on the refugee's race, religion, nationality, political opinion, or membership of a particular social group (UNHCR 2011). Gender is not named as a ground for protection.

15 For more on the role and function of Guidelines, see IRB 2021.

16 For instance, the absence of state protection and the possibility of internal flight are to be considered in decisions on gender-based claims.

17 Immigration and Refugee Board of Canada (IRB) adjudicators are independent decision makers; they cannot be forced or pressured to issue a specific decision on

any given case. This independence is meant to shield refugee decisions from the influence of policy and political considerations. However, as I show throughout this book, political and administrative calculations have consistently, albeit indirectly, impacted refugee adjudications.

18 UNHCR Executive Committee, "Refugee Women and International Protection" No. 39, 1985. https://www.unhcr.org/publications/refugee-women-and-international-protection.

19 For Nada's own account of her refugee case and feminist beliefs, see Nada 1993.

20 The topic of domestic abuse produced an especially complex discussion; in particular, legal scholars debated whether Canada may grant protection to women against forms of violence that pertain to Canada itself (see Macklin 1995). Eventually, the question was resolved by making the absence of state protection against domestic abuse a condition for granting refugee status in these cases (Trueheart 1993).

21 *Immigration Act*, SC 1976–77, c 52, s 1.

22 Those opposing the gender-based refugee policy were also concerned that expanding refugee protection based on gender could potentially lead to demands for more expansions, such as on the basis of sexual orientation, poverty, or famine (Scanlan 1993). Of course, without the hindsight of history, opponents could not imagine that in a matter of years persecution based on sexual orientation and gender identity would be widely acknowledged in refugee jurisprudence.

23 Not all advocates replicated this reasoning. Groups such as the Canadian Council for Refugees and the National Action Committee on the Status of Women held more radical positions that did not wish to appease the restrictionist sentiments of the time. In fact, these groups criticized the limitations of the *Gender Guidelines* in offering meaningful protection to women (see, for instance, J. Miller 1993b; Ulbrich 1993).

24 The IRB had already announced that it was considering a draft policy paper on the topic of gender-based claims (A. Thompson 1993b). This paper laid the foundation for the *Gender Guidelines* (J. Miller 1993a).

25 "IRB Acceptance Rates-Response," 1995, RG 76-B-1, box 1993/1994, file 8620–19, vol 8, Refugee and Displaced Persons – General Immigration and Refugee Board, Department of Employment and Immigration fonds, Library and Archives Canada.

Chapter 4: The Losing Game of Protection

Acknowledgment: Parts of this chapter were previously published in *Feminist Legal Studies* and are reproduced here with the permission of the publisher, Springer Nature. For the full article, see Masoumi 2019.

1 The Immigration and Refugee Board of Canada (IRB) released an updated version of the original 1993 *Guideline 4: Women Refugee Claimants Fearing Gender-related Persecution*, March 9, 1993 (*Gender Guidelines*), on November 13, 1996. The IRB has recently revised and released this Guideline as *Chairperson's Guideline 4-*

Gender Considerations in Proceedings Before the Immigration and Refugee Board, July 18, 2022, https://irb.gc.ca/en/legal-policy/policies/Pages/GuideDir04.aspx.

2 Sam Ifejika (1993) suggested that while positive decisions had to be explained, negative decisions were not scrutinized (Vincent 1992c).

3 Interview with former adjudicator, 11 November 2016.

4 The IRB's annual reports were deeply transformed by this new reporting format. For instance, the IRB (1997, 1998, 1999, 2000) began to report costs per claim for the first time. Even the language used in the reports shifted dramatically. In a matter of a few years, the use of terms such as "dividends" and "investments" became commonplace in the IRB's reports (see, for example, IRB 1997, 6).

5 The additional resources were requested to respond to a surge of appeals that visa officers had created and passed along to the IRB. See Letter from Robert Desperrier to Hallam Johnson, 1995, RG 76-B-1, box 1993/1994, file 8620–19, vol 8, Refugee and Displaced Persons – General Immigration and Refugee Board, Department of Employment and Immigration fonds, Library and Archives Canada (LAC).

6 Letter from Hallam Johnson to Robert Desperrier, 1995, RG 76 B-1, Box 1993/1994, File 8620-19, Volume 8, Refugee and Displaced Persons- General-Immigration and Refugee Board, Department of Employment and Immigration fonds, Library and Archives Canada, Ottawa, Canada.

7 Before single-person panels were regularized by the *Immigration and Refugee Protection Act*, SC 2001, c 27 [*IRPA*] in 2001, these adjudications were contingent on the consent of claimants. Today, all IRB decisions are made by one adjudicator. For more on the gradual normalization of single-person adjudications over the 1990s, see IRB 2000.

8 Interview with former adjudicator, October 6, 2016.

9 *IRPA*.

10 These statistics were acquired through an access to information and privacy request (Doc. A-2018–00418/SD) to the IRB.

11 This unpublished report was acquired through personal contact with the author, Paul St. Clair. St. Clair is a long-time refugee advocate and settlement worker at CultureLink, with specialized focus on Roma migrants and refugees. He has been intimately involved in advocacy for Roma refugees and the appeal of the Lead case. Parts of this report have been published online by the *Hungarian Free Press* and are available publicly. https://hungarianfreepress.com/2017/08/25/hungarian-roma-refugees-in-canada-the-lead-case-its-aftermath-and-the-future-parts-2-3/.

12 Visa requirements were eventually imposed on Hungarians in 2001. For more on the geopolitics of visa requirements in relation to Hungary and the Czech Republic, see *Hungarian Free Press* 2017; Levine-Rasky 2016; Levine-Rasky, Beaudoin, and St Clair 2014.

13 See *Geza v Canada (Minister of Citizenship and Immigration)*, [2006] 4 FCR 377, 2006 FCA 124; reversing *Geza v Canada (Minister of Citizenship and Immigration)*, [2005] 3 FCR 3, 2004 FC 1039 (Federal Court), paras 7–8, also cited in Macklin 2013.

14 Like guidelines, persuasive decisions, and jurisprudential guides, Lead cases provide direction to, and facilitate the work of, claim adjudicators.
15 Before the Lead case, Roma Hungarians were processed in normal adjudication proceedings.
16 Much remains unknown about how the Lead case was developed. According to the unpublished report by St. Clair (*Hungarian Free Press* 2017), more than half of the communications between the IRB, the Department of Immigration, and other government departments pertaining to the development of the Lead case were not released even during the appeal proceedings due to national security concerns.
17 Travel costs were covered by Ontario Legal Aid (*Hungarian Free Press* 2017).
18 *Kozak v Canada (Minister of Citizenship and Immigration)*, 2006 FCA 124, para 65.
19 For a detailed account of this chilling case, see Mitrovica 2017.

Chapter 5: Pivoting on Gay

1 Justin Trudeau was the first sitting prime minister to march in Pride Parade, in 2016. For more on this, see N. Thompson 2016.
2 *Immigration and Refugee Protection Act*, SC 2001, c 27 [*IRPA*].
3 *Convention Relating to the Status of Refugees*, July 28, 1951, 189 UNTS 150 (entered into force April 22, 1954) *[Refugee Convention]; Convention against Torture and Other Cruel, Inhuman or Degrading Treatment or Punishment*, December 10, 1984, 1465 UNTS 85 (entered into force June 26, 1987). Before the *IRPA*, the cases involving these issues fell under the purview of the Department of Immigration rather than the Immigration and Refugee Board of Canada (IRB) (2002); as a result, they were not decided by politically independent adjudicators.
4 Two-person panels were only advantageous for claimants when the residing adjudicators were of differing opinions; when the two adjudicators concurred, there was no particular advantage to claimants. For administrative ease, adjudicators were often scheduled in common pairings that at times involved like-minded decision makers. Durable pairings of like-minded adjudicators were of little advantage to claimants' chances of acceptance or the IRB's rates of output. Interview with former adjudicator, November 11, 2016.
5 Interview with refugee advocate, July 15, 2016.
6 The IRB administrators had long been in favour of an internal appeal division and had begun conceptualizing the appeal process since the late 1990s. Interview with former adjudicator, November 11, 2016.
7 Interview with refugee advocate, July 15, 2016.
8 Although the delay in establishing the Refugee Appeal Division (RAD) lightened the IRB's (2002, 10) work, it was not fully endorsed by the board. In fact, the decision to postpone the RAD was made without consultation with the IRB officials; by the time the announcement was made by the Liberal government, the IRB had already devoted precious resources to the development of the new division.

9 For example, claimants from designated countries of origin were excluded from appeals to the RAD.

10 For more information on the IRB's appeal procedures, see "Filing a Claim," *Immigration and Refugee Board of Canada*, https://irb-cisr.gc.ca/en/filing-refugee-appeal/Pages/refugee1.aspx.

11 These relations were negotiated and clarified over the course of several years in a memorandum of understanding between the IRB, the Canada Border Services Agency, and the Department of Immigration. See IRB 2005, 5.

12 *Agreement between the Government of Canada and the Government of the United States of America for Cooperation in the Examination of Refugee Status Claims from Nationals of Third Countries*, December 5, 2002, https://www.canada.ca/en/immigration-refugees-citizenship/corporate/mandate/policies-operational-instructions-agreements/agreements/safe-third-country-agreement/final-text.html.

13 The *Safe Third Country Agreement* was successfully challenged in the Federal Court by a coalition of refugee advocacy organizations in 2020. However, the federal government appealed the decision in 2021, and the earlier ruling was overturned by the Federal Court of Appeal. Hence, the *Agreement* remains in place today. For more on this, see Sevunts 2021.

14 For instance, in 2001, 13,497 refugee claimants entered Canada from the United States, and only a few hundred moved from Canada to the United States to make refugee claims (see Hyndman and Mountz 2007).

15 *Balanced Refugee Reform Act*, SC 2010, c 8.

16 *Protecting Canada's Immigration System Act*, SC 2012, c 17.

17 For example, the immigration minister was afforded the authority to designate "safe" countries, and the minister of public safety and emergency preparedness was given the power to designate "irregular" arrivals. Claimants arriving "irregularly" or from "safe" countries were then subject to differential procedures that restricted their access to rights and mobility. The designation of "safe" countries will be discussed more fully in the next chapter. For more on "irregular" arrivals, see "First Designation of Irregular Arrivals," *Steven Meurrencs Immigration Law*, December 5, 2012, https://meurrensonimmigration.com/first-designation-of-irregular-arrival/.

18 *Chairperson's Guideline 9: Proceedings before the IRB Involving Sexual Orientation and Gender Identity and Expression*, May 1, 2017 (*SOGIE Guidelines*). These Guidelines have been revised and released as *Chairperson's Guideline 9: Proceedings before the IRB Involving Sexual Orientation, Gender Identity and Expression, and Sex Characteristics* on December 17, 2021, https://irb.gc.ca/en/legal-policy/policies/Pages/GuideDir09.aspx/.

19 *Canadian Human Rights Act*, RSC 1985, c H-6; Bill C-23, *An Act to Modernize the Statutes of Canada in Relation to Benefits and Obligations*, SC 2000, c. 12; *Civil Marriage Act*, SC 2005, c 33.

20 For a more detailed discussion of LGBT rights in Canada, see "Rights of LGBTI Persons," *Government of Canada*, https://www.canada.ca/en/canadian-heritage/services/rights-lgbti-persons.html.

21 This, of course, does not mean that every instance of same-sex contact was necessarily prosecuted with severity. Rather, as Lyle Dick (2009) notes, the actual interest in prosecution was determined by a host of legal and extrajudicial factors, including, for instance, the overarching culture of the time as well as the personal sentiments of presiding officials on questions of sexual non-normativity.

22 *Immigration Act*, RS 1927, c. 93.

23 For more on the gay liberation movement and its impact on lesbian and gay rights in Canada, see Smith 1999.

24 *Immigration Act*, SC 1976–77, c 52, s 1.

25 During this period, same-sex couples continued to push the boundaries of existing regulations, and bureaucrats accommodated same-sex spousal sponsorships through unconventional legal avenues, such as by recourse to humanitarian and compassionate grounds. For a more detailed discussion of same-sex spousal sponsorships, see LaViolette 2004.

26 See the United Nations High Commissioner for Refugees (UNHCR), *Guidelines on International Protection no. 9: Claims to Refugee Status based on Sexual Orientation and/or Gender Identity within the context of Article 1A(2) of the 1951 Convention and/or Its 1967 Protocol Relating to the Status of Refugees*, HCR/GIP/12/09, October 23, 2012, http://www.unhcr.org/509136ca9.pdf.

27 *Canada (Attorney General) v Ward*, [1993] 2 SCR 689.

28 Interview with former adjudicator, November 11, 2016.

29 For more on how affect and intuition influence sexual orientation and gender identity and expression (SOGIE) refugee credibility assessments, see Murray 2014.

30 In one particularly animated story, a former decision maker (interviewed October 6, 2016) recounted the heavy flirtation between an openly gay language interpreter and a claimant in front of a disapproving same-sex partner during a hearing. For the decision maker, witnessing these interactions eliminated any doubt about the credibility of the two claimants' homosexuality.

31 Interview with former adjudicator, November 11, 2016.

32 Author's observation of consultation session, November 25, 2016.

33 *SOGIE Guidelines*, section 2 (emphasis added).

34 After the UNHCR identified single gay, bisexual, and transgender men as a particularly vulnerable group among Syrian refugees, Canada prioritized resettling these groups. These initiatives, however, were criticized for neglecting and deprioritizing other vulnerable SOGIE populations, such as those from Turkey and Iran (see Molnar 2018).

35 According to the terms of the *Refugee Convention*, a refugee is a person who is outside of their country of nationality or habitual residence and is unable or un-

willing to return to this country due to a well-founded fear of persecution. In other words, persons who reside in their own countries are not within the *Convention*'s definition of a refugee.

36 For more on this project, see Ibbitson 2017a.

37 For example, the increase in the number of SOGIE claims from Nigeria in the late 2010s sparked an investigation by authorities from the IRB and the Department of Immigration (see Molnar 2018).

38 This data was obtained by *Xtra Magazine* through an access to information and privacy request to the IRB. For the full database, see "IRB Data Release: SOGI and General Claim Decisions 2011–2015," https://docs.google.com/spreadsheets/d/1LDFqkYJCpOTO_B-oItLlmH3vQoYrnSF3Nl_o5q9tZ7o/edit#gid=604097886.

39 This data was obtained by *Xtra Magazine* through an access to information and privacy request to the IRB. See "IRB Data Release."

40 Post-colonial, transnational, and historical studies of sexuality have long demonstrated the role of colonial systems in cultivating heterosexist and transphobic violence in the colonized world. For a few examples, see Najmabadi 2005; Human Rights Watch 2008; Wesley 2014; Kizito 2017.

Chapter 6: Protection on Life Support

1 For a summary of Jason Kenney's voting history on sexual rights as a member of parliament, see "Voting Records: Jason Kenney," *Campaign Life Coalition*, https://www.campaignlifecoalition.com/voting-records/view/mp/province//id/155/name/jason-kenney#bio.

2 This data was obtained by *Xtra Magazine* through an access to information and privacy request to the Immigration and Refugee Board of Canada (IRB). For the full database, see "IRB Data Release: SOGI and General Claim Decisions 2011–2015," https://docs.google.com/spreadsheets/d/1LDFqkYJCpOTO_B-oItLlmH3vQoYrnSF3Nl_o5q9tZ7o/edit#gid=604097886.

3 *Chairperson's Guideline 9: Proceedings before the IRB Involving Sexual Orientation and Gender Identity and Expression*, May 1, 2017 (*SOGIE Guidelines*). These guidelines have been revised and released as *Chairperson's Guideline 9: Proceedings before the IRB Involving Sexual Orientation, Gender Identity and Expression, and Sex Characteristics* on December 17, 2021, https://irb.gc.ca/en/legal-policy/policies/Pages/GuideDir09.aspx/.

4 Between 2001 and 2012, the IRB was legislated to expand its protection mandate, accept the transfer of new tasks (such as pre-removal risk assessments), create an entirely new division to process appeals, radically change its scheduling practices, and define a cooperative relation with the newly created Canada Border Services Agency.

5 Interviews with former adjudicators, October 6, 2016, and November 11, 2016.

6 Interview with former adjudicator, October 6, 2016.

7 The new case management system diverted claims to four hearing streams based on their complexity. Easy and straightforward claims were directed to short hearings, while more complex cases were given longer hearing times.
8 Interview with former adjudicator, October 6, 2016.
9 Interview with former adjudicator, October 6, 2016.
10 The imposition of visa requirements against countries such as Hungary and Zimbabwe, the Department of Immigration's strategies for stopping unauthorized travellers abroad, and the implementation of the *Safe Third Country Agreement*, December 5, 2002, https://www.canada.ca/en/immigration-refugees-citizenship/corporate/mandate/policies-operational-instructions-agreements/agreements/safe-third-country-agreement.html significantly dropped the number of incoming claims in Canada (IRB 2003, 23; 2004, 7; 2005, 24–25).
11 Speculations ran high as to the reason for the delays. While some criticized the Conservatives for wishing to evade the pool of candidates that had been screened by the previous Liberal government, others accused the government of intentionally sabotaging the IRB in order to establish a system that could be controlled more directly by political authorities (Campion-Smith 2007).
12 Following years of criticism, Judy Sgro, the Liberal minister of immigration, had reformed the appointment process in 2004. Under the reformed system, candidates were first screened by an independent advisory committee consisting of lawyers, academics, immigration advocates, and human resources experts. A second panel of IRB officials, appointed by the chairperson, then selected adjudicators from the pool of qualified candidates. The minister's role was limited to appointing the recommended persons (Campion-Smith 2007; Keung 2007). The Conservatives planned to increase the ministerial control over appointments by condensing the process into a single round of selection, conducted by a panel half of whose members were to be directly appointed by the minister.
13 Politicized appointment processes reorient adjudicators' accountability from the IRB's administration to political parties or even specific politicians and afford adjudicators undue protection irrespective of their performance, responsiveness, and productivity (interview with former adjudicator, November 11, 2016).
14 Jean-Guy Fleury's frustration with appointment delays was well known (Keung 2007). In the month prior to his resignation, Fleury had raised the issue with a parliamentary immigration committee and met with the minister eight times just to discuss appointments (Galloway 2006).
15 Five members of the appointment advisory committee also stepped down to protest the announced changes (Campion-Smith 2007).
16 For instance, while the IRB (2009, 16) was funded to process twenty-five thousand claims, it received thirty-six thousand cases in 2008–09.
17 Interview with former adjudicator, October 6, 2016.

18 The role of refugee hearing officers (RHOs) (also titled refugee protection officers) had long been a topic of controversy at the IRB. As early as the early 1990s, RHOs were criticized for undermining the non-adversarial nature of the adjudication process by their aggressive styles of cross-examination and problematic practices in disseminating information (see Hathaway 1993). Hence, the elimination of their role was not purely motivated by budgetary concerns.
19 Interview with former adjudicator, October 6, 2016.
20 Experiences of trauma can impact claimants' ability to retrieve, recall, and narrate details of their cases with consistency (interview with refugee lawyer, November 30, 2016; interview with refugee support worker, September 15, 2016). In these cases, submission of supplementary documentation, such as psychiatric reports, are key to establishing the credibility of claimants. While some lawyers are savvy at recognizing their clients' limitations and gathering supplementary documentations on their behalf, claimants without capable legal representation do far worse in a system that places great emphasis on the real-time interactions of the hearing.
21 Interview with former adjudicator, October 6, 2016.
22 For instance, the IRB began to introduce streamlined pre-hearing readiness protocols (see IRB 2003, 18, 24).
23 Interview with former adjudicator, October 6, 2016. Shorter written reasons were thought to help adjudicators finalize claims more quickly and minimize the chances of error – hence, eliminating the possible grounds for future appeals.
24 Interview with former adjudicator, October 6, 2016. For more on the managerialization of refugee protection in Canada, see Soennecken 2013.
25 The workloads were controlled, in part, through imposition of visa requirements.
26 *Protecting Canada's Refugee System Act,* SC 2012, c 17. For example, those making refugee claims at Canadian ports of entry had only fifteen days to complete and submit their basis of claim forms, compared to twenty-eight days in the previous legislation. The truncated timelines hindered claimants' access to the Canadian regime of refugee protection as well as their chances of success. The shorter timelines gave claimants considerably less time to seek and procure proper legal representation, gather evidence and documentation, and complete their forms in detail. For more on this, see Canadian Bar Association 2012.
27 IRB officials frequently reported that the legislated timelines were grossly out of touch with the realities of refugee claim processing (IRB 2014, 15; 2015, 2). The timelines, for instance, did not account for the learning curve of new adjudicators, delays in front-end security screenings by other departments, or basic human resource issues such as increases in vacation allocations (IRB 2014, 15).
28 These also included claims that were sent back from Federal Court for reassessment (IRB 2016, 19).

29 Despite this, the volume of incoming claims continued to exceed processing capacities, and the number of claims waiting review grew (IRB 2016, 19).

30 *North American Free Trade Agreement*, December 17, 1992, Can TS 1994 No 2, (1993) 32 ILM 289 (entered into force January 1, 1994).

31 For fuller accounts of these conditions, see Jimenez 2008; Valpy 2009.

32 The visa requirement was announced on very short notice, allowing a grace period of only forty-eight hours for those already in transit (O'Neil 2009); any longer notice, Jason Kenney had argued, would create a "rush for the border" (Clark 2009, A1). Imposing visas on hundreds of thousands of Mexicans who travelled to Canada as students, tourists, and businesspeople was, of course, a costly political and administrative endeavour. Displeased by the news and yet unwilling to risk the loss of Canadian tourism, Mexican officials reciprocated by imposing visas on Canadian diplomats only (Barrio-Terrazas 2009). To cope with the volume of applications, fourteen visa officers had to be flown from Ottawa, and several Mexicans were hired locally to assist the overstretched visa officers in the Canadian embassy in Mexico City (Cryderman 2009). The messy scramble to administer visas, nonetheless, caused an assortment of administrative troubles for international students (Cryderman 2009; Willick 2009); damaged the image of Canada in Mexico (Simpson 2009); and caused controversy – in one case, a prominent Supreme Court of Mexico justice was refused entry to Canada (*Toronto Star* 2009). Ultimately, the increased administrative cost of visa processing and the loss of tourism revenues in Canada outweighed any financial value gained from cutting the number of Mexican refugee claims (Simpson 2010).

33 Like the infamous Lead case, Persuasive decisions are administrative devices that are meant to lighten the work of refugee status determination by providing replicable guiding reasoning on cases of similar circumstances.

34 To establish absence of protection in Mexico, claimants were required to demonstrate sustained, yet unsuccessful, effort in securing the help of Mexican authorities. It was, for example, considered insufficient for claimants to state that they had sought support from "some member of the police force." For more on this, see Jimenez 2008.

35 *Guideline 4: Women Refugee Claimants Fearing Gender-related Persecution*, March 9, 1993. The IRB has recently revised and released this Guideline as *Chairperson's Guideline 4- Gender Considerations in Proceedings Before the Immigration and Refugee Board*, July 18, 2022, https://irb.gc.ca/en/legal-policy/policies/Pages/GuideDir04.aspx.

36 Interview with refugee lawyer, November 30, 2016.

37 Interview with refugee lawyer, November 30, 2016.

38 Fast-tracking systems had long been used by the IRB to increase the productivity of claim processing. Historically, these systems were created internally by the IRB and were applied to claims that were largely believed to be well founded.

39 Designated countries of origin (DCO) claims that were made at ports of entry were to be heard within thirty days. Other DCOs had forty-five days before their hearing.

40 Federal appeals of refugee decisions have several significant limitations. First, Federal Courts can only consider appeals based on judicial grounds. Therefore, claimants are required to demonstrate evidence of judicial error at the IRB to be considered for an appeal. Second, Federal Courts cannot rule on the substance of cases as refugee adjudication remains under the exclusive authority of the board. This means, for example, that claimants cannot appeal the assessments of their credibility in court. Third, federal appeals require a leave to appeal. Leaves, in turn, are rarely granted. As a result, most appellants are never permitted to appeal their cases.

41 The DCO was protested passionately by refugee advocates and successfully challenged in the Federal Court in 2015 (see Levine-Rasky, Beaudoin, and St. Clair 2014; Keung 2015). The Conservative government then initiated an appeal to sustain the DCO. However, after the election of the Liberals, the appeal proceedings were dropped and all countries were removed from the DCO list in 2019 (see Canadian Broadcasting Corporation 2016; Government of Canada 2019a).

42 This data was obtained by *Xtra Magazine* through an access to information and privacy request to the IRB. For the full database, see "IRB Data Release: SOGI and General Claim Decisions 2011–2015," https://docs.google.com/spreadsheets/d/1LDFqkYJCpOTO_B-oItLlmH3vQoYrnSF3Nl_o5q9tZ7o/edit#gid=604097886.

43 *SOGIE Guidelines*.

44 Before any person is deported from Canada, risk assessments are made to ensure that the deportee is not sent to dangerous conditions. These assessments are particularly important for claims from highly volatile national contexts. These assessments do not provide secure status in Canada but only protect prospective deportees from likely danger after deportation.

45 Grise's family was only issued visas after thirty-four hundred dollars, which was raised by advocates, was paid to the federal government to cover the cost of the deportation that had sent Grise to her death (Keung 2009).

Conclusion

1 For a fuller account of the Irish migration to Toronto due to the Great Hunger, see "Great Famine History," *Canada Ireland Foundation*, http://irelandparkfoundation.com/famine-memorial/great-famine-history/.

2 See United Nations High Commission for Refugees (UNHCR), "Figures at a Glance," 2020, https://www.unhcr.org/figures-at-a-glance.html.

3 For more on the refugee situation in Lebanon, see Karasapan and Shah 2021.

4 *Convention Relating to the Status of Refugees*, July 28, 1951, 189 UNTS 150 (entered into force April 22, 1954).

5 *Protocol Relating to the Status of Refugees,* January 31, 1967, 606 UNTS 267 (entered into force October 4, 1967). For the list of signatories, see "State Parties to the 1951 Convention relating to the Status of Refugees and the 1967 Protocol," *United Nations High Commissioner for Refugees,* https://www.unhcr.org/protect/PROTECTION/3b73b0d63.pdf.

6 The terms of the United Nations Relief and Works Agency for Palestine Refugees in the Near East only apply to Palestinians who reside in one of the specified areas of operation (Jordan, Syria, Lebanon, the West Bank, and the Gaza Strip). Hence, Palestinians who are outside this geographical region are not protected by the agency (Knudsen 2009).

7 For a discussion of how this has affected Syrian refugees in Lebanon, see Janmyr 2016.

8 For an example of this in relation to Afghan refugees in the 1980s, see Gallagher 1989.

9 *Immigration Act,* SC 1976–77, c 52, s 1.

10 See UNHCR, "Figures at a Glance."

11 *Protecting Canada's Immigration System Act,* SC 2012, c 17.

12 *Agreement between the Government of Canada and the Government of the United States of America for Cooperation in the Examination of Refugee Status Claims from Nationals of Third Countries,* December 5, 2002, https://www.canada.ca/en/immigration-refugees-citizenship/corporate/mandate/policies-operational-instructions-agreements/agreements/safe-third-country-agreement/final-text.html.

13 Deportations were eventually put on hold given the increasingly unsafe conditions in Haiti and due to strong mobilization for deportation relief by advocates (Olson 2018; Canadian Broadcasting Corporation 2019).

14 For instance, as Susan Kneebone (2009) reports, in 2002, Canada accepted 55 percent of the refugee claims it processed, a rate considerably higher than those of the United States, the United Kingdom (approximately 30 percent), Australia, Belgium, Sweden (20–25 percent), and Greece (2 percent). For several decades, American law defined refugees as persons fleeing "from a Communist-dominated country or area, or from any country within the general area of the middle East." In fact, it was not until 1980 that the United States began to adopt a more politically neutral definition in line with the international law. Yet, as Michael Teitelbaum (1984) notes, refugee admissions in the United States continued to reflect American political interests well after 1980.

15 For more information on the asylum process in the United States, see "The Affirmative Asylum Process," *US Citizenship and Immigration Services,* https://www.uscis.gov/humanitarian/refugees-asylum/asylum/affirmative-asylum-process.

16 For more information on the Australian system, see "Asylum Seekers and Refugees Guide," *Australian Human Rights Commission,* https://www.humanrights.gov.au/our-work/asylum-seekers-and-refugees/asylum-seekers-and-refugees-guide#process.

17 In 2017, the appeal case of an Afghan Hazara asylum seeker in the Federal Court revealed that parts of the negative decision issued by the Refugee Review Tribunal had been cut and pasted from other refugee applications. For more on this case, see N. Robinson 2017.

18 For more on the evasive nature of state departments, see Abrams 1988.

Appendix B: Written Interview with an IRB Manager

1 Portions of this text have been removed and other parts have been anonymized to protect the interviewee's identity.

References

Abrams, Philip. 1988. "Notes on the Difficulty of Studying the State (1977)." *Journal of Historical Sociology* 1 (1): 58–89.

Abu-Laban, Yasmeen. 1998. "Welcome/Stay Out: The Contradiction of Canadian Integration and Immigration Policies at the Millennium." *Canadian Ethnic Studies Journal* 30 (3): 190–213.

Anderson, Benedict. 1991. *Imagined Communities: Reflections on the Origin and Spread of Nationalism.* London: Verso.

Anderson, Christopher G. 2010. "Restricting Rights, Losing Control: The Politics of Control over Asylum Seekers in Liberal-Democratic States – Lessons from the Canadian Case, 1951–1989." *Canadian Journal of Political Science* 43 (4): 937–59.

Arendt, Hannah. (1951) 1973. *The Origins of Totalitarianism.* New York: Harcourt Brace Jovanovich.

Arhin, Antonella. 2013. "Roma in Canada: Migratory Trends, Issues and Perceptions." In *Roma Migration to and from Canada: The Czech, Hungarian, and Slovak Case,* edited by Zsuzsanna Vidra, 53–86. Budapest: Centre for Policy Studies, Central European University.

Arizona Daily Star. 1993. "Women and Asylum." February 6, 20a.

Aucoin, Peter. 1995. *The New Public Management: Canada in Comparative Perspective.* Montreal: Institute for Research on Public Policy.

Balibar, Etienne. 1991. "The Nation Form." In *Race, Nation, Class: Ambiguous Identities,* edited by E. Balibar and I.M. Wallerstein, 86–105. New York: Verso.

Barrio-Terrazas, Francisco. 2009. "Keeping Mexico Close to Canada." *National Post,* July 21, A10.

Bashford, Alison, and Jane McAdam. 2014. "The Right to Asylum: Britain's 1905 Aliens Act and the Evolution of Refugee Law." *Law and History Review* 32 (2): 309–50.

Bauder, Harald. 2008. "The Economic Case for Immigration: Neoliberal and Regulatory Paradigms in Canada's Press." *Studies in Political Economy* 82 (1): 131–52.

Beaudoin, Julianna, Jennifer Danch, and Sean Rehaag. 2015. "No Refuge: Hungarian Romani Refugee Claimants in Canada." Osgoode Hall Law School Legal Studies Research Paper no. 12. https://digitalcommons.osgoode.yorku.ca/cgi/viewcontent.cgi?referer=https://www.google.ca/&httpsredir=1&article=1090&context=olsrps.

Berg, Laurie, and Jenni Millbank. 2009. "Constructing the Personal Narratives of Lesbian, Gay and Bisexual Asylum Claimants." *Journal of Refugee Studies* 22 (2): 195–223.

Biehl, Kristen S. 2015. "Governing through Uncertainty: Experiences of Being a Refugee in Turkey as a Country for Temporary Asylum." *Social Analysis* 59 (1): 57–75. doi:10.3167/sa.2015.590104.

Bielski, Zosia. 2017. "After A Lifetime of Hiding, Gay Refugees Seeking Protection in Canada Are Expected to Prove Their Identity." *Globe and Mail*, April 30. https://www.theglobeandmail.com/life/relationships/after-lifetime-of-hiding-gay-refugees-to-canada-expected-to-prove-theiridentity/article34858343/.

Bohmer, Carol, and Amy Shuman. 2008. *Rejecting Refugees: Political Asylum in the 21st Century*. London: Routledge.

Bourdieu, Pierre. 1993a. "Some Properties of Fields." In *Sociology in Question*, translated and edited by Richard Nice, 72–77. London: Sage.

–. 1993b. *The Field of Cultural Production: Essays on Art and Literature*. Edited and introduced by Randal Johnson. New York: Columbia University Press.

–. 1996. *The Rules of Art: Genesis and Structure of the Literary Field*. Translated by Susan Emanuel. Stanford, CA: Stanford University Press.

Braganza, Chantal. 2018. "How the Federal Government May Be Creating Refugee Backlogs." *TV Ontario*, July 17. https://tvo.org/article/current-affairs/how-the-federal-government-may-be-creating-refugee-backlogs.

British Broadcasting Corporation. 2016. "Australia Asylum: Why Is It Controversial?" *BBC News*, August 3. http://www.bbc.com/news/world-asia-28189608.

Broadbent, Edward. 1992. "Prisoners in Their Own Homes." *Globe and Mail*, December 21, A17.

Broeders, Dennis. 2010. "Return to Sender?" *Punishment & Society* 12 (2): 169–86.

Brown, Wendy. 2015. *Undoing the Demos: Neoliberalism's Stealth Revolution*. Brooklyn, NY: Zone Books.

Brubaker, Rogers. 1992. *Citizenship and Nationhood in France and Germany*. Cambridge, MA: Harvard University Press.

Cabot, Heath. 2014. *On the Doorstep of Europe: Asylum and Citizenship in Greece*. Philadelphia: University of Pennsylvania Press.

Campbell, Meagan. 2017. "Haitian Asylum Seekers Are About to Test Canada's Refugee System in a Big Way." *Maclean's*, December 18. https://www.macleans.ca/news/canada/haitian-asylum-seekers-are-about-to-test-canadas-refugee-system-in-a-big-way/.

Campion-Smith, Bruce. 2007. "Board Changes Spark Worried about Refugees." *Toronto Star*, March 3. https://www.thestar.com/news/2007/03/03/board_changes_spark_worries_about_refugees.html.

Canada Border Services Agency (CBSA). 2022. "Annual Detention Statistics: 2012-2022." https://www.cbsa-asfc.gc.ca/security-securite/detent/stat-2012-2022-eng.html.

Canadian Bar Association. 2012. *Bill C-31: Protecting Canada's Immigration System Act*. Ottawa: Canadian Bar Association. https://www.cba.org/CMSPages/GetFile.aspx?guid=293bebf9-5237-4106-a26a-7d4241501a38#:~:text=Bill%20C%2D31%20restricts%20access,or%20have%20no%20credible%20basis.

Canadian Broadcasting Corporation. 2016. "Liberals Drop Legal Appeal of Unconstitutional Conservative Refugee Measure." January 4. https://www.cbc.ca/news/politics/liberals-drop-legal-appeal-of-unconstitutional-conservative-refugee-measure-1.3389336.

–. 2019. "Haitian Asylum Seeker 'Living in Hell' 6 Months after Deportation from Quebec." February 17. https://www.cbc.ca/news/canada/montreal/haitian-asylum-seeker-deported-1.5023211.

Canadian Council for Refugees (CCR). 1996. "Refugees and Identity Documents." http://ccrweb.ca/en/refugees-and-identity-documents.

–. 2003. "Comments on the Occasion of the Tenth Anniversary of the Immigration and Refugee Board Gender Guidelines." http://ccrweb.ca/sites/ccrweb.ca/files/static-files/gendergcom.htm.

–. 2005. "Closing the Front Door on Refugees: Report on the First Year of the Safe Third Country Agreement." https://ccrweb.ca/sites/ccrweb.ca/files/static-files/closingdoordec05.pdf.

–. 2009. "Brief History of Canada's Responses to Refugees." https://ccrweb.ca/sites/ccrweb.ca/files/static-files/canadarefugeeshistory4.htm.

–. 2016. "Immigration Detention Statistics." https://ccrweb.ca/sites/ccrweb.ca/files/immigration-detention-statistics-2015.pdf.

–. N.d. "Safe Third Country." http://ccrweb.ca/en/safe-third-country.

Capra, Fritjof, and Ugo Mattei. 2015. *The Ecology of Law: Toward a Legal System in Tune with Nature and Community.* Oakland, CA: Berrett-Koehler.

Cardozo, Andrew. 1993. "Refuge for Abused Women." *Toronto Star*, February 17, A19.

–. 2018. "Challenging the Myths: The Truth about Canadian Refugee Law." https://carl-acaadr.ca/challenging-myths/.

Carver, Natasha. 2016. "'For Her Protection and Benefit': The Regulation of Marriage-Related Migration to the UK." *Ethnic and Racial Studies* 39 (15): 2758–76.

Cernetig, Miro. 1994. "Ottawa Accused of Fast-Tracking Unsavoury Immigrants." *Globe and Mail*, August 30, A2.

Chan, Arlene. 2017. "Chinese Immigration Act." In *The Canadian Encyclopedia*. Toronto: Historica Canada. https://www.thecanadianencyclopedia.ca/en/article/chinese-immigration-act.

Chen, Brandon, and Jamie Chai Yun Liew. 2017. "Refugees Once Again Have Full Health Benefits, But Some Practitioners Still Don't Know That." *CBC News*, May 9. https://www.cbc.ca/news/opinion/refugee-health-care-1.4105120.

Citizenship and Immigration Canada. 2013. "Backgrounder – Designated Countries of Origin" [archived]. *Government of Canada*. https://www.canada.ca/en/immigration-refugees-citizenship/news/archives/backgrounders-2012/designated-countries-origin-2.html.

–. 2017. "Designated Countries of Origin Policy." *Government of Canada*. https://www.canada.ca/en/immigration-refugees-citizenship/services/refugees/claim-protection-inside-canada/apply/designated-countries-policy.html.

Clark, Campbell. 2009. "Minister Calls for Overhaul of Canada's Refugee System." *Globe and Mail*, July 15. https://www.theglobeandmail.com/news/national/minister-calls-for-overhaul-of-canadas-refugee-system/article1201539/.

Connell, Raewyn, Barbara Fawcett, and Gabrielle Meagher. 2009. "Neoliberalism, New Public Management and the Human Service Professions: Introduction to the Special Issue." *Journal of Sociology* 45 (4): 331–38.

Cryderman, Kelly. 2009. "Visa Rules Threaten Student Exchange Programs." *Calgary Herald*, July 16, B1.

Da, Wei Wei. 2002. "Chileans in Canada: Contexts of Departure and Arrival." In Latin American Research Group, *Social Cohesion and International Migration in a Globalizing Era: Transnational Solidarities and Newcomer Incorporation in Canada*. Toronto: York University. https://www.yorku.ca/cohesion/LARG/PDF/Chile-WWD-2002.pdf.

Dauvergne, Catherine. 2004. "Refugee Law and the Measure of Globalisation." *Law in Context* 22 (2): 62–82.

Day, Ancela. 2009. "Refusing the Refugees Taking the Trade: Canada's Unspoken Policy on Mexican Immigrants." *Canadian Dimension* 43 (5): 28–30.

Dench, Janet. N.d. "A Hundred Years of Immigration to Canada 1900–1999 (Part 2)." *Canadian Council for Refugees*. http://ccrweb.ca/en/hundred-years-immigration-canada-part-2.

Dick, Lyle. 2009. "The 1942 Same-sex Trials in Edmonton: On the State's Repression of Sexual Minorities, Archives, and Human Rights in Canada." *Archivaria* 68: 183–217.

DiMaggio, P.J., and W.W. Powell. 1983. "The Iron Cage Revisited: Institutional Isomorphism and Collective Rationality in Organizational Fields." *American Sociological Review* 48 (2): 147–60.

Dirks, Gerald E. 1984. "A Policy within a Policy: The Identification and Admission of Refugees to Canada." *Canadian Journal of Political Science* 17 (2): 279–307.

–. 1995. *Controversy and Complexity: Canadian Immigration Policy during the 1980s.* Montreal and Kingston: McGill-Queen's University Press.

Dobbin, Frank, Lauren B. Edelman, John W. Meyer, and Ann Swidler. 1988. "The Expansion of Due Process in Organizations." In *Institutional Patterns and Organizations: Culture and Environment,* edited by Lynne G. Zucker, 71–98. Cambridge, MA: Ballinger.

Dobbin, Frank, John R. Sutton, John W. Meyer, and Richard Scott. 1993. "Equal Opportunity Law and the Construction of Internal Labor Markets." *American Journal of Sociology* 99 (2): 396–427.

Douzinas, Costas. 2000. *The End of Human Rights: Critical Legal Thought at the Turn of the Century.* Oxford: Hart.

Edelman, Lauren B. 1990. "Legal Environments and Organizational Governance: The Expansion of Due Process in the American Workplace." *American Journal of Sociology* 95 (6): 1401–40.

–. 1992. "Legal Ambiguity and Symbolic Structures: Organizational Mediation of Civil Rights Law." *American Journal of Sociology* 97 (6): 1531–76.

Edelman, Lauren B., Steven E. Abraham, and Howard S. Erlanger. 1992. "Professional Construction of Law: The Inflated Threat of Wrongful Discharge." *Law and Society Review* 26 (1): 47–84.

Edelman, Lauren B., Howard S. Erlanger, and John Lande. 1993. "Internal Dispute Resolution: The Transformation of Civil Rights in the Workplace." *Law and Society Review* 27 (3): 497–534.

Edwards, Steven. 2009. "Spike in Refugee Claims Shows 'Systematic Abuse,' Kenney Says." *The Ottawa Citizen,* March 25, A5.

Evans Cameron, Hilary. 2016. "When in Doubt: The Law of Fact-Finding in Canadian Refugee Status Determination." JSC diss., Faculty of Law, University of Toronto.

Fadi, Hanna. 2005. "Punishing Masculinity in Gay Asylum Claims." *Yale Law Journal* 114 (4): 913–20.

Fekete, Jason. 2009. "Citizenship Program Needs to Focus on Canadian 'Values': Kenny." *American Renaissance,* April 16.

Feldman, Ilana. 2008. *Governing Gaza: Bureaucracy, Authority, and the Work of Rule.* Durham, NC: Duke University Press.

Ferlie, Ewan. 1996. *The New Public Management in Action.* Oxford: Oxford University Press.

Fernandez, Keith J. 2021. "Top 10 LGBT+ Friendly Countries for Expats." *Expatica,* May 28. https://www.expatica.com/moving/location/lgbt-friendly-countries-9880/.

Ferreira da Silva, Denise. 2001. "Towards a Critique of the Socio-Logos of Justice: The Analytics of Raciality and the Production of Universality." *Social Identities* 7 (3): 421–54.

Foot, Richard. 2006. "Singh Case." *The Canadian Encyclopedia*. Toronto: Historica Canada. https://www.thecanadianencyclopedia.ca/en/article/singh-case.

Foucault, Michel. (1965) 1988. *Madness and Civilization: A History of Insanity in the Age of Reason*. Translated by Richard Howard. New York: Vintage Books.

–. (1976) 1990. *The History of Sexuality*. Volume 1: *An Introduction*. Translated by Robert Hurley. New York: Vintage Books.

–. (1975) 1995. *Discipline and Punish: The Birth of the Prison*. Translated by Alan Sheridan. New York: Vintage Books.

–. (1978–79) 2008. *The Birth of Biopolitics: Lectures at the Collège de France, 1978–79*. Translated by Graham Burchell. New York: Palgrave MacMillan.

Friedland, Roger, and Robert R. Alford. 1991. "Bringing Society Back In: Symbols, Practices, and Institutional Contradictions." In *The New Institutionalism in Organizational Analysis*, edited by W.W. Powell and P.J. DiMaggio, 232–66. Chicago: University of Chicago Press.

Fuglerud, Øivind. 2004. "Constructing Exclusion. The Micro-Sociology of an Immigration Department. *Social Anthropology* 12 (1): 25–40.

Gallagher, Dennis. 1989. "The Evolution of the International Refugee System." *International Migration Review* 23 (3): 579–98.

Galloway, Gloria. 2006. "Immigration Board Short of Staff as Backlog Grows." *Globe and Mail*, October 18, A7. https://www.theglobeandmail.com/news/national/immigration-board-short-of-staff-as-backlog-grows/article18174913/.

Gargiulo, Enrico. 2017. "The Limits of Local Citizenship: Administrative Borders within the Italian Municipalities." *Citizenship Studies* 21 (3): 327–43.

Geist, Michael. 2015. "Signing vs. Ratifying: Unpacking the Canadian Government Position on the TPP." *Centre for Law, Technology and Society, University of Ottawa*. https://techlaw.uottawa.ca/news/signing-vs-ratifying-unpacking-canadian-government-position-tpp-0.

Girard, Raphael. 2019. "Asylum Policy in Canada." *Canadian Immigration Historical Society Bulletin* 88: 1–5.

Globe and Mail. 1951. "General Refugee Pact Regarded as Unlikely." July 5, 2.

–. 1968. "At Home – Some Beginnings." December 5, 6.

–. 1978. "New Immigration Act Tightens Entry Rules." April 11, 8.

–. 1992. "News Index: Monday February 17, 1992." February 17, A2.

–. 2008. "Mexico's Good Fight." October 21. https://www.theglobeandmail.com/opinion/mexicos-good-fight/article1323383/.

Glynn, Irial. 2011. "The Genesis and Development of Article 1 of the 1951 Refugee Convention." *Journal of Refugee Studies* 25 (1): 134–48.

Goldblatt, Murray. 1969. "Jews' Status in Question: New Refugee Definition Urged by MacEachen." *Globe and Mail*, May 28, 31.

Goldenziel, Jill I. 2016. "The Curse of the Nation-State: Refugees, Migration, and Security in International Law." *Arizona State Law Journal* 48: 579–636.

Goldring, Luin, and Patricia Landolt. 2013. "The Conditionality of Legal Status and Rights: Conceptualizing Precarious Non-Citizenship in Canada." In *Producing and Negotiating Non-Citizenship: Precarious Legal Status in Canada*, edited by Luin Goldring and Patricia Landolt, 3–28. Toronto: University of Toronto Press.

Government of Canada. 2019a. "Canada Ends the Designated Country of Origin Practice." May 17. https://www.canada.ca/en/immigration-refugees-citizenship/news/2019/05/canada-ends-the-designated-country-of-origin-practice.html.

–. 2019b. "Archived- Designated Countries of Origin Policy." May 17. https://www.canada.ca/en/immigration-refugees-citizenship/services/refugees/claim-protection-inside-canada/apply/designated-countries-policy.html.

Gray, John. 1995. *Liberalism*. 2nd ed. Minneapolis: University of Minnesota Press.

Green, Mendel. 1993. "Racism Allegations Are Just Rubbish." *Toronto Star*, August 30, A12.

Green, Richard. 1987. "Give Me Your Tired, Your Poor, Your Huddled Masses (of Heterosexuals): An Analysis of American and Canadian Immigration Policy." *Anglo-American Law Review* 16: 139–59.

Greenaway, Norma. 2009. "Deportation Order Ended in Death." *The Vancouver Sun*, October 26, B2.

Greenwood, Royston, Amalia M. Diaz, Stan X. Li, and Jose C. Lorente. 2010. "The Multiplicity of Institutional Logics and the Heterogeneity of Organizational Responses." *Organization Science* 21 (2): 521–39.

Greenwood, Royston, Mia Raynard, Farah Kodeih, Evelyn. R. Micelotta, and Michael Lounsbury. 2011. "Institutional Complexity and Organizational Responses." *Academy of Management Annuals* 5 (1): 317–71.

Grossberg, Lawrence. 1986. "On Postmodernism and Articulation: An Interview with Stuart Hall." *Journal of Communication Inquiry* 10 (2): 45–60.

Gupta, Akhil. 2012. *Red Tape: Bureaucracy, Structural Violence, and Poverty in India*. Durham, NC: Duke University Press.

Haddad, Emma. 2008. *The Refugee in International Society: Between Sovereigns*. Cambridge, UK: Cambridge University Press.

Hall, Stuart. 1980. "Race, Articulation and Societies Structured in Dominance." In *Sociological Theories: Race and Colonialism*, edited by Colette Guillaumin, 305–43. Paris: United Nations Educational, Scientific and Cultural Organization.

–. 1985. "Signification, Representation, Ideology: Althusser and the Post-Structuralist Debates." *Critical Studies in Mass Communication* 2 (2): 91–114.

–. 1997. "The Work of Representation." In *Representation: Cultural Representations and Signifying Practices*, edited by Stuart Hall, 1–47. London: Sage, in association with the Open University.

Hamilton Spectator. 1993a. "Deportation Order for Abused Woman under Review." February 11, A5.

–. 1993b. "Women Refugee Claimants Gain Deportation Reprieve." February 13, A10.

–. 2001. "Encoding/Decoding." In *Media and Cultural Studies: KeyWorks*, edited by Meenakshi Gigi Durham and Douglas M. Kellner, 163–73. Oxford: Blackwell.

Hamlin, Rebecca. 2014. *Let Me Be a Refugee: Administrative Justice and the Politics of Asylum in the United States, Canada, and Australia*. Oxford: Oxford University Press.

Harris, Kathleen. 2016. "Mexican Visa Lift Expected to Cost Canada $262M over a Decade." *CBC News*, December 1. https://www.cbc.ca/news/politics/mexico-visa-immigration-canada-mccallum-1.3875483.

Hartman, Yvonne. 2005. "In Bed with the Enemy: Some Ideas on the Connections between Neoliberalism and the Welfare State." *Current Sociology* 53 (1): 57–73.

Hathaway, James C. 1993. *Rebuilding Trust: Report of the Review of Fundamental Justice in Information Gathering and Dissemination at the Immigration and Refugee Board of Canada*. Ottawa: Immigration and Refugee Board.

Hawkins, Freda. 1988. *Canada and Immigration: Public Policy and Public Concern*. Montreal and Kingston: McGill-Queen's University Press.

Haynes, Janet M. 2018. "Safe Country Agreement: Closing the Doors on Refugee Women Seeking Protection." *Families in Society* 95 (2): 140–48.

Hilgers, Mathieu, and Eric Mangez. 2015. "Introduction to Pierre Bourdieu's Theory of Social Fields." In *Bourdieu's Theory of Social Fields: Concepts and Applications*, edited by Mathiew Hilgers and Eric Mangez, 1–36. London: Routledge.

Hindess, Barry. 2000. "Citizenship in the International Management of Populations." *American Behavioral Scientist* 43 (9): 1486–97.

Hobbes, Thomas. (1651) 1996. *Leviathan*. Edited by J.C.A. Gaskin. Oxford: Oxford University Press.

Hoffman, Michael. L. 1951. "Security Blocks Plans to Protect Stateless People." *Globe and Mail*, July 10, 3.

Hoy, Benjamin. 2018. "Policing Morality: Regulating Sexuality across the Canada-United States Border." *Canadian Historical Review* 99 (1): 30–62.

Human Rights Watch. 2008. *This Alien Legacy: The Origins of "Sodomy" Laws in British Colonialism*. https://www.hrw.org/sites/default/files/reports/lgbt1208_webwcover.pdf.

Hungarian Free Press. 2017. "Hungarian Roma Refugees in Canada – The Lead Case, Its Aftermath and The Future (Parts 2 & 3)." August 25. https://hungarianfreepress.com/2017/08/25/hungarian-roma-refugees-in-canada-the-lead-case-its-aftermath-and-the-future-parts-2-3/.

Hyndman, Jennifer, and Alison Mountz. 2007. "Refuge or Refusal: The Geography of Exclusion." In *Violent Geographies: Fear, Terror, and Political Violence*, edited by Derek Gregory and Allan Pred, 77–92. New York: Routledge.

Ibbitson, John. 2017a. "How Canada Has Been Secretly Giving Asylum to Gay People in Chechnya Fleeing Persecution." *Globe and Mail*, September 1. https://www.theglobeandmail.com/news/canada-chechnya-gay-asylum/article36145997/.

–. 2017b. "Russia to Probe Canada's Aid to Gay Chechens Fleeing Persecution." *Globe and Mail,* September 5. https://www.theglobeandmail.com/news/politics/russia-to-probe-canadas-aid-to-gay-chechens-fleeing-persecution/article36180629/.

Ifejika, Sam. 1993. "Refugee from Racism on the Refugee Board." *Toronto Star,* August 11, A19.

Immigration and Refugee Board of Canada (IRB). 1990. *Annual Report for the Year Ending December 31, 1989.* Ottawa: Immigration and Refugee Board.

–. 1991. *Annual Report for the Year Ending December 31, 1990.* Ottawa: IRB.

–. 1992. *Annual Report for the Year Ending December 31, 1991.* Ottawa: IRB.

–. 1993. *Annual Report for the Year Ending December 31, 1992.* Ottawa: IRB.

–. 1994. *Annual Report for the Year Ending December 31, 1993.* Ottawa: IRB.

–. 1995. *Annual Report for the Year Ending December 31, 1994.* Ottawa: IRB.

–. 1996. *Performance Report for the Period Ending March 31, 1996.* Ottawa: IRB.

–. 1997. *Performance Report for the Period Ending March 31, 1997.* Ottawa: IRB.

–. 1998. *Performance Report for the Period Ending March 31, 1998.* Ottawa: IRB.

–. 1999. *Performance Report for the Period Ending March 31, 1999.* Ottawa: IRB.

–. 2000. *Performance Report for the Period Ending March 31, 2000.* Ottawa: IRB.

–. 2001. *Performance Report for the Period Ending March 31, 2001.* Ottawa: IRB.

–. 2002. *Performance Report for the Period Ending March 31, 2002.* Ottawa: IRB.

–. 2003. *Performance Report for the Period Ending March 31, 2003.* Ottawa: IRB.

–. 2004. *Performance Report for the Period Ending March 31, 2004.* Ottawa: IRB.

–. 2005. *Performance Report for the Period Ending March 31, 2005.* Ottawa: IRB.

–. 2006. *Performance Report for the Period Ending March 31, 2006.* Ottawa: IRB.

–. 2007. *Performance Report for the Period Ending March 31, 2007.* Ottawa: IRB.

–. 2008. *Performance Report for the Period Ending March 31, 2008.* Ottawa: IRB.

–. 2009. *Performance Report for the Period Ending March 31, 2009.* Ottawa: IRB.

–. 2010. *Performance Report for the Period Ending March 31, 2010.* Ottawa: IRB.

–. 2013. *2012–2013 Part III – Departmental Performance Report.* Ottawa: IRB.

–. 2014. *Performance Report for the Period Ending March 31, 2014.* Ottawa: IRB.

–. 2015. *Performance Report for the Period Ending March 31, 2015.* Ottawa: IRB.

–. 2016. *Performance Report for the Period Ending March 31, 2016.* Ottawa: IRB.

–. 2017. *Departmental Results Report 2016–2017.* Ottawa: IRB.

–. 2019. "About the IRB." https://irb-cisr.gc.ca/en/board/Pages/index.aspx.

–. 2021. "Policy Instruments." https://irb.gc.ca/en/legal-policy/policies/Pages/index.aspx.

Ivanyi, Peter. 2009. "The Real Refugee Scandal." *National Post,* March 26, A19.

Janmyr, Maja. 2016. "Precarity in Exile: The Legal Status of Syrian Refugees in Lebanon." *Refugee Survey Quarterly* 35 (4): 58–78.

Jimenez, Marina. 2007. "Immigration Board Head Abruptly Resigns Amid Changes." *Globe and Mail,* February 28. https://www.theglobeandmail.com/news/national/immigration-board-head-abruptly-resigns-amid-changes/article1071792/.

–. 2008. "9000 'Ordinary People' Flee Mexican Drug War." *Globe and Mail*, October 19. https://www.theglobeandmail.com/news/national/9000-ordinary-people-flee-mexican-drug-war/article1064573/

Jones, Stephen. 2017. "Pitiful Plight of Refugees Locked Up in Australian Island 'Internment Camps' Who Have Provoked Trump's Wrath." *Mirror*, February 2. https://www.mirror.co.uk/news/world-news/pitiful-plight-refugees-locked-up-9743949.

Jordan, Sharalyn R. 2009. "Un/Convention(al) Refugees: Contextualizing the Accounts of Refugees Facing Homophobic or Transphobic Persecution." *Refuge* 26 (2): 165–82.

Jubany, Olga. 2011. "Constructing Truths in a Culture of Disbelief: Understanding Asylum Screening from within." *International Sociology* 26 (1): 74–94.

Kapur, Ratna. 2006. "Human Rights in the 21st Century: Take a Walk on the Dark Side." *Sydney Law Review* 28 (4): 665–87.

Karasapan, Omer, and Sajjad Shah. 2021. "Why Syrian Refugees in Lebanon Are a Crisis within a Crisis." *Brooklings*, April 15. https://www.brookings.edu/blog/future-development/2021/04/15/why-syrian-refugees-in-lebanon-are-a-crisis-within-a-crisis/.

Kelley, Ninette, and Michael J. Trebilcock. 1998. *The Making of the Mosaic: A History of Canadian Immigration Policy*. Toronto: University of Toronto Press.

Keung, Nicholas. 2007. "Refugee Chair Quits in 'Frustration.'" *Toronto Star*, February 28. https://www.thestar.com/news/2007/02/28/refugee_chair_quits_in_frustration.html.

–. 2009. "Mexican Woman Deported to Her Death." *Toronto Star*, October 23. https://www.thestar.com/news/gta/2009/10/23/mexican_woman_deported_to_her_death.html.

–. 2010. "When Their Home Is No Safe Haven." *Toronto Star*, March 7. https://www.thestar.com/news/insight/2010/03/07/when_their_home_is_no_safe_haven.html.

–. 2013. "Roma Refugees: Canadian Billboards in Hungary Warn of Deportation." *Toronto Star*, January 25. https://www.thestar.com/news/canada/2013/01/25/roma_refugees_canadian_billboards_in_hungary_warn_of_deportation.html.

–. 2015. "Court Rules Denial of Appeals for 'Safe Country' Refugees Unconstitutional." *Toronto Star*, July 24. https://www.thestar.com/news/immigration/2015/07/23/court-strikes-down-ottawas-safe-country-list-for-refugees.html.

–. 2017. "Refugee Board Creates Guidelines for Deciding LGBTQ Claims." *Toronto Star*, May 5. https://www.thestar.com/news/immigration/2017/05/05/refugee-board-creates-guidelines-for-deciding-lgbtq-claims.html.

Kim, Jaeeun. 2011. "Establishing Identity: Documents, Performance, and Biometric Information in Immigration Proceedings." *Law & Social Inquiry* 36 (3): 760–86. doi:10.2307/23011889.

Kinsman, Gary, and Patrizia Gentile. 2010. *The Canadian War on Queers: National Security as Sexual Regulation*. Vancouver: UBC Press.

Kizito, Kalemba. 2017. "Bequeathed Legacies: Colonialism and State Led Homophobia in Uganda." *Surveillance & Society* 15 (3–4): 567–72.

Kneebone, Susan. 2009. "Introduction: Refugee and Asylum Seekers in the International Context: Rights and Realities." In *Refugees, Asylum Seekers and the Rule of Law: Comparative Perspectives*, edited by Susan Kneebone, 1–31. Cambridge, UK: Cambridge University Press.

Knudsen, Are. 2009. "Widening the Protection Gap: The 'Politics of Citizenship' for Palestinian Refugees in Lebanon, 1948–2008." *Journal of Refugee Studies* 22 (1): 51–73.

Koshy, Susan. 1999. "From Cold War to Trade War: Neocolonialism and Human Rights." *Social Text* 58: 1–32.

Landau, Loren B., and Roni Amit. 2014. "Wither Policy? Southern African Perspectives on Understanding Law, 'Refugee' Policy and Protection." *Journal of Refugee Studies* 27 (4): 534–52.

Landsberg, Michele. 1992. "Immigration Keeps Terrorists, Kicks Women Out Our Door." *Toronto Star*, December 1, C1.

Lane, Jan-Eric. 2000. *New Public Management: An Introduction*. London: Routledge.

LaViolette, Nicole. 2004. "Coming Out to Canada: The Immigration of Same-Sex Couples under the Immigration and Refugee Protection Act." *McGill Law Journal* 49: 969–1003.

Lee, Edward Ou Jin, and Shari Brotman. 2011. "Identity, Refugeeness, Belonging: Experiences of Sexual Minority Refugees in Canada." *Canadian Review of Sociology / Revue canadienne de sociologie* 48 (3): 241–74.

Lee-An, Jiyoung. 2020. "'Fake' or 'Real' Marriage? Gender, Age, 'Race' and Class in the Construction of Un/desirability of Marriage Migrants in South Korea." *Studies in Social Justice* 14 (1): 125–45.

Levine-Rasky, Cynthia. 2016. *Writing the Roma*. Halifax: Fernwood.

Levine-Rasky, Cynthia, Julianna Beaudoin, and Paul St. Clair. 2014. "The Exclusion of Roma Claimants in Canadian Refugee Policy." *Patterns of Prejudice* 48 (1): 67–93.

Li, Peter S. 2001. "The Racial Subtext in Canada's Immigration Discourse." *Journal of International Migration and Integration* 2 (1): 77–97.

Lipsky, Michael. 1980. *Street-Level Bureaucracy: Dilemmas of the Individual in Public Services*. New York: Russell Sage Foundation.

Locke, John. (1689) 1988. *Two Treatises of Government*. Edited by Peter Laslett. Cambridge, UK: Cambridge University Press.

Loescher, Gil. 1993. *Beyond Charity: International Cooperation and the Global Refugee Crisis*. New York: Oxford University Press.

Macklin, Audrey. 1995. "Refugee Women and the Imperative of Categories." *Human Rights Quarterly* 17: 213–77.

–. 2003. *The Value(s) of the Canada-US Safe Country Agreement*. Ottawa: Caledon Institute of Social Policy. https://papers.ssrn.com/sol3/papers.cfm?abstract_id=557005.

–. 2013. "A Safe Country to Emulate? Canada and the European Refugee." In *The Global Reach of European Refugee Law,* edited by H. Lambery, J. McAdam, and M. Fullerton, 99–130. Cambridge, UK: Cambridge University Press.

Madokoro, Laura. 2016. *Elusive Refuge: Chinese Migrants in the Cold War.* Cambridge, MA: Harvard University Press.

–. 2022. "Eurocentrism and the International Refugee Regime." *Journal of Modern European History* 20 (1): 34–39.

Mahoney, James, and Kathleen Ann Thelen. 2010. *Explaining Institutional Change: Ambiguity, Agency, and Power.* Cambridge, UK: Cambridge University Press.

Malkki, Liisa. 1992. "National Geographic: The Rooting of Peoples and the Territorialization of National Identity among Scholars and Refugees." *Cultural Anthropology* 7 (1): 24–44.

Markowitz, Arthur A. 1973. "Humanitarianism versus Restrictionism: The United States and the Hungarian Refugees." *International Migration Review* 7 (1): 46–59.

Marks, Stephen P. 1981. "Emerging Human Rights: A New Generation for the 1980s?" *Rutgers Law Review* 33: 435–52.

Marshall, Thomas H. (1950) 2009. "Citizenship and Social Class." In *Inequality and Society: Social Science Perspectives on Social Stratification,* edited by J. Manza and M. Sauder, 148–54. New York: W.W. Norton.

Marx, Karl. (1844) 2002. "On the Jewish Question." In *Citizenship: Critical Concepts,* edited by B.S. Turner and P. Hamilton, 278–94. New York: Routledge.

Masoumi, Azar. 2019. "The Politics of 'Doing Exactly Nothing': Feminist Legal Change and Bureaucratic Administration of Refugee Protection." *Feminist Legal Studies* 27: 243–61.

–. 2020. "The Battle of Numbers: Refugee Protection, Race, and Neoliberal Politics of Bureaucratic Efficiency." *Oñati Socio-Legal Series* 10 (6): 1084–1106.

Mayblin, Lucy. 2017. *Asylum after Empire: Colonial Legacies in the Politics of Asylum Seeking.* London: Roman and Littlefield.

Mayeda, Andrew. 2007. "Critics Say PM Is Staging Refugee Board Power Grab." *Ottawa Citizen,* February 28, A3.

McCluskey, Martha T. 2003. "Efficiency and Social Citizenship: Challenging the Neoliberal Attack on the Welfare State." *Indiana Law Journal* 78: 783–876.

McShane, King G. 2006a. "Substantive Law." In *The Canadian Encyclopedia.* Toronto: Historica Canada. https://www.thecanadianencyclopedia.ca/en/article/substantive-law.

–. 2006b. "Procedural Law." In *The Canadian Encyclopedia.* Toronto: Historica Canada. https://www.thecanadianencyclopedia.ca/article/procedural-law.

Mehta, Uday. 1990. "Liberal Strategies of Exclusion." *Politics and Society* 18 (4): 427–54.

Meyer, J.W., and Brian Rowan. 1977. "Institutionalized Organizations: Formal Structure as Myth and Ceremony." *American Journal of Sociology* 83 (2): 340–63.

Millbank, Jenni. 2003 "Gender, Sex and Visibility in Refugee Claims on the Basis of Sexual Orientation." *Georgetown Immigration Law Journal* 18 (1): 77–110.

Miller, Alice. 2005. "Gay Enough: Some Tensions in Seeking the Grant of Asylum and Protecting Global Sexual Diversity." In *Passing Lines: Sexuality and Immigration,* edited by Brad Epps, Keja Valens, and Bill Johnson Gonzalez, 137–88. Cambridge, MA: Harvard University Press.

Miller, Jacquie. 1993a. "Canada Moves to Assist Women Refugees." *Hamilton Spectator,* February 2, A7.

–. 1993b. "Refugee Women May Get a Break." *Hamilton Post,* March 10, A1.

Mitrovica, Andrew. 2017. "No Refuge: For Challenging a Policy That Discriminated against Certain Refugees, a Federal Employee's Career Was Ruined. Despite Being Cleared, He Still Awaits Justice." *The Walrus,* October 12. https://thewalrus.ca/no-refuge/.

Molnar, Petra. 2018. "LGBTQ+ Refugees in Canada." In *The Canadian Encyclopedia.* Toronto: Historica Canada. https://www.thecanadianencyclopedia.ca/en/article/lgbtq2-refugees-in-canada.

Mongia, Radhika V. 2007. "Historicizing State Sovereignty: Inequality and the Form of Equivalence." *Comparative Studies in Society and History* 49 (2): 384–411.

–. 2018. *Indian Migration and Empire: A Colonial Genealogy of the Modern State.* Durham, NC: Duke University Press.

Mountz, Alison. 2010. *Seeking Asylum: Human Smuggling and Bureaucracy at the Border.* Minneapolis: University of Minnesota Press.

Mukhtar, Maria, Jennifer Dean, Kathi Wilson, Effat Ghassemi, and Dana H. Wilson. 2016. "'But Many of These Problems Are About Funds…': The Challenges Immigrant Settlement Agencies (ISAs) Encounter in a Suburban Setting in Ontario, Canada." *Journal of International Migration and Integration* 17 (2): 389–408.

Murphy, Jessica. 2017. "Canada Has Quietly Granted Asylum to LGBT Chechens." *BBC News,* September 7. https://www.bbc.com/news/world-us-canada-41075528.

Murray, David. 2011. "Becoming Queer Here: Integration and Adaptation Experiences of Sexual Minority Refugees in Toronto." *Refuge* 28 (2): 127–35.

–. 2014. "To Feel the Truth: Discourse and Emotion in Canadian Sexual Orientation Refugee Hearings." *Journal of Language and Sexuality* 3 (1): 6–27.

–. 2016. *Real Queer? Sexual Orientation and Gender Identity Refugees in the Canadian Refugee Apparatus.* New York: Rowman and Littlefield.

Nada. 1993. "A Refugee's View: Blame Women's Oppression on Politics Not Culture." *Hamilton Spectator,* March 12, A7.

Najmabadi, Afsaneh. 2005. *Women with Mustaches and Men without Beards: Gender and Sexual Anxieties of Iranian Modernity.* Berkeley: University of California Press.

Neuwirth, Jessica. 1992. "A Test of Canada's Gender Equality." *Christian Science Monitor,* November 18, 18.

Nolan, Tami P. 1992. "Refugee Board Antics Reflect Badly on Canada." *Hamilton Spectator,* February 22, A7.

O'Leary, Barry. 2008. "'We Cannot Claim Any Particular Knowledge of the Ways of Homosexuals, Still Less of Iranian Homosexuals': The Particular Problems Facing Those Who Seek Asylum on the Basis of their Sexual Identity." *Feminist Legal Studies* 16 (1): 87–95.

Olson, Isaac. 2018. "Canada Urged to Put Hold on Sending Asylum Seekers Back to Haiti amid Violent Protests." *CBC News*, July 11. https://www.cbc.ca/news/canada/montreal/haiti-advocates-hold-asylum-seeker-deportation-1.4742056.

O'Neil, Peter. 2009. "Canada Clamps Down on Refugee Claims." *Canwest News Service*, July 13.

Ong, Aihwa. 2003. *Buddha Is Hiding: Refugees, Citizenship, the New America*. Berkeley: University of California Press.

Oziewicz, Estanislao. 1993. "Why a Change of Heart Does Not Change Policy." *Globe and Mail*, February 5, A13.

Park, Hijin. 2015. "Producing Refugees and Trafficked Persons: Women, Unaccompanied Minors, and Discourses of Criminalized Victimhood." In *Engendering Transnational Voices: Studies in Family, Work, and Identity*, edited by Guida Man and Rina Cohen, 255–72. Waterloo, ON: Wilfrid Laurier University Press.

Pateman, Carole. 1988. *The Sexual Contract*. Cambridge, UK: Polity.

Pedraza, Francisco I. 2014. "The Two-Way Street of Acculturation, Discrimination, and Latino Immigration Restrictionism." *Political Research Quarterly* 67 (4): 889–904.

Plaut, W. Gunter. 1985. *Refugee Determination in Canada: Proposals for a New System: A Report to the Honourable Flora MacDonald, Minister of Employment and Immigration*. Ottawa: Minister of Supply and Services Canada.

Povinelli, Elizabeth A. 1998. "The Cunning of Recognition: Real Being and Aboriginal Recognition in Settler Australia." *Australian Feminist Law Journal* 11 (1): 3–27.

Rajaram, Prem Kumar. 2013. "Historicising 'Asylum' and Responsibility." *Citizenship Studies* 17 (6–7): 681–96.

Rau, Krishna. 2018. "Lesbian, Gay, Bisexual and Transgender Rights in Canada." In *The Canadian Encyclopedia*. Toronto: Historica Canada. https://www.thecanadianencyclopedia.ca/en/article/lesbian-gay-bisexual-and-transgender-rights-in-canada.

Razack, Sherene. 1995. "Domestic Violence as Gender Persecution: Policing the Borders of Nation, Race, and Gender." *Canadian Journal of Women and the Law* 8: 45–88.

–. 1998. *Looking White People in the Eye*. Toronto: University of Toronto Press.

–. 1999. "Making Canada White: Law and the Policing of Bodies of Colour in the 1990s." *Canadian Journal of Law & Society* 14 (1): 159–84.

Refugee Council. N.d. "The Truth about Asylum." *Refugee Council*. https://www.refugeecouncil.org.uk/information/refugee-asylum-facts/the-truth-about-asylum/.

Rehaag, Sean. 2008. "Patrolling the Borders of Sexual Orientation: Bisexual Refugee Claims in Canada." *McGill Law Journal* 53: 59–102.

Reuters. 1996. "Canada Demands Visas after Chilean 'Refugee' Wave." June 6.

Rinehart, Dianne. 1994. "Reform Fears on Immigration Called off Base." *Winnipeg Free Press,* August 30, A2.

Ritzer, George. (1993) 2013. *The McDonaldization of Society.* Thousand Oaks, CA: Sage.

Robinson, Cabeiri D. 2012. "Too Much Nationality: Kashmiri Refugees, the South Asian Refugee Regime, and a Refugee State, 1947–1974." *Journal of Refugee Studies* 25 (3): 344–65.

Robinson, Daniel J., and David Kimmel. 1994. "The Queer Career of Homosexual Security Vetting in Cold War Canada." *Canadian Historical Review* 85 (3): 319–45.

Robinson, Natasha. 2017. "Refugee Review Tribunal 'Cut and Pasted' Paragraphs from Separate Asylum Seeker Applications." *ABC News,* September 12. https://www.abc.net.au/news/2017-09-12/refugee-review-tribunal-found-to-have-transposed-paragraphs/8899510.

Rozakou, Katerina. 2017. "Nonrecording the 'European Refugee Crisis' in Greece: Navigating through Irregular Bureaucracy." *Focaal* 77: 36–49.

Saltsman, Adam. 2014. "Beyond the Law: Power, Discretion, and Bureaucracy in the Management of Asylum Space in Thailand." *Journal of Refugee Studies* 27 (3): 457–76.

Samuel, Sigal. 2018. "There's a Perception That Canada Is Being Invaded." *The Atlantic,* May 26. https://www.theatlantic.com/international/archive/2018/05/theres-a-perception-that-canada-is-being-invaded/561032/.

Sarick, Lila. 1995. "Chilean Refugee Claims Show Sharp Increase." *Globe and Mail,* August 25, A8.

Satzewich, Vic. 2015. *Points of Entry: How Canada's Immigration Officers Decide Who Gets In.* Vancouver: UBC Press.

Scalettaris, Giulia. 2020. "The Afghan Ministry of Refugees: An Unruly Trainee in State Capacity Building." *Third World Quarterly* 41 (1): 151–67.

Scanlan, David. 1993. "Women in Hiding: Groups Urge Compassion for Abused Refugees." *Kitchener-Waterloo Record,* January 26, C3.

Scott, James C. 1998. *Seeing Like a State: How Certain Schemes to Improve the Human Condition Have Failed.* New Haven, CT: Yale University Press.

Scott, Marian. 2009. "Sometimes a Safe Haven." *Montreal Gazette,* June 20, B1.

Scott, William R. 1991. "Unpacking Institutional Arguments." In *The New Institutionalism in Organizational Analysis,* edited by W.W. Powell and P.J. DiMaggio, 164–82. Chicago: University of Chicago Press.

Sevunts, Levon. 2021. "Federal Court of Appeal Upholds Safe Third Country Agreement." *Radio Canada International,* April 15. https://www.rcinet.ca/en/2021/04/15/federal-court-of-appeal-upholds-safe-third-country-agreement/.

Showler, Peter. 2009. "No Quick Fix for Refugees." *Ottawa Citizen*, May 15, A15.

Sidhu, Ravinder, and Sandra Taylor. 2007. "Educational Provision for Refugee Youth in Australia: Left to Chance?" *Journal of Sociology* 43 (3): 283–300.

Silverstein, Paul A. 2005. "Immigrant Racialization and the New Savage Slot: Race, Migration, and Immigration in the New Europe." *Annual Review of Anthropology* 34: 363–84.

Simcox, David. 1997. "Major Predictors of Immigration Restrictionism: Operationalizing 'Nativism.'" *Population & Environment* 19 (2): 129–43.

Simpson, Jeffrey. 2009. "How We Might Make Up with Our Mexican Amigo." *Globe and Mail*, August 1. https://www.theglobeandmail.com/opinion/how-we-might-make-up-with-our-mexican-amigo/article1345075/.

–. 2010. "While Mexicans Fume, Our Reputation and Revenues Take a Hit." *Globe and Mail*, February 2. https://www.theglobeandmail.com/opinion/while-mexicans-fume-canadas-reputation-and-revenues-take-a-hit/article1364615/.

Small, Peter, and Donovan Vincent. 1992. "Lawyers Back Demand for Immigration Probe." *Toronto Star*, November 20, A7.

Smith, Miriam Catherine. 1999. *Lesbian and Gay Rights in Canada: Social Movements and Equality-Seeking: 1971–1995*. Toronto: University of Toronto Press.

Soennecken, Dagmar. 2013. "The Managerialization of Refugee Determination in Canada." *Droit et Société* 84 (2): 291–311.

Soguk, Nevzat. 1999. *States and Strangers: Refugees and Displacement of Statecraft*. Minneapolis: University of Minnesota Press.

Streeck, Wolfgang, and Kathleen Ann Thelen. 2005. *Beyond Continuity Institutional Change in Advanced Political Economies*. Oxford: Oxford University Press.

Suleiman, Jaber. 2006. "Marginalised Community: The Case of Palestinian Refugees in Lebanon." *Development Research Centre on Migration, Globalisation and Poverty, University of Sussex*. https://assets.publishing.service.gov.uk/media/57a08c4be5274a31e0001112/JaberEdited.pdf.

Sutton, John R., Frank Dobbin, John W. Meyer, and W. Richard Scott. 1994. "The Legalization of the Workplace." *American Journal of Sociology* 99 (4): 944–71.

Swink, Arwen. 2005. "Queer Refuge: A Review of the Role of Country Condition Analysis in Asylum Adjudications for Members of Sexual Minorities." *Hastings International and Comparative Law Review* 29: 251–66.

Tatum, Dillon S. 2018. "Discourse, Genealogy and Methods of Text Selection in International Relations." *Cambridge Review of International Affairs* 31 (3–4): 344–64.

Taylor, Lesley C. 2008. "Reprieve for Abused Mexican Women." *Toronto Star*, June 25, A1.

Teitelbaum, Michael S. 1984. "Immigration, Refugees, and Foreign Policy." *International Organization* 38 (3): 429–50.

Thobani, Sunera. 2000. "Closing Ranks: Racism and Sexism in Canada's Immigration Policy." *Race & Class* 42 (1): 35–55.

–. 2007. *Exalted Subjects: Studies in the Making of Race and Nation in Canada*. Toronto: University of Toronto Press.

Thompson, Allan. 1993a. "Ottawa Studies Refugee Claims for Women at Risk." *Toronto Star*, January 28, A3.

–. 1993b. "Persecuted Women May Be Accepted as Refugees." *Toronto Star*, January 30, A1.

–. 1993c. "Women Fleeing Abuse to Qualify as Refugees." *Toronto Star*, February 11, A4.

–. 1993d. "Women Refugees Pushed Aside, Advocates Say." *Toronto Star*, May 15, D5.

–. 1994. "Bad Apples on Refugee Fast Track." *Toronto Star*, August 30, A9.

Thompson, Nicole. 2016. "Trudeau Was First Sitting Prime Minister to March in Pride Parade." *Canadian Press*, July 3. https://toronto.ctvnews.ca/trudeau-was-first-sitting-prime-minister-to-march-in-pride-parade-1.2970978#:~:text=Trudeau%20marched%20in%20the%20Toronto,and%20waved%20a%20rainbow%20flag.&text=PRESS%2FAdrian%20Wyld)-,Trudeau%20marched%20in%20the%20Toronto%20Pride%20Parade%20on%20July%203,and%20waved%20a%20rainbow%20flag.

Todd, Rosemary. 1992. "Broadbent Urges Change to Rules on Refugee Status." *Hamilton Spectator*, November 26, C5.

Tomkinson, Sule. 2015a. "Studying Refugee Decision-making: Difficulties in Accessing the Research Site and Strategies for Resolution." *Refugee Review* 2 (1): 151–60.

–. 2015b. "Doing Fieldwork on State Organizations in Democractic Settings: Ethical Issues of Research in Refugee Decision Making." *Forum: Qualitative Social Research* 16 (1): Art. 6.

–. 2018. "Who Are You Afraid of and Why? Inside the Black Box of Refugee Tribunals." *Canadian Public Administration* 61 (2): 184–204.

Toronto Star. 2009. "Fixing the Refugee Mess." October 28. https://www.thestar.com/opinion/editorials/2009/10/28/fixing_the_refugee_mess.html.

Torpey, John. 2000. *The Invention of the Passport: Surveillance, Citizenship, and the State*. Cambridge, UK: Cambridge University Press.

Trueheart, Charles. 1993. "Canada Opens Doors to Refugee Claims Based on Gender." *Washington Post*, February 27, A17.

Ulbrich, Jeffrey. 1993. "Saudi Woman Who Refuses Veil Wins Right to Refuge in Canada." *Associated Press*, February 4.

UNHCR (United Nations High Commissioner for Refugees). 2011. "The 1951 Convention Relating to the Status of Refugees and Its 1967 Protocol." http://www.unhcr.org/about-us/background/4ec262df9/1951-convention-relating-status-refugees-its-1967-protocol.html.

Valpy, Michael. 1993. "The Women Persecuted for Being Women." *Globe and Mail*, March 11, A2.

–. 2009. "Facing Death Threats, a Respected Officer Fled a State of Corruption." *Globe and Mail,* October 14. https://www.theglobeandmail.com/opinion/oct-15-letters-to-the-editor/article1203472/.

Vincent, Donovan. 1992a. "Former Member Calls for Probe of Refugee Board." *Toronto Star,* November 21, A6.

–. 1992b. "A Member of Canada's Immigration and Refugee Board Has Resigned." *Toronto Star,* November 20, A2.

–. 1992c. "Refugee Board Member Quits to Protest Racism in Ministry." *Toronto Star,* November 19, A1.

–. 1993. "Refugee Board Head Rejects Racism Claim." *Toronto Star,* February 16, A2.

Vucetic, Srdjan. 2011. "Genealogy as a Research Tool in International Relations." *Review of International Studies* 37 (3): 1295–1312.

Walters, William. 2012. *Governmentality: Critical Encounters.* London: Routledge.

Weber, Max. (1922) 1978. "Chapter XI: Bureaucracy." In *Economy and Society: An Outline of Interpretive Sociology,* translated and edited by Guenther Roth and Claus Wittich, 956–1005. Berkeley: University of California Press.

Wesley, Saylesh. 2014. "Twin-Spirited Woman: Sts'iyóye Smestíyexw Slhá:li." *Transgender Studies Quarterly* 1 (3): 338–51.

Wheelwright, Julie. 1993. "One Giant Step for Women in Search of Asylum." *The Guardian,* March 22, A11.

Whelan, Daniel J., and Jack Donnelly. 2007. "The West, Economic and Social Rights, and the Global Human Rights Regime: Setting the Record Straight." *Human Rights Quarterly* 29 (4): 908–49.

Williams, Jacqueline. 2017. "Australia Refugee Camp on Manus Island Is Closing, Detainees Say." *New York Times,* May 16. https://www.nytimes.com/2017/05/16/world/australia/refugee-manus-island-papua-new-guinea.html.

Willick, Frances. 2009. "Experts Split on Mexican Visas." *Windsor Star,* July 15, A1.

Winnipeg Free Press. 1995. "Board's Acceptance Percentage in Dispute." March 15.

Wright, Teresa. 2019. "Refugee Advocates 'Shocked and Dismayed' over Asylum Changes in Budget Bill." *CBC News,* April 9. https://www.cbc.ca/news/politics/refugee-asylum-federal-budget-1.5091397?fbclid=IwAR1jME5CdOhLsYJu-7Ac5MKU1W52sI7YOqDcRC-Nlc-Xfk6YPycJES-oeo4.

York, Geoffrey. 1993a. "Domestic Abuse Accepted for Refugee Status." *Globe and Mail,* March 10, A1.

–. 1993b. "Policy Shift Too Late for Women." *Globe and Mail,* February 3, A4.

Zabjek, Alexandra. 2009. "Mexican Refugees Flocking to Canada to Escape Violence at Home." *Canwest News Service,* March 2.

Zeleza, Paul Tiyambe. 2007. "The Struggle for Human Rights in Africa." *Canadian Journal of African Studies / La Revue canadienne des études africaines* 41 (3): 474–506.

Zetter, Roger, and Martyn Pearl. 2000. "The Minority within the Minority: Refugee Community-Based Organisations in the UK and the Impact of Restrictionism on Asylum-Seekers." *Journal of Ethnic and Migration Studies* 26 (4): 675–97.

Zilio, Michelle. 2018a. "Immigration Advocates Urge Ottawa Not to Scrap Refugee Determination System." *Globe and Mail,* June 26. https://www.theglobeandmail.com/politics/article-immigration-advocates-urge-ottawa-not-to-scrap-refugee-determination/.

–. 2018b. "Asylum-Seeker Surge at Quebec Border Choking Canada's Refugee System, Data Show." *Globe and Mail,* September 11. https://www.theglobeandmail.com/politics/article-asylum-seeker-surge-at-quebec-border-choking-canadas-refugee-system/.

Index

Note: "(f)" after a page number indicates a figure.

Printed and bound in Canada by Friesens
Set in Myriad and Sabon by Artegraphica Design Co.
Copy editor: Stacy Belden
Proofreader: Caitlin Gordon-Walker
Indexer: Margaret de Boer
Cover designer: Will Brown